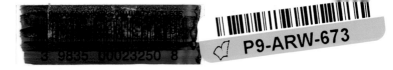

REAGAN'S LEADERSHIP AND THE ATLANTIC ALLIANCE

VIEWS FROM EUROPE AND AMERICA

Pergamon Titles of Related Interest

Denoon CONSTRAINTS ON STRATEGY: THE ECONOMICS OF WESTERN SECURITY

Dougherty/Pfaltzgraff SHATTERING EUROPE'S DEFENSE CONSENSUS

Goldstein FIGHTING ALLIES: TENSIONS WITHIN THE ATLANTIC SYSTEM

Reychler/Rudney DIRECTORY GUIDE OF EUROPEAN SECURITY AND DEFENSE RESEARCH

Windass AVOIDING NUCLEAR WAR

Related Journals
(Free specimen copies available upon request)

DEFENSE ANALYSIS

REAGAN'S LEADERSHIP AND THE ATLANTIC ALLIANCE

VIEWS FROM EUROPE AND AMERICA

Walter Goldstein

Developed with the support of the
Standing Conference of Atlantic Organizations

PERGAMON-BRASSEY'S
International Defense Publishers, Inc.

Washington New York London Oxford
Beijing Frankfurt São Paulo Sydney Tokyo Toronto

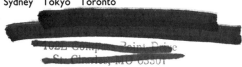

Pergamon Press Offices:

U.S.A. (Editorial)	Pergamon-Brassey's International Defense Publishers, 1340 Old Chain Bridge Road, McLean, Virginia 22101
(Orders & Inquiries)	Pergamon Press, Maxwell House, Fairview Park, Elmsford, New York 10523, U.S.A.
U.K. (Editorial)	Brassey's Defence Publishers, 24 Gray's Inn Road, London WC1X 8HR
(Orders & Enquiries)	Brassey's Defence Publishers, Headington Hill Hall, Oxford OX3 0BW, England
PEOPLE'S REPUBLIC OF CHINA	Pergamon Press, Qianmen Hotel, Beijing, People's Republic of China
FEDERAL REPUBLIC OF GERMANY	Pergamon Press, Hammerweg 6, D-6242 Kronberg, Federal Republic of Germany
BRAZIL	Pergamon Editora, Rua Eça de Queiros, 346, CEP 04011, São Paulo, Brazil
AUSTRALIA	Pergamon Press (Aust.) Pty., P.O. Box 544, Potts Point, NSW 2011, Australia
JAPAN	Pergamon Press, 8th Floor, Matsuoka Central Building, 1-7-1 Nishishinjuku, Shinjuku-ku, Tokyo 160, Japan
CANADA	Pergamon Press Canada, Suite 104, 150 Consumers Road, Willowdale, Ontario M2J 1P9, Canada

First printing 1986

Library of Congress Cataloging-in-Publication Data

Reagan's leadership and the Atlantic Alliance.

"Developed with the support of the Standing Conference
of Atlantic Organizations."
Papers presented at the 13th Annual Meeting of the
Standing Conference of Atlantic Organizations, Wingspread
House, Racine, Wis., July 1985, sponsored by the
Johnson Foundation and the Information Directorate of
NATO.
1. United States--Foreign relations--1981- --
Congresses. 2 Reagan, Ronald--Congresses. 3. United
States--Foreign relations--Europe--Congresses.
4. Europe--Foreign relations--United States--Congresses.
I. Goldstein, Walter, 1930- . II. Standing
Conference of Atlantic Organizations. Meeting (13th :
1985 : Wingspread House) III. Johnson Foundation
(Racine, Wis.) IV. North Atlantic Treaty Organization.
Information Directorate.
E876.R422   1986   327.73   86-8121
ISBN 0-08-033982-4

Printed in the United States of America

CONTENTS

Foreword: The Reagan Years and the Atlantic Alliance

The chapters in this book were drawn from the papers presented to the Standing Conference of Atlantic Organizations (SCAO) at its thirteenth annual meeting in July 1985. The meeting was held at Wingspread House in Racine, Wisconsin. It was jointly sponsored by the Johnson Foundation and the Information Service directorate of NATO.

The conference examined a subject of topical concern on both sides of the Atlantic: the likely thrust of U.S. foreign policy in the second term of President Reagan's administration. Relations within the Atlantic Alliance and European responses to U.S. policy initiatives provided the principal themes for discussion. The question before the conference was whether Reagan would maintain the policy priorities that had been established in previous years or whether the onset of basic changes should be anticipated. The maintenance of good relations within the Atlantic Alliance has been a leading priority for the United States, and for its European allies, in the thirty-five years since the NATO treaty was signed. The collective security arrangements of the Western world clearly depend upon the effective operation of the Alliance and the stalwart guarantee by the United States to underwrite the defense of Western Europe. The issue to be determined, therefore, was whether U.S. policy was likely to change in the four years of Reagan's second term, and how the European allies might react to any foreseeable changes.

The papers presented at Wingspread were written by distinguished American participants, most of whom had combined a career in diplomatic or government service with an eminent record in scholarly research. The discussants on each paper were Europeans. They included parliamentarians from France, West Germany, and the Netherlands, SCAO members from the United Kingdom and Norway, and two members of NATO headquarters staff in Brussels. The session on the Strategic Defense Initiative (SDI) was ably handled by two young researchers with considerable technical talent. The fifth paper, on the roles in foreign policy played by the U.S. Congress, was written by an Oxford don after the meeting had adjourned. The editor of the book wrote a much needed paper on American economic leadership in world affairs and a summary chapter of conclusions.

SCAO was first established as an organization in 1973 at the Rockefeller Foundation center at Bellagio, on Lake Como, with support provided by the German Marshall Fund. Its task is to bring together the voluntary organizations in the member countries of NATO as a working unit and to strengthen policy linkages between North America and Western Europe. SCAO's member organizations include the Atlantic Treaty Association, the English-Speaking Union, and twenty other groups. Twelve annual conferences have been held by SCAO since the first meeting in Bellagio in 1973. The themes have varied from "Youth and Security Values in the Alliance," at Wilton Park in Britain, in 1978, to a comparison between European and American political systems, in Berlin in 1979. The geographical focus shifted after the oil crises of the 1970s to "Western Interests Outside the NATO Area," at the Akademie für Politische Wissenschaft at Tutzing in Bavaria in 1981, to the politics of defense strategy at the College d'Europe, at Bruges in 1982, and "The Perceptions of a Middle Power: Canada," in Toronto in 1983.

SCAO has met three times in the United States, thanks to the generous hospitality of the Johnson Foundation and its staff at Wingspread. The first meeting, in 1977, questioned if the Western world had lost some of its will to survive. The second discussed the dynamics of the American political system in the election year of 1980. The third meeting produced the papers in this book. Forty participants came in 1985 from the NATO countries, and a number of them were drawn from college student groups. Some represented constituent member organizations of SCAO; others were invited because of the expert contribution that they could make in leading the discussion.

It is worth noting that the agenda for these three SCAO conferences has moved with the times, shifting in emphasis as new crises have emerged within the Alliance. In 1977 the discussion focused on four topics: (1) the critical state of the world economy following the first oil shock and the abandonment of the Bretton Woods scheme to stabilize world currencies; (2) the capacity of the U.S. political system to recover from the effects of the Vietnam war and Watergate; (3) the rise of the Soviet Union as a military superpower, as General Scowcroft had put it, that maintained global ambitions and mounting strategic capabilities; and (4) the changing relationships within the Atlantic Alliance once the European Economic Community (EEC) had gained roughly equal strength to the economy of the United States. The discussion in 1977 concluded, optimistically, that the East–West balance could be firmly maintained and that the survival capabilities of the Western world could be reinforced by such institutions as NATO and the European Community.*

In 1980, prior to the election of President Reagan, attention focused on the differences between the American and the European systems, looking particularly at the checks and balances that make the decision-making process in the United States so difficult to understand in Europe. European participants questioned American colleagues about whether a change of the party in power would weaken leadership in the Congress and the executive branch. The discussion also produced a better understanding of American assessments of the Atlantic Alliance and of the importance that was still accorded to NATO security doctrines by both political parties in the United States, by President Carter and the mass media.

The third conference convened in 1985 to assess the record of the first Reagan administration and the prospects for its second term. Tensions had increased between East and West to a greater extent than had been anticipated in the 1970s, and the accomplishments of détente had been critically questioned. The Soviet invasion of Afghanistan had been followed by the suppression of Solidarity in Poland and of the dissidents' movement in the Soviet Union, in contravention of the Conference on Security and Cooperation in Europe (CSCE) agreements of 1975. On the Western side, there had been a failure to ratify the SALT II treaty and a stormy debate over the deployment of cruise and Pershing missiles in Western Europe, in response to the Soviet deployment of SS-20s. Reagan's proposal for a Strategic Defense Initiative had worried many European allies, and it was questioned whether the resumption of arms control negotiations between the superpowers in Geneva would ever be productive. Speculation ran rife over the style of Soviet leadership that had emerged under Mikhail Gorbachev and over the prospects that could reasonably be expected from his summit meeting with Ronald Reagan. Little evidence has actually been seen of a change in Soviet policies to match the Kremlin's efforts to project a more attractive style, and discussion naturally concentrated on American attitudes and capacities for change in the near future.

SCAO was highly fortunate in lining up four accomplished Americans to produce papers for the conference. The first, Robert Osgood, had recently retired from a senior position in the Policy Planning Council of the State Department. Formerly he had worked in the National Security Council in the Nixon–Kissinger White House. As the author of widely quoted books on American diplomacy, Professor Osgood has now returned to the School of Advanced International Studies of the Johns Hopkins University

---

*The papers were published as a book, *The Western World and the Will to Survive* (Racine, WI: The Johnson Foundation, 1977).

in Washington, D.C. Osgood emphasized that pragmatic realism and a cautious conduct of policy have characterized the Reagan administration, even at those times when the idealistic or threatening rhetoric of its leaders had disturbed public opinion among many of America's closest allies. Though there appeared to have been a switch during President Reagan's first term from President Carter's emphasis on human rights and orderly superpower relations, what appeared to be major policy changes were in fact disguised continuity. There had been a continuous policy pattern in containing the Soviet Union and in closely cooperating with the Atlantic Alliance. The rhetoric of confrontation and competition in superpower negotiations might have been misleading, but no basic modification in policy had been adopted. Osgood believed that these trends would survive through Reagan's second term.

The second paper came from Martin Hillenbrand, formerly the U.S. Ambassador to the Federal Republic of Germany (FRG) and now the Dean Rusk Professor of International Relations at the University of Georgia. He drew upon his long diplomatic experience to develop the theme that American relations with the Alliance had always been subject to change. If future changes were not correctly handled, however, there could be a drifting apart of the North American and European member countries. Trade rivalries had become more intense, weapons systems had become highly expensive, and disagreements flourished not only over nuclear but also over outer space and conventional armament programs. There were diverging assessments, too, of the strategic intentions and capabilities of the Soviet Union. A new generation of leaders had taken positions of responsibility in many Western countries, and they had no personal memories of the tense conditions in which NATO had first been established. Their increasing concern with the Pacific rim, Central America, and the Caribbean was significant, but it would not necessarily lead to a weakening of transatlantic ties.

John Rielly, the president of the Chicago Council on Foreign Relations, provided a well-documented and reassuring interpretation of American public opinion. Mass opinion had been much less volatile in its attitudes toward the Soviet Union and the Atlantic Alliance than the rhetoric of some political leaders might have suggested. Rielly found that there were no strong public pressures on the administration to abandon previous policies. Public opinion supported the coupling of the U.S.-based nuclear deterrent with a strong conventional defense in the NATO area, and negotiations on arms control measures with the Soviet Union were strongly favored. Though the doctrines of détente no longer reflected the preferred expression of American sentiment, opinion polls showed that strong majorities still placed Europe at the center of American foreign policy concerns and firmly supported the continuing presence of American troops in Europe. The majority mood held to a belief that was described by Rielly as "conservative internationalism," though it had been challenged by a revival of vocal expressions of "nationalist unilateralism." The conflict between the two ideologies was reflected in the discrepancy between the style and performance of President Reagan and his administration in his first term. In most cases, however, the more vocal advocates of unilateral nationalist action had failed to sway foreign policy.

The fourth paper, on U.S. defense policy, provided a brilliant analysis of SDI by Gil Klinger, a recent graduate of the Kennedy School of Government at Harvard University and now a research analyst at the Rand Corporation. His presentation was informed and objective, giving equal emphasis to the possibilities and the difficulties to be overcome before research could move forward to the stage of deployment. The impression was that, given time and money, defenses of specific and limited strategic objectives should be possible; but that the president's original aspiration to remove all threats of a nuclear exchange with an effective defense of the civil population was very far away indeed. Another of the young participants, Steve Smith of the University of East Anglia, was equally brilliant but more skeptical in drawing attention to the many hurdles that SDI would have to overcome. Many of the European discussants suggested that this ambitious project, whether it was successful or not, could upset the East–West balance and undermine Western reliance on the U.S. nuclear deterrent.

The conference concluded with a summary of the various points of view that are reproduced in this book. It was presented by SCAO's rapporteur, Walter Goldstein, professor of public policy at the Rockefeller College of the State University of New York at Albany. His summary generated a lively exchange between European and American participants. The former were a little more anxious and doubting about the trends that U.S. foreign policy might follow in the last years of President Reagan's leadership. They saw increasing attention to Pacific rather than Atlantic issues, and they questioned the effects that the SDI emphasis on ballistic missile defense (BMD) might exert on the arms reduction negotiations in Geneva. In contrast, the Americans saw little danger of diminishing concern with the Atlantic Alliance or of a declining emphasis on the priority accorded to the maintenance of Western unity. What they foresaw was that the U.S. Congress would combat more and more of the president's initiatives, as his "lame duck" term wound to a close, and that it would fight him relentlessly on matters relating to fiscal policy, the financing of the deficit, and the high level of defense spending that Reagan has continually urged.

The conflict between the Congress and the president is an issue that worries and perplexes many of the NATO allies. No similar division of power is to be found in their own political systems. It was for this reason that the editor chose to include in this book a paper that was submitted after the conference adjourned. It was written by David Robertson, a Fellow of St. Hugh's College in Oxford, who has written several books on the dynamics of electoral and legislative politics. He had been awarded a research grant to study in Washington, and his paper reflects an Englishman's surprise at the political warfare waged between the White House and the Congress to control the deliberation of foreign policy. It serves a useful purpose in analyzing the skirmishing and the blocking tactics that both sides pursue when new initiatives are tested to change U.S. defense policy, the negotiating positions staked out for arms control talks, or the U.S. contribution to the Alliance. The paper provides a valuable prognosis of the congressional battles that Reagan will have to fight as he completes his eight years in office.

To round out the evaluation of Reagan's administration, the editor contributed two papers that were clearly required. The first considers the economic and monetary leadership that the United States provides for the Western Alliance system. The second draws together the conclusions that were reached by the American and the European participants. Though the summarizing judgments are those of Walter Goldstein as an individual participant, he has tried to capture the full range of views that were expressed by the contributors to the volume.

Considerable numbers of books have been published on NATO politics and the thrust of American diplomacy in recent years. It is hoped that this volume will do more than add just another title to the list. The talent gathered together by SCAO from both sides of the Atlantic in its 1985 meeting was impressive. The authors are remarkably well informed and outspoken. That they disagree with each other over critical matters of Western strategy is obviously to be welcomed. So, too, is their final conclusion: that the cohesion of the Alliance is likely to remain strong and that American leadership is so well trusted that the Alliance can only gain from a frank discussion of policy disagreements. The vigor of the discussion justifies the decision to publish this book, and it lends strength to SCAO's basic purpose: to provide a critical meeting place for the voluntary organizations that are concerned with Atlantic policy issues. It is a tribute to the editor's skills that he has managed to put these views together in a readable and rewarding publication.

Sir Frank Roberts

Acknowledgements

As the editor of the book I would like to acknowledge the assistance I received in putting together this project.

Rita Goodman, Vice-President of the Johnson Foundation, made most of the arrangements for the SCAO conference at Wingspread in 1985. As in our previous visits, in 1977 and 1980, she provided a generosity in hospitality and an efficiency in management that remain unmatched in the travels that I have made with SCAO across Europe and North America.

The staff of NATO's Information Directorate in Brussels gave helpful advice and logistic support well beyond the course of duty. They managed to encourage our efforts while avoiding the slightest expression of policy influence. Their example could serve as a model for public agencies charged with promoting academic and policy research.

Working with SCAO members and officers was usually a delight, although occasionally infuriating, and most of them were willing to rewrite their manuscript drafts several times over. Sir Frank Roberts sustained a firm direction and an intellectual enthusiasm in the SCAO debates, which he has chaired for many years . . . except when irreverence overtook him and left him convulsed with laughter. Inga Haag, the distinguished *directrice* of SCAO, ran the proceedings with such charm and competence that participants forgot they were supposed to be bored at some point. Colleagues from Belgium, Britain, Canada, France, Germany and the United States spoke so well for their national positions that conflict across the conference table seemed to be inevitable at times. On second thought, it was suggested that if national governments could only speak as capably, there would be more understanding and greater humor in the discourse of the Alliance.

A brief history of SCAO is given by Sir Frank Roberts in the Foreword. He points out that the SCAO was founded to encourage an informal and constructive debate on Alliance policy choices. Aided by such skillful friends, it was a pleasant assignment to put together the papers in this debate on Atlantic policy. In doing so I was encouraged by my friendly guru at Pergamon-Brassey's, Frank Margiotta; by Maxine Morman, of the staff at Rockefeller College of the State University of New York; and most of all, by my wife, Batya, without whose good cheer the project would have become more onerous.

Walter Goldstein
Albany, New York
April, 1986

1
Introduction: Continuity and Change in American Foreign Policy

Sir Frank Roberts

The aim of this book is to determine whether emerging forces of continuity or change, over the next few years, will modify the formulation of U.S. foreign policy and the special regard America holds for the Atlantic Alliance. In recent years, allies and adversaries alike have been somewhat confused by the changing appearances of American policy. The replacement of the Carter by the Reagan administration raised questions on both sides of the Atlantic regarding America's leadership role and its policy priorities. The time has come to ask which way policy is likely to change in President Reagan's second term. Will he hew to the principles of continuity that were established during the thirty-five years of NATO's evolving consensus, or will he institute changes that could lead to a basic revision of Alliance strategy? Henry Kissinger once suggested that the United States must attend to global responsibilities, whereas the European allies are largely concerned with regional interests. Will this divergence lead to greater difficulties within the Alliance in future years? Or will the Reagan second term reaffirm the consensus procedures and the collective principles embodied in the NATO treaty? That is the subject that preoccupies the American authors of these papers and the European commentators who responded to them.

World affairs have become increasingly complex in the 1980s. Economic tensions have become more troubling, and differences have appeared within the Alliance regarding the behavior of the Soviet Union and the costs that should be paid to preserve the East–West balance of power. Western disagreements have multiplied over North–South relations, the conduct of foreign economic policy, and the role that might one day be played by China, Japan, and other powers outside the Atlantic area. In the first two decades of the cold war, there was an appearance of simplicity; though the perception of threat was high, it was assumed that the global management of conflict could be accomplished within a bipolar system. The management of power today is multipolar and more diffuse. No one is sure what structures of world order will emerge as the world moves toward the 1990s.

In the early days of the Alliance, the principal concern focused on how best to deal with the Soviet Union, the single power center of the Communist bloc. Strong Communist parties had emerged in France and Italy, the entente created during the writing of the UN charter had dissolved, and the nuclear arms buildup had begun to accelerate. Following the Soviet blockade of Berlin and the Communist takeover in Prague, it was feared that Stalin might not be satisfied with the division of Europe and of Germany and that he might be tempted to move further west. At that time the overwhelming superiority of Soviet conventional forces in Europe was balanced only by the American atom bomb. Soviet power had not yet confronted the formidable strength of the Western market system, and the Soviet version of Marxist–Leninist ideology still attracted many followers in Europe and the Third World. Only the United States enjoyed the necessary economic and military power to restore stability to Western Europe and, through the Marshall Plan and NATO, to provide the collective security guarantee that was incorporated in the Atlantic Alliance. Spurred on by great European leaders such as Bevin, Adenauer, de Gasperi, and Schumann, the United States found its own historic leadership in Truman, Marshall, Acheson, and Eisenhower. They succeeded in replacing the traditions of isolationism with a determined drive to create a balance of power in the Atlantic and in the Pacific. They set out to revive the European and the Japanese economies with assistance programs that combined great generosity with long-term self-interest. East–West relations were managed through a strategic commitment to containment. Any further Soviet expansion was blocked, and the postwar patterns of settlement were solidified, notwithstanding the angry rhetoric of John Foster Dulles to roll back the Communist occupation of Eastern Europe. The upheavals in Budapest in 1956 and in Prague in 1968 exposed his rhetoric once and for all as empty words.

Europe became dependent on the United States economically as well as militarily, and the Bretton Woods financial system facilitated the stabilizing of world trade and the raising of living standards. North–South problems in those postwar years concentrated on the process of decolonization. The former British Empire was transformed into a commonwealth of independent but freely associated nations, and the former French empire in Black Africa (although not in Southeast Asia or Arab North Africa) became a closely knit francophone community. The Soviet Union was not at that time a global military power; under Stalin's reign it attended to its own vital interests nearer home. Nor could it then, or later, proffer to the developing nations of the Third World the economic advantages that flowed from the trade and investment benefits offered by the developed industrial countries of the West and, later, Japan. The Soviet contribution to the Third World, which even Soviet theory considered unripe for socialism, still less communism, was restricted to anti-imperialist propaganda and the supply of armaments.

The thrust of postwar American policies was to contain the Soviet Union, to revive the enormous strength of Western Europe and Japan, and to encourage the former colonies to achieve independence. By and large the policies succeeded. But over the last twenty-five years they have had to be adapted to changes in the world scene, whether in North–South, East–West, or West–West relationships. Soviet policies, of course, have had to change too, most notably under Khrushchev in the 1950s and 1960s, and maybe they are going to change again under Gorbachev. It is striking that changes in the patterns of East–West relations have been relatively less volatile than those in North–South or even West–West relations, and that the standoff between the superpowers and their alliances has remained stable in recent decades.

That the forces of change in West–West relations have not undermined the patterns of stability can be largely attributed to the success of the Western, predominantly the American, policies adopted from 1947 onward. Western Europe and Japan developed phenomenally successful economies, and they began to realize unprecedented industrial growth. Their growth in GNP generated new challenges to American foreign and economic policy. Moreover, it became obvious that the Soviet economic and ideological model carried no attraction for the electorates of industrial societies in the Western world. The economic principles of Marxism lost credibility, and the failure to achieve industrial growth became the Achilles heel of the Soviet Union. Confronted with the ruthless but failing politics of the Soviet system, it was logical that Western society should lose some of the sense of fear that had primed public support for a buildup of defense and deterrence capabilities.

As a second consequence of success, Western Europe, especially after the establishment of the EEC, joined Japan as strong trading rivals and economic competitors to the United States. This eventuality had been foreseen by American leaders, but they had hoped that a partnership agreement would be built across the Western world. This has not yet been achieved. An effective merging of political, burden-sharing, global, and regional concerns proved to be impractical. A heavy price had to be paid to manage the commercial competition that came to challenge the power of the American economy. The terms of world trade changed as the European Community began to rival the power of the United States and as Japan, with the growth of the Pacific rim, threatened the ascendancy of the Atlantic area in the world economy.

A close and trilateral grouping of power brought the United States, Western Europe, and Japan together in an interdependent relationship. The original economic dependence on the United States has been replaced by new modes of competition. But this has led in turn to a series of bitter disputes with the EEC over agricultural products or steel exports, or with Japan over cars and electronics equipment. Friction has also appeared in East–West trade over U.S. restrictions on high-technology exports to the Soviet bloc or the financing of the Siberian gas pipeline. Competition in the Western market-economy system requires greater interdependence on the one side, while fostering rivalries on the other with American multinational companies and agricultural exporters. These economic strains and stresses require constant attention if they are not to aggravate divisions among allied governments and among large sections of the electorate on both sides of the Atlantic.

Perhaps the greatest changes since the 1950s have been seen in North–South relationships and in the politics of the Third World. The last vestiges of colonialism have been swept aside, except perhaps in the Soviet Union itself, and relations between excolonial countries and their former colonial masters have been largely smoothed out. The one exception, South Africa, is potentially explosive, but the crisis there does not in fact present a colonial problem. Although many former colonies have called themselves socialist regimes, few have opted for the Soviet model or for dependence upon Soviet protection. Indonesia and Egypt are outstanding examples of important Third World countries that threw off the Communist embrace.

Economic development has been the main concern of the Third World countries, and it is notable that the most successful of them adopted a market economy and encouraged incoming foreign investment. The best examples are to be found in Hong Kong, Singapore, Malaysia, South Korea, and Taiwan in Southeast Asia; in Mexico and Brazil in Latin America; and in Nigeria, Kenya, and the Ivory Coast in Africa. The oil-rich countries of the Middle East prospered considerably in the 1970s, building new oil installations and investing their revenues in the West. A few important countries, above all India, tried to follow a middle course, both in economic planning and in exploring the political prospects of nonalignment. Soviet success in the Third World has been limited to Cuba, Vietnam, Ethiopia, South Yemen, and Angola, but these countries' present leaning toward the Soviet Union has not helped their economic growth or their political development. Syria and Libya are certainly not reliable Soviet allies, and their social systems do not follow the principles of socialism in the Soviet sense. Afghanistan has yet to be chalked up as a Soviet success, even after many years of Soviet occupation.

The great majority in what is now the diverse grouping of Third World countries is united only in its determination not to be drawn into East–West conflicts and to remain detached from the struggles of NATO and the Warsaw Pact. The developing countries tried for some years to join together, despite their different economic and political interests, to persuade the Organization for Economic Cooperation and Development (OECD) countries to adopt a New International Economic Order to correct the increasing imbalances in North–South trade. Unfortunately, the interdependence of the world trade system does not allow for the market intervention they seek, and the leading capitalist countries have declined to support their ambitious design.

A new factor emerged in the 1970s, as Third World countries came to realize that the Soviet Union had drawn level as a military superpower with the United States and that it was now able to exert its influence on a global scale. This development stood in contrast with the stalemate that has prevailed for so many years in Europe, dividing the ideological and military alignments of NATO from the Warsaw Pact countries. Europe remained stable but divided, while wars raged in Korea, Vietnam, and the Indian subcontinent, and between Israel and its Arab neighbors, Iran and Iraq. Numerous revolutions and civil wars seized hold in Asia, Latin America, and Black Africa, but not even in Korea and Vietnam were the superpowers drawn into direct conflict with each other. Even though there were no agreed lines of demarcation, as in Europe, the Soviet Union was not inclined to actively participate in what it still describes as "national liberation movements" that swept across the developing world.

Soviet policy since the Cuban crisis in 1962 has been marked by caution in such dangerous areas as Central America and the Middle East. It has looked for targets of opportunity in Africa and especially in Afghanistan. But the U.S. administration, once it had recovered from the Vietnam trauma, determined to assert its diplomatic and even its military force in areas vital to the Western economies, such as the Middle East and sub-Saharan Africa. The response of the United States and its European allies may have caused some surprise to the Soviet leaders. They believed, as Lenin himself had prophesied, that the struggle between the capitalist and the Communist systems would be decided in the world outside Europe. They still assumed that the road to Paris led through Shanghai, Calcutta, and Cairo. Events have not proved them right, even in Shanghai. Furthermore, if the struggle is indeed to be decided outside Europe, the force of economic and political advantage strongly lies with the West.

Changes in the Communist world have achieved remarkable proportions, too, but the Soviet achievement of nuclear parity with the United States and the Soviet Union's record in outer space have changed the strategic prospects of both superpowers. The considerable growth in the Soviets' naval and military strength has modified the global balance of power. It is of a different order from the standoff seen at the time of the Berlin crises of 1948 and 1959–1961 or of the Cuban missile confrontation of 1962. NATO can no longer rely upon a clear nuclear superiority to balance the Soviet superiority in conventional forces and even at sea NATO's superiority is now marginal.

As a consequence, far more attention is paid today to procedures of crisis management between the superpowers, and less confidence subsists within the Western alliance regarding the American nuclear guarantee of Europe's defense. There has been greater popular unease about the possible "early first use" of the American nuclear deterrent and about the U.S. contingency plans to initiate a limited nuclear war on European soil. This has been to the advantage of the Soviet Union, whose leaders are less influenced by alliance concerns or popular opinion. But it has also modified Marxist–Leninist doctrines about the inevitability of a war to destroy capitalist society. Doctrine now turns to the concept of peaceful existence, though it obviously does not imply that ideological neutrality or an eventual convergence of the two social systems will bring an end to the struggle between the superpowers. Moreover, the position of the Soviet Union has been gravely challenged as the ideological leader of the Communist world by the emergence of China, by the quarrel with Yugoslavia, and by movements of Eurocommunism in Italy, Spain, and even France.

A matter of much greater importance to the Soviet Union, as the self-appointed base of Marxist–Leninist orthodoxy, has been the undeniable evidence of weaknesses in the Soviet economy and its failure to modernize the high-technology, agriculture, and service sectors, and the poor productivity of its light industries and consumer manufacturing. In all these spheres, it has lagged far behind the market economies of the West, even in a decade of oil shocks and trade recession, and it even fell behind its own allies in Eastern Europe. Under Brezhnev and his immediate and ailing successors, Soviet society appeared to be stagnant and inflexible, unable to cope with its weakness except in handling military procurements. Action to cope with these problems has been proclaimed a first priority by the new and younger leadership of Gorbachev.

Weaknesses have become increasingly obvious in Eastern Europe, where Soviet control, although still effective, has become more difficult to exercise. Solidarity in Poland provided the best example of the new troubles to be faced. Nationalist unrest has been influenced to some extent by the continuing review process launched by the CSCE. Taking a longer view, nationalist rivalries within the Soviet Union are also beginning to develop, and, in the years ahead, ethnic tension might gravely intensify among the Soviet population.

The Soviet leadership can no longer operate according to its own timetable or its own reading of the correlation of forces that prompt political and economic change. The new Soviet leaders will probably heed arguments favoring the caution and prudence that have traditionally moved Soviet decision making. This caution has been reinforced by the determined re-armament program of the Reagan administration and by the superiority of U.S. military technology demonstrated in the SDI for ballistic missile defense.

Of course, the Soviet Union's economic weaknesses should not be exaggerated, given its vast size and resources. As was wisely said about Russia a century ago, it is never as strong or as weak as it sometimes looks. During the era that saw Khrushchev's "liberalizing" tendencies at home and the boisterous claims of "camaraderie" abroad, the Kremlin became dangerously overconfident in its dealings with the Kennedy administration. That led to the most serious crises in East–West relations, over the Berlin Wall in 1961 and the Cuban missile confrontation in 1962.

The changed relationships within the Western alliance and within the so-called Third World over the past twenty-five years have generated several surprises. They left the United States the leading superpower, but it was no longer unchallenged even within the Western world. In comparison, East–West relations have not greatly moved, though the Soviet Union managed to assert itself as an equal superpower in military terms. However, the Soviets' achievements in military strength have to be balanced against their failures in economic and ideological advance and the loss of China as a close associate. Clearly, the United States has remained the more important superpower, while at the same time the increase in Soviet military might has strengthened the determination of NATO to modernize its forces and to bolster the Western policy of containment.

It is time to ask how the changes in the world scene have succeeded in moving the United States, itself, to react. There have been elements of change as well as of continuity in U.S. policies. Which have predominated, American critics at home and overseas have asked, as the chafings and maneuvering of policies unrolled? In recent years Helmut Schmidt has been strongly critical of U.S. policies, charging that they too often ignored the outside world. Immediately after 1945 the principal emphasis was placed on cooperation with the Soviet Union. This suddenly changed into something close to all-out hostility during the early period of the cold war, between 1946 and 1953, largely in response to Stalin's actions in Prague, Berlin, and Korea. It was claimed at the time that there was not a stone in the NATO defense wall that Stalin himself had not provided.

High hopes of cooperation returned during Khrushchev's first years, starting with the Austrian State Treaty and the Soviet reconciliation with Yugoslavia. Hopes were rudely dashed in Budapest and Warsaw in 1956, and in the Berlin Wall and the Cuban missile crises in the 1960s. This led to the high-water mark of American interventionism, a step far removed from the old isolationism, with John Kennedy's proclamation that he was a Berliner and that wherever liberty was in danger, America would come to the rescue. The vigorous buildup of American deterrent forces was followed by an era of East–West détente, in which important nuclear agreements were signed, the German policy of Ostpolitik began, and the situation in Berlin was stabilized.

But in the 1960s American intervention in the war in Vietnam failed, with a consequent weakening of America's resolve to act as the world's policeman. Withdrawal symptoms were correctly interpreted by the Soviet Union, enabling them to extend without serious risk their own influence in southern Africa, the horn of Africa, and Afghanistan. But the late 1960s and early 1970s were also the years of the skillful diplomacy of Nixon and Kissinger. They exploited the Sino–Soviet rupture, and they extended American influence in the Middle East, especially in Egypt, at the expense of the Soviet Union. These achievements were won despite the Watergate catastrophe and the forced resignation of Richard Nixon. The policy of détente with the Soviet Union was sustained by President Ford in his summit meeting with Brezhnev at Vladivostok. Secretary Kissinger's tactics were less effective, however, in handling crises in Cyprus and the Indian subcontinent, or in dealing with America's restless allies in Europe itself. The allies were increasingly concerned by the U.S. handling of the economic consequences of the breakdown of the Bretton Woods system and of the oil shocks of the 1970s. The European case was not improved by the tendency in many countries to demand stronger American leadership and to then complain whenever it was exercised. It appeared that there was almost equal anxiety when the United States was at odds with the Russians and when it moved to establish better terms with them.

During the last two presidencies, of Carter and Reagan, European attitudes have reflected this ambivalence all too vividly. Carter was held to be too naive in handling East–West relations, and his chief adviser, Zbigniew Brzezinski, was compared unfavorably with Henry Kissinger. The failure to secure ratification of the SALT II treaty created alarm and despondency in Europe. President Carter was blamed for the neutron bomb fiasco and for a shifting of the balance of military power in Russia's favor. He was accused of attaching undue importance to human rights issues and failing to anticipate the revolution in Iran. The strongest criticism was voiced against his failure to release the imprisoned hostages in the U.S. Embassy in Teheran.

With the entry of the Reagan administration in 1981, U.S. policy appeared to move into a fundamental change and it was indeed so presented to public opinion. The rapid buildup of American military strength was justified by Reagan's denunciation of the "empire of evil." At the same time, the United States adopted economic policies that showed scant regard for the financial turmoil that beset so many of its allies, leaving their unemployment and currency arrangements in disarray. Yet another criticism surfaced in the European parliaments. This focused on the growing trend in the United States to resort to unilateral action. Concern was expressed about U.S. action in Central America. There was real anger, even among America's closest allies, when the United States exerted pressure on NATO members to suspend their profitable contracts to build the Siberian gas pipeline, yet, at the same time, promoted its own wheat sales with the Soviet Union. The U.S. intervention in Lebanon, followed by rapid withdrawal, undermined confidence in U.S. leadership. The quick success of the American intervention in Grenada drew popular applause in the United States but considerable criticism in Europe, especially in Britain. This was naturally resented by many Americans, because the United States had supported, at some political cost, the British invasion of the Falkland Islands. Behind all these criticisms lay dissatisfaction in Europe not so much with the substance as with the presentation of American global policy.

A more serious matter began to divide the Atlantic Alliance, and it reflected the growing divergence between American and European assessments of the Soviet threat. Opinion polls showed that Europeans still regarded détente as a realistic policy objective, while opinion in the United States disagreed. Though Europeans denounced the Soviet suppression of Solidarity and of the dissidents in the Soviet Union, they believed that a more tolerable relationship could be built between the democratic and the Communist regimes in Europe. This should include improved relations between West and East Germany and a better position in Berlin. European countries had to cooperate and trade with their neighbors in the Soviet Union and Eastern Europe, whereas the United States lived with no comparable pressures, in either social or commercial terms. The United States had, however, borne the main brunt of securing Western interests in the world outside the NATO defense area. Americans felt they had been cheated by the Russians during the period of détente. The Soviets had increased their military spending and nuclear strength in the 1970s, while the Americans had in effect stood still. Many Americans held that détente was a one-way street that favored the Russians, whereas the Europeans saw it as an essential accompaniment to defense and deterrence.

An outside observer might conclude from this review that there had been mounting discord within the Western Alliance and that détente had lost its support in the United States. Fortunately, this has not been the case. Opinion polls in Europe, and election results in countries such as West Germany and Britain, have reflected strong majority support for NATO and the U.S. connection. Even France under Mitterand has moved a considerable way in this direction. The polls have not supported the well-publicized views of peace movements, left-wing groups, or environmental enthusiasts. Major decisions taken by NATO, most recently to station U.S. cruise and Pershing missiles in Europe, were endorsed by most European electors. Transatlantic unity was sustained, partly because the military threat from the Soviet Union had increased and partly because the behavior of the Soviet Union in Afghanistan and in Poland had been so aggressive.

Basically, there was sustained confidence in the Alliance and in U.S. leadership. Although America's allies could never be taken for granted, the fact is that no American administration over the past forty years has attempted to change the policies of collective security and containment. A strong pattern of bipartisan support was built under Truman in the late 1940s, and it has never wavered. Even during the period of withdrawal and reluctance to undertake any new commitments, following the Vietnam War, there was no sign of a return to traditional isolationism. NATO has remained at the center of U.S. foreign policy, and the American military presence in Europe has been firmly maintained. Containment of the Soviet Union, although interpreted in different ways, has remained the guiding principle in East–West relations. Contacts with Moscow, though frequently limited to crisis management, have always been maintained, and arms control negotiations have been (and are today) being pursued, even in what has seemed to be an unpromising climate. President Reagan appeared to open his first term in a mood of relentless hostility to the Soviet Union, but he decided in his second term to schedule a series of summit meetings with Mikhail Gorbachev. Whatever may eventually come of his SDI, it is clear that he regards it as a step away from dependence upon the threat of mutual nuclear extinction.

Examples of continuity in U.S. foreign policy and of consistency with previous doctrines of Alliance unity can be cited in other fields. The Truman Doctrine of 1947 still moves U.S. policy toward Turkey and Greece, despite their own bilateral disputes. American support for Israel has not been swayed by the need to secure U.S. and Western interests in the Arab world, especially in Egypt and Saudi Arabia. The support has survived many differences with Israeli governments, not least over the Israeli incursion into Lebanon. President Carter has not, in my view, been given sufficient credit for the Camp David accords between Israel and Egypt or for his resolution in deterring possible Soviet moves in the Persian Gulf. His declaration of the Carter Doctrine justified the extension of American military protection and the provision of armed forces in the Gulf area. America's readiness to accept global responsibilities was further demonstrated in its involvement in the search for diplomatic solutions, first in Zimbabwe and now in Namibia and South Africa, even though Black Africa had never previously featured highly among American priority areas of concern. In Western Europe itself, American encouragement for a closer union, above all in the expanding European Community, has remained constant. So has American concern for development programs throughout the Third World, in spite of the more stringent and realistic approach taken to providing aid or supporting the UN and other organizations active in development work.

It will be clear, therefore, that I subscribe to Robert Osgood's thesis (chapter 2) that U.S. policies on essential issues over the past twenty-five years have focused more on continuity than change, despite the habit of incoming administrations of proclaiming a complete reversal of the policies of their predecessors. This may be a matter of regret in Moscow but not in NATO capitals. Because these policies have imposed far-reaching responsibilities and great burdens of military and economic expenditure upon the American people, it was most reassuring to hear John Rielly's well-documented message (chapter 11), that American public opinion has been resolute in endorsing Reagan's policies.

European participants in the Wingspread conference were usefully reminded of these underlying truths, though we are often distracted from them by day-to-day discords. Obviously, there is no cause to become complacent or to assume the indefinite continuation of present policy commitments, even though continuity is clearly in the national interest of the United States and its NATO allies. Martin Hillenbrand alerted SCAO to the many issues that could further divide the Atlantic Alliance (chapter 4), and Gil Klinger warned that there were still many unsolved problems in SDI (chapter 13). These were timely and valuable contributions to a lively debate. As the rapporteur of the conference, Walter Goldstein summarized (chapter 16) the points on which the participants agreed, however critically, with the principal finding: that most Alliance members believed that President Reagan's second term would preserve the principles of continuity embodied in U.S. foreign policy, and that the maintenance of Alliance unity would enjoy a high priority in the conduct of American diplomacy. Despite all the criticisms that were expressed, this was the optimistic conclusion SCAO finally affirmed.

2
Reagan's Foreign Policy in a Postwar Perspective

Robert E. Osgood

The place of the Reagan administration in postwar foreign policy can best be judged by assessing its impact on the leading continuities and changes in policy. The postwar policy of the United States contains great continuities but these continuities are combined with a pattern of discontinuity and this gives an erratic quality to the conduct of policy. Moreover, these continuities are modified by the impact of changes in the domestic and international environment of foreign relations that constrain the exercise of American power.

In its first term, the Reagan administration, following a familiar pattern of revival in the wake of retrenchment, essentially restored the central continuities against the weight of disillusionment and dissent generated by the war in Vietnam. In its second term, the administration faces new opportunities, despite new obstacles, to stabilize these continuities by adjusting the main lines of postwar policy to major domestic and international constraints that have emerged in the last two decades.

Whether it succeeds in this stabilization will depend as much on the somewhat unpredictable vicissitudes of Soviet behavior and international developments as on official intentions or even official performance. Equally, success or failure will depend on whether the nation, in its approach to foreign affairs, is prepared to come to terms with the constraints on American power while retaining the will to use this power discriminately.

The problem of adjusting the main lines of American policy to the growing constraints on American power is most acute with respect to the so-called Third World, but it has implications for relations with Western Europe as well. For, if one regards America's expanded global commitments as analogous to the holdings of an empire, it is clear that there is an integral relationship between the core and the extended empire. As in the case of the British Empire, the fate and fortunes of one react upon the other.

CONTAINMENT: THE CORE OF CONTINUITY

Even before the end of World War II the American public and its leaders had abandoned historic isolationism because they became convinced by U.S. involvement in two world wars in a quarter of a century that American security depended on the security of Western Europe and the Pacific. But, to support this expanded conception of security, Americans did not look toward projecting military power abroad. Rather, they counted on the Soviet Union, Great Britain, and even Nationalist China as partners in a global condominium against the revival of German and Japanese aggression (not Soviet expansionism), within their historic spheres of paramountcy. At the same time, the United States confined its security responsibilities to the Western hemisphere and the Atlantic and Pacific ocean barriers — all under the aegis of the United Nations and in accordance with the principles of the UN Charter and the Atlantic Charter that preceded it.

It took overwhelming evidence that Moscow was the opponent, not the supporter, of this new international order to transform the American postwar role from regional partner and impartial mediator of Soviet–British differences to major antagonist in a bilateral power struggle. Soviet troops remained in Azerbaijan until the United States exerted pressure in 1946; the Soviets pressed Turkey for bases, territorial concessions, and revision of the Montreux convention governing passage through the Dardanelles straits; the Soviets satellized all of Eastern Europe and they tried to dismantle the German industrial economy while resisting the negotiation of peace treaties to establish a new international order in Central Europe. Then came Britain's sudden withdrawal from its security commitments to Greece in the midst of the Greek civil war, which threatened to create another Communist satellite in that strategic position. To counter these crises took the creation of a Western defense treaty (the Brussels Pact) against the Soviets by the European victors and the 1947 economic crisis in Europe, which jeopardized the simultaneous achievement of defense and economic recovery. The Berlin blockade of 1949 completed the transformation by implementing the American role with the first overseas military commitment, the North Atlantic Treaty, precisely the kind of "entangling alliance" that Americans had sworn to avoid ever since the achievement of independence.

In this transformation of America's world role lie the origins and the principal perceptual and prescriptive elements of the grand strategy of containment, which has been the core of postwar American foreign policy. Containment, as defined by George Kennan, Dean Acheson, and others in the formative period 1947–1949, had committed the United States to preventing the forcible expansion of Soviet (and, until the 1973 Sino–American rapprochement, Chinese) influence and control by economically and militarily strengthening vulnerable countries and regions and by exerting countervailing pressure by military and other means against Communist force and subversion wherever they occur. The success of containment over a number of years (the number, originally conceived as around a decade, has been indefinitely extended) was expected to lead to the moderation of Soviet policy, the erosion of Soviet despotism and of the Soviet imperial domain, and perhaps the eventual collapse or reform of the whole Soviet system. Although faith in these happy endings has grown faint and remote, Acheson's objective of "negotiating from strength" on the basis of a military equilibrium, little more than a slogan in his time, has emerged in the era of arms negotiations as the popular and seemingly indispensable consolation for the continuing burdens of coexistence, especially the defense burden.

Containment is not the whole of American foreign policy. One significant part of postwar policy, for example, has developed outside the context of the cold war: American international trade and monetary policy. Nor is containment a set of prescriptions for dealing with all the contingencies that may arise. No strategy could usefully compress all the conflicting objectives and diverse circumstances relevant to the implementation of containment into a comprehensive plan. But, as a central design for combining the elements of American power to support a set of geopolitical and other interests, based on a coherent set of assumptions about the principal adversaries and allies and informed by certain established values, modes of behavior, and lessons of history, containment is as much a grand (that is to say, national, as opposed to just military, economic, or diplomatic) strategy as any great power or empire has pursued in peacetime. And it has been pursued with notable consistency throughout fundamental changes in the international environment.

Among the elements of consistency are the priorities of vital foreign interests. Aside from the Western hemisphere (where the Monroe Doctrine, in practice, has applied only to Central America and the Caribbean), the top priority remains, as at the end of World War II, the security of Western Europe and Japan. Between these vital interests there can be no doubt that the former still comes first, despite the astonishing economic ascendance of the Pacific Basin and the growing attention that East Asia has attracted. This is a function not only of historical ties and political affinity but also of the simple fact that Western Europe, an appendage of the Eurasian landmass containing divided Germany and isolated Berlin, is more vulnerable to Soviet aggression than the islands of Japan. Next in importance to the major democratic, industrial–technological allies in Europe and Asia is the Middle East, now extended to encompass Southwest Asia, which, at the outset of the cold war, long before the Organization of Petroleum Exporting Countries (OPEC) and the collapse of the shah's Iran or, for that matter, even the creation of Israel, was perceived to be integrally related to the security of Europe and of intrinsic economic and geopolitical importance.

More surprising, however, than the continuous application of containment to these areas of obvious geopolitical importance, which comprise the core of the American "empire," is the consistent application of containment to the vast heterogeneous colonial and postcolonial areas that comprise the extended empire in the Third World. For here containment has repeatedly been applied, especially through economic aid, arms aid, military intervention, and limited wars, to counter putative Communist threats (although only in the Cuban missile crisis a *direct* threat of *Soviet* arms) against countries that are *intrinsically* of less than vital interest to American security. It is a demonstration of the comprehensiveness as well as the consistency of containment that the politically turbulent, unstable Third World, despite the secondary or negligible geostrategic importance of the points of containment's application, has been the scene of America's greatest foreign troubles and controversies and the only scene of its military interventions and wars.

The continuity of containment in the Third World manifests the enduring intensity of a determining concept, rooted in the lessons of history, that underlies containment: the concept that the defenders of the international status quo and peace must deter or defeat piecemeal aggression by revisionist, expansionist powers, lest one conquest, whatever its intrinsic importance, lead to a succession of conquests, which, eventually, must be opposed at the risk of world war. The strength of this concept, derived from the period between the two world wars and, as a lesson against the appeasement of piecemeal aggression, encapsulated in the legend of Munich (largely true in its original context), lies in its fusion of a very expansive conception of American security interests with the transcendent goal of international order. Combining the appeals of American nationalism and idealism and translated into the theory of falling dominoes, the lesson of piecemeal interwar aggression has infused the power politics of containment with a distinctive intensity and persistence, without which it would be difficult to explain much of the history of postwar American foreign policy, including the Vietnam War.

Containment as a strategy of realpolitik has always gone against the grain of both American nationalism and American idealism, since it is so negative and defensive in connotation, lacks the convincing promise of victory over evil, and defines American policy in terms of managing, rather than transcending, power. Coupled with an underlying concept of international order, however, containment has had a compelling attraction. For this concept, in terms of which Americans have seen themselves discharging the global mission that the Soviets and international communism prevented the original United Nations from performing, has provided the indispensable moral sanction for containment. Consequently, although official spokesmen for American policy have always studiously avoided the word, containment in practice has been the foundation of a pervasive and enduring foreign policy consensus among those who influence, articulate, or run America's foreign relations.

This consensus has not prevented some fundamental controversies over the implementation of containment. The controversies centered upon military policy and commitments, precipitated by the Taft ring-wing neo-isolationists and the Wallace left-wing neo-isolationists before the Korean War; the "loss of China" and the conduct of the Korean War; the commitment of American troops to defend the forward line in Western Europe; the domestic sources of foreign adversities, evoked by McCarthyism; the bomber and missile gaps, antiballistic missiles (ABMs), and arms control; and, of course, the war in Vietnam. Equally significant have been the continual but less focused differences arising from the tension between anticommunism or anti-Sovietism and the liberal vision of America as the opponent of poverty, oppression, weapons, and war, a tension that periodically produces political eruptions, which are most severe inside the Democratic party.

The mark of the strength of the postwar consensus, however, is that, in spite of the controversies and tensions, containment in its principal outlines has been supported with remarkable consistency throughout a succession of crises and basic changes in international politics. Nevertheless, there is now a common supposition that Vietnam shattered this consensus and therefore destroyed the continuity of containment. Indeed, the Carter administration came into office articulating this supposition as the basis of its political mandate. Although President Carter himself turned to the revival of containment in the wake of the Iranian hostage crisis and after the Soviet invasion of Afghanistan, and President Reagan came into office with a mandate to banish the "Vietnam syndrome" and restore America's military strength and the will to use it, the supposition of a basic discontinuity in American foreign policy persists among the intelligentsia who interpret the twists and turns of America's foreign career.

To place the current of the Reagan administration's foreign relations in the stream of American foreign policy, one must first assess the place of Vietnam in this stream. For there can be no doubt that Vietnam is one of those formative episodes, like the Berlin airlift, the Greek–Turkish aid program, the Korean War, Sputnik, and the Cuban missile crisis, that have left a lasting impact on American foreign policy. And it is certain that the Reagan administration was both a reaction to and an influence on the legacy of that most traumatic of American wars.

THE PATTERN OF OSCILLATION

The place of Vietnam in postwar foreign policy must be assessed not only in relation to the continuities of this policy but also in relation to a pattern of apparent discontinuity, a repeated oscillation of effort and mood, which, paradoxically, is a continuing feature of American foreign policy in the cold war. Some characterize this oscillation as an alternation between extroversion and introversion; but a less extreme and more accurate designation of the polarity is the augmentation and retrenchment of containment, since the oscillation of effort and mood has never altered the nation's steadily increasing involvement in international affairs in support of containment.

This oscillation between the augmentation and the retrenchment of containment is driven by three forces: (1) the steady geographical expansion of U.S. security interests and commitments, formal or not, that support foreign interests against threats to them; (2) the perceived and, in a sense, actual gap between commitments and the power to support them that results from a chronic lag of resources, especially in military capabilities, behind the commitments; and (3) an alternation between relative complacency and alarm about the Soviet (until the 1970s, the Sino–Soviet) threat.

These sources of oscillation result from a tendency that marks the dynamics of other great powers and empires: the tendency of commitments to outrun resources in the pursuit of security. They result from periodic East–West crises, as the contending superpowers established spheres of influence in the developed regions and extended their reach into the undeveloped and less stable areas of the world. But the oscillation is amplified by some distinctive features of the American approach to foreign relations: the historic reluctance to sustain security investments at a high rate in peacetime, the surprised and militant reaction to adversaries who disturb the assumptions that sanction this reluctance, and the longing to return to "normalcy" after each exertion in response to a disturbance. It is also amplified by distinctive American democratic institutions: the organized popular base of foreign policy, the pervasive role of the media, and the dominant role of presidential elections, especially when they correspond to a shift in mood and effort.

The resulting pattern of oscillation is a central theme in America's postwar foreign relations, as successive new administrations, and sometimes the same administration, have sought to narrow the gap between commitments and power by various strategies of augmentation or retrenchment. The commitments–power gap was created at the outset of the cold war with the unprecedented extension of U.S. commitments in the period 1947–1950, while the postdemobilization defense budget was frozen at around $13 billion. The Korean War precipitated the first material augmentation of containment: a fourfold increase in defense spending and the creation of an American-commanded allied armed force to protect Europe, followed by the emplacement of six American divisions on German soil and West Germany's incorporation into NATO. But the war-born alarm soon subsided, and President Eisenhower came into office with a mandate to support containment more effectively at less cost and less risk of involving American forces in local wars. To achieve this goal of retrenchment, his administration declared greater dependence on nuclear retaliation as a substitute for local resistance, reinforced deterrence with a network of alliances in Asia and the northern tier of the Middle East, and engaged in the first incipient détente with the Soviet Union: the 1957 summit meeting, where the short-lived "spirit of Geneva" was born.

Retrenchment was followed by alarm, however, with the Soviet orbiting of Sputnik, the concomitant fear of an imminent missile gap, Khrushchev's instigation of the Berlin crisis of 1958–1961, the shooting down of the American U-2 spy plane over Russia, growing troubles with Castro, the onset of the Congo crisis, and Nasser's turn to Moscow for arms. The shock of these events prepared the way for President Kennedy to come into office proclaiming his determination to restore American power and prestige. To augment containment he strengthened America's already superior strategic strike force, proclaimed top priority for the creation of limited-war capabilities to fight "wars of national liberation," and launched the Alliance for Progress, a program of economic and sociopolitical development to strengthen the underdeveloped areas of Latin America against Castroism.

However, the seeming success of augmentation, manifested in the military buildup and the successful surmounting of crises in Berlin, Cuba, and the Congo, set the stage for retrenchment again. The Cuban missile crisis became the catalyst for a turn toward arms control and the atmospheric nuclear test ban, and for another try at détente, encouraged by the Soviets for their own reasons: catching up with American strategic power, tending to troubles in Eastern Europe, and waging a mounting conflict with China. On a wave of complacency, President Johnson took office determined to avoid foreign distractions while he concentrated on domestic social and economic improvements. But America's escalating intervention in the Vietnam War, undertaken more to vindicate the interwar lessons by preventing falling dominoes than to support any intrinsic security interests, thwarted his design.

But the Vietnam War, unlike the Korean War, did not precipitate a shift to the augmentation of containment. Materially and politically, it was a great distraction from global containment efforts and the source of further expansion of the gap between commitments and military capabilities. The nation's reaction against the exorbitant costs of a losing war for abstract anti-Communist axioms, seemingly unrelated to intrinsic interests, assured a deeper plunge into retrenchment. It fell to President Nixon and Henry Kissinger to extricate the country from the war and then to implement retrenchment while trying to limit it. They achieved this task with remarkable success, although the achievement began to unravel during President Ford's administration.

President Nixon, responding to popular and congressional pressure, aimed to close the interests–power gap at a reduced level of military effort and foreign military involvement. With the Nixon Doctrine, he put vulnerable Third World countries on notice that they would have to rely more on their own efforts than on U.S. intervention for security, and he expanded arms aid as a stimulus to self-reliance. To support America's growing security concerns in the Middle East, as the British relinquished their historic role, he elevated the shah's Iran into a regional security surrogate. To blunt the Soviet threat, he and Kissinger orchestrated a global détente with Moscow, based on rapprochement with the People's Republic of China, the pursuit of strategic arms limitations (SALT) on the basis of acknowledged military parity, and a somewhat uneven effort to use SALT and expanded grain trade as a lever to secure Soviet restraint in the Third World.

Once again, however, American retrenchment was accompanied by Soviet expansion. Moscow, continuing its massive military buildup, albeit within the bounds of SALT I, seemed determined to go far beyond the American conception of parity (that is, equal capacity to deliver unacceptable retaliatory destruction) to achieve counterforce superiority. With the unexpected sudden collapse of the Portuguese empire, it seemed to be in a position for the first time to extend its influence, with the help of Cuban troops and East European technicians, into a huge region not adjacent to the homeland, beginning with the victory of the People's Liberation Army in Angola in 1975. But this time, unlike the provocation at the end of the Eisenhower administration, these blows to America's global influence and prestige, far from fueling another shift to augmentation, touched off America's most sweeping retrenchment effort, a delayed reaction to the shock of Vietnam, when Jimmy Carter assumed the presidency on a platform of moral redemption and retreat from containment. Warning against the "inordinate fear of communism" that had led the country "to embrace any dictator who joined us in our fear," Carter promised to reduce the defense budget even more substantially while concentrating on the "global agenda" of international reform to address the needs of the Third World in the presumably dominant North–South axis of international politics.

Within a year, however, the Carter administration began shifting from the retrenchment to the augmentation of containment in response to the resurgent fear of Soviet expansion and the commitments–power gap that had grown during the 1970s. The stimulus for this shift was what Zbigniew Brzezinski called the "arc of crisis" — Soviet alignment with Mengistu's Marxist–Leninist regime in Ethiopia, Soviet establishment of a military client in South Yemen, Soviet alliance with North Vietnam, and, finally, the invasion of Afghanistan to replace an unreliable puppet regime — together with the Iranian revolution and the protracted hostage crisis.

In response to the resurgent fear of Soviet military strength and expansion, the Carter administration reversed the decade-long decline of real defense expenditures, appealed for a steady increase in NATO defense expenditures by all its members, agreed to emplace new intermediate-range missiles in Europe, announced the Carter Doctrine proclaiming an American commitment to defend the oil fields of the Gulf, called for a Rapid Deployment Force to support the doctrine, imposed a grain embargo and other sanctions on the Soviet Union, and moved toward a "strategic relationship" with the People's Republic of China.

Ronald Reagan, like John F. Kennedy, rode into office on a wave of public support for the augmentation of containment, while his predecessor tried to justify the case for retrenchment. Because of his promises to restore the military balance and the national economy, to revive the nation's confidence in the justice of its foreign mission, and to reassert the support of foreign commitments, Reagan's electoral mandate was to revitalize containment in a second and even more ambitious peacetime augmentation. But he would have to discharge this mandate under domestic and international constraints on American power that Kennedy did not have to consider.

In reviewing this pattern of oscillation, one can see that although the level and intensity of U.S. commitment to its major allies have been far steadier than those to Third World areas, American policies toward the European allies were affected by the cycles of augmentation and retrenchment even when the triggering events were located in the Third World. When America's Third World (in NATO parlance, out-of-area) involvements posed the threat of distracting American concerns from Europe, interfering with Europe's special East–West interests (for example, trade), or entangling the allies in American conflicts, these cycles had the most intense effect on transatlantic relations.

The pattern of oscillation has been even more closely correlated to shifting estimates of relative Soviet military strength. In a sense, the East–West military relationship has become the central political issue of the cold war. Thus, surges of increased defense expenditures have been the primary means of augmenting containment, and arms control has become the primary means of retrenchment. Both have a direct impact on U.S.–European relations because of Europe's sense of vulnerability and helplessness and its dependence on America's nuclear protectorate.

It was feared that America's Third World involvement would impair U.S.–European relations and result in a reduction of American resources in Western Europe. But this has not happened, except in the minds of those who consider the American security efforts on behalf of NATO and Japan excessive anyway.

One thing is clear about the impact of the Third World on U.S.–European relations. Whatever the specific European concerns about a particular shift toward augmentation or retrenchment, the pattern of oscillation itself is vastly disturbing for Europeans who feel that their very survival and their peace of mind depend on the will of the United States.

CONSTRAINTS ON AMERICAN POWER

The regularity of the pattern of oscillation in American postwar policy naturally leads to the presumption that yet another period of retrenchment will follow the post-Vietnam Reagan period of augmentation—perhaps even in Reagan's second term—unless or until some real or imagined East-West crisis revives national alarm about the Soviet threat. But the future, beginning with the role of Reagan's second administration, is more complicated than a simple extrapolation from the past. Two very large factors affecting the implementation of containment, in addition to President Reagan himself, complicate the pattern of U.S. foreign relations: the mounting constraints on American and on Soviet power.

The basic constraints on American power have been emerging for decades and have little to do with the impact of the Vietnam War, but the war is a powerful catalyst accentuating the effect of these constraints. The constraints are so familiar that a list will suffice. Some of them impinge directly on U.S. and NATO defense efforts and the cohesion of the Western alliance:

- Loss of American primacy and leverage in the international economic system
- Loss of American strategic military superiority and the Soviet achievement of parity-plus
- The concomitant problem of maintaining the credibility, especially in allied eyes, of extended nuclear deterrence, that is, the deterrence of an attack upon Western Europe by virtue of the American pledge to initiate the use of nuclear weapons against a conventional attack that cannot be conventionally withstood
- Rise in the Western democracies of the organized antinuclear, antidefense movement
- Onset of domestic and international economic maladies: inflation, unemployment, deficits, trade imbalances, and the structural deficiencies of the European economies
- The growing role of arms negotiations as a sanction for defense policies, coupled with the great difficulty of achieving arms agreements that directly affect the military balance

The constraints on American power in the Third World are equally limiting:

- Disorder of much of the Third World that springs from the instability of regimes; increased incidence of local national conflicts and the growth of crosscutting ethnic and religious ferment; rise of terrorism; volatility of shifting alignments and coalitions, notably in the Middle East; and absence of a political and social infrastructure for economic stability and political cohesion

- Propensity toward xenophobic nationalism that often takes the form of anti-Americanism
- Vulnerability of some remaining friendly oligarchic regimes to revolutionary anti-American replacements
- Overwhelming debts and their possibly adverse internal and external political consequences

These multiple constraints are not just problems. They are conditions that restrict American influence and access, and they reduce American scope for diplomatic maneuver and political leverage. Vietnam has had the same effect.

Indirectly, Vietnam has contributed to the spread of nuclear pacifism in the United States and Western Europe. The organized dissent that the war evoked found a congenial medium of expression in the peace movement and also in the ecology, antiracist, and feminist movements in the United States. Exported to the publics, media, and universities of Western Europe, organized antinuclear sentiment found more fertile soil and had more influence on government policies than in the United States. Its influence emerged with surprising force during the intermediate nuclear force (INF) deployment crisis. Despite the failure of its anti-INF program and its subsequent incoherence and political inefficacy, especially in West Germany, where it might have had the greatest effect, the peace movement remains a factor that governments must take into account in handling military and East–West issues. This is particularly true with respect to arms control, which has become an indispensable sedative to calm nuclear anxieties and gain acceptance for defense programs, and which will continue to play a key role in U.S.-European relations.

A more pervasive and enduring influence of the Vietnam War on American foreign policy has been exerted through its impact on two American institutions, Congress and the professional military. Vietnam dissent stimulated a reassertion of the congressional role in foreign policy and a host of legislative restrictions on presidential conduct of foreign relations (of which the War Powers Resolution is the most prominent) that seem likely to confuse and impede executive initiatives and programs, especially in foreign assistance, defense programs, and use of force, long after their bitter origins have faded from memory. The trauma of a lost war has reinforced the familiar reluctance of the military to use force except under the most favorable and therefore least likely conditions: advance assurance of popular support; an enemy that eschews guerilla and revolutionary warfare; precise and unchanging political objectives that can be readily achieved by military victory in a short, decisive war; no sanctuaries to protect the enemy's logistics and staging areas; and no local political considerations to interfere with military operations. This all-or-nothing attitude is institutionalized in military training, organization, operational doctrine, and weapons and equipment, which, as before the Vietnam War, are designed to fight a conventional war in Europe rather than a variety of possible small wars in the Third World.

Vietnam's most direct effect upon U.S. foreign policy, however, has been its impact on public and official attitudes toward the use of force in the Third World specifically and, more problematically, toward an active global involvement in general. The common interpretation of this impact is that it has "shattered" the whole postwar "consensus" that has undergirded containment. Obviously, considering the continuity of American policy toward East–West relations and the principal American allies, this is, at the least, a geographical exaggeration. But is it accurate even with respect to the use of force in the Third World?

In the narrowest sense the war did not show anything about the American approach to the use of force except under the distinctive conditions of this particular war, which are unlikely to be replicated. It showed that there is a limit to the effectiveness of American armed forces against a militant revolutionary country fighting a civil war against a weak and fragmented regime; and that there is a limit to the price Americans are willing to pay, particularly in terms of casualties and the duration of the war, to vindicate the postwar consensus about stopping piecemeal Communist aggression. It shows the limits of this price when the war is fought for intrinsically far less than vital interests in order to establish the independence of an alien government that probably could not have sustained itself, despite the military victories achieved on its behalf, unless the United States were willing to bolster and protect it indefinitely.

Something like this proposition may stick in the national consciousness as the decisive lesson of Vietnam. If so, it will constitute a significant qualification to the open-ended conception of containment that prevailed before. It will make containment more selective and discriminating.

The selective nature of the perceived lessons of Vietnam, however, is further indicated by what we know about the aftermath of the war. The North Vietnam victory has brought great physical suffering and oppression to South Vietnam and, indirectly, even greater suffering and oppression to the Cambodian people. This verifies the moral import of the postwar consensus that piecemeal aggression must be opposed. Although North Vietnam quickly extended its rule to Cambodia and Laos, dominoes did not fall beyond these historic Vietnamese targets. Indeed, the outcome of the war created barriers to dominoes falling. Most significantly, it strengthened

ASEAN as the Third World's most effective regional organization and a counterpoise to Vietnamese (or, for that matter, Soviet and Chinese) expansion, with an incipient military security role. The North Vietnamese victory did enable the Soviets to pick up an important strategic asset in Cam Ranh Bay, but it also consolidated the Sino–Soviet split, triggered the Sino–American alignment, and arrayed Chinese military and diplomatic influence against further Vietnamese expansion. America's loss of the war — and, even more, its public reaction to the loss — did diminish its reputation in some foreign quarters as an invincible and prudent protector of freedom. It may have encouraged the Soviets to capitalize on the opportunities of the 1970s to project their influence in the arc of crisis. But the war did not do permanent damage to America's position in the world. It did not transform the bipolar global balance of power. Subsequent developments have proved American resilience and the continuity of containment.

It seems more accurate, therefore, to speak of the qualification, the refinement and moderation, of the postwar consensus underlying containment than to pronounce its destruction. One does not need the polls that purport to measure opinions of the mass public to see that containment is now regarded more selectively, especially with respect to the direct use of American armed force. This applies to prevailing perceptions of the interests for which the United States might use force, the nature and magnitude of the Soviet threat to these interests, the kinds of contingencies that might justify intervention, and the efficacy or utility of American armed force in small wars and lesser military encounters. Nevertheless, as American involvement in Central America shows, containment and its basic rationale are very much intact, in opposition to the establishment of Communist, or Marxist–Leninist, regimes in countries that might become agents of Soviet interests. The domestic political process, as on previous occasions, reflects differences about how to implement containment but not about the need to do so.

If containment is now more discriminating, and its discrimination reflects the complexities and constraints of the international environment, this may mean that the containment consensus is stronger, not weaker. But it could also mean simply that, although the nation wants containment, it is no longer willing to pay the price for it. In this case, the containment consensus will prove to be an empty abstraction when the next real crisis that requires the use of force occurs.

CONSTRAINTS ON SOVIET POWER

Whether post-Vietnam qualifications to the containment consensus are adapted to the real conditions of American security or are merely a hollow echo of the pre-Vietnam consensus will depend a great deal upon the nature of Soviet behavior. Heretofore, the Soviets have displayed a talent for alarming the United States into sudden augmentations of containment. Perhaps the American reaction has been hyperbolic because of a preceding neglect of defense or unrealistic expectations of Soviet restraint; but, in part, the reaction has been due to the simple fact that what the Soviets regard as normal behavior, like taking advantage of détente to catch up with Western positions of influence in the Third World, is regarded as a threat to world peace by the United States. A combination of sobered American expectations and moderated Soviet behavior, in both cases strengthened by the lessons of the rise and fall of détente, would go far to overcome the extremities of the postwar pattern of oscillation.

If there is a moderation of Soviet behavior, it will not be because of a change of basic strategy, which still aims to replace U.S. global influence with its own, but, as in the case of containment, because Moscow, in pursuing its grand strategy, must come to terms with the growing constraints on its power. In the past decade the constraints on Soviet power have become as familiar as those on American power, and need only to be listed:

- Politically insoluble industrial, technological, and agricultural inefficiency
- Geostrategic encirclement of the Soviet heartland by prospering, technologically advanced Western democracies allied to the United States, together with an alienated, modernizing China, which confronts the Soviets with the prospect of a two-front war
- Problems of contiguous empire in Eastern Europe because of political dissidence, national disaffection, economic stagnation, demands for Soviet help, and the attraction of Western societies
- A growing burden of extended empire in the Third World because of costly subsidies, unreliability of clients and their record of defection, inability to compete with Western political uses of economic aid, loss of ideological appeal, absence of the Soviet economic model's attraction, and emergence of anti-Communist, anti-Soviet insurgencies
- Political turbulence and volatility of the Third World, which impedes stable alignments and effective diplomatic intervention, and which makes even indirect military intervention risky
- Islamic opposition to Soviet ideology and power, accentuated by the Soviet effort to suppress Afghanistan
- The prospect of American counterintervention and the continuing Soviet avoidance of local involvements that might lead to a direct military encounter with U.S. armed forces

Only in the steady generation and maintenance of military power — nuclear, conventional, and chemical; intercontinental, European, and Third World — does the Soviet Union excel. But under the constraints of using this enormous panoply of armed force, the Soviets must exploit their asset primarily as a political and psychological lever.

Moscow is not about to surrender its contiguous empire or retrench its extended empire. No matter what renewed efforts it may devote to revitalizing the Soviet economy (a goal it is unlikely to achieve), Moscow will not diminish its foreign concerns. It remains determined to gain parity with the United States and then surpass it in the global "correlation of forces." To this end it will continue to exploit every opportunity to diminish American influence and advance its own where the risks and costs seem minimal, whether in the uses of nuclear intimidation and indigenous nuclear pacifism to neutralize Western Europe and divide the European allies from their transatlantic protector, or in supporting, directly or through proxies, anti-American regimes and movements in the Third World.

Nevertheless, faced with the aggregate of formidable constraints on Soviet power, which have grown in proportion to the steady geographical expansion of Soviet global commitments and involvements, there is evidence that Moscow feels even more overcommitted than Washington. This sense of overcommitment reinforces the inherent Soviet caution in implementing expansionist propensities.

Therefore, it is not unrealistic to ask whether constraints on both of the superpowers may not provide the basis for the kind of moderation of their competition that would foster the stabilization of containment. To answer this question we must first consider the requirements of stabilized containment and then turn to an assessment of the Reagan administration to determine the prospects of its adapting containment to these requirements.

REVISED REQUIREMENTS OF CONTAINMENT

In the central international system of U.S.-Soviet and U.S.-allied relations, the stabilization of containment requires a less erratic approach to U.S.-Soviet relations and a far less fluctuating defense effort. It requires an arms control approach of realistic, limited expectations, serving as a complement, not an alternative, to defense policies, and yet an approach that can justifiably alleviate the nuclear anxieties of democratic nations. These requirements are integrally related to the crux of America's foreign strength: the maintenance of allied cohesion and cooperation, notwithstanding the differentiation of national perspectives and their articulation by increasingly security-conscious publics. Of course, this entails far more than a military requirement, but the military requirement is nonetheless of primary political significance. It is a long-standing requirement that recent military and political developments have made more urgent, and that is to substantially reduce the dependence of NATO's deterrence on the first use of nuclear weapons.

It is in the Third World that the requirements of containment have changed the most. There the classic concept of containment must now be qualified by recognition of the more complicated realities of the structure and dynamics of contemporary international politics, as well as by the lessons of Vietnam, with which they coincide. The constraints on both of the superpowers in the Third World, particularly those that spring from the diffusion of power, the instability of regimes, and the volatile, unstructured nature of intraregional politics, refute the image of dominoes and the assumption that one fallen domino necessarily leads to another. It should be clear that the domino analogy, shown to be of limited applicability even in the wake of the United States' worst defeat, is a misleading simplification (though never completely wrong) of a much more varied and complicated dynamic of countervailing forces. It is equally misleading to think of the Third World as a homogeneous area of underdeveloped nationalists, full of "vacuums" waiting to be filled by one superpower or the other. It is more like a disparate, fragmented aggregation of heterogeneous countries and groups of countries and shifting indigenous balances of power, sustained or upset by independent-minded regimes that the superpowers can influence only marginally for limited ends.

These realities do not mean that the Third World will cease to be the most volatile and dangerous arena in the cold war. Quite the contrary. The Third World will be full of "low-intensity conflicts," small interstate wars, state and substate terrorism, subversion, and insurgency. Third World governments will seek aid for their faltering economies and hard-pressed military establishments, and they will seek extraregional help against their regional adversaries. But, at the same time, they will seek to limit their dependence on their helpers by keeping their diplomatic options open and sometimes playing off one superpower against the other. And always they will be conscious of the utility of appealing to the sensitivities of world opinion to constrain superpower intervention.

For the implementation of containment this means that U.S. military security will depend less on waging large-scale conventional wars or conventional revolutionary wars, as in Korea and Indochina respectively, than on supporting local forces indirectly and conducting raids, rescues, and counterterrorist, peacemaking, or peacekeeping operations. Even more, containment will depend on all those measures short of armed force that one might call *micropolitics*: military assistance, economic aid, covert action, internal political persuasion, preventive diplomacy, diplomatic mediation, propaganda, and public diplomacy.

These are challenging requirements, which will be particularly difficult to meet because they call for major institutional adjustments on the part of Congress and the military. But they are quite different from the kinds of challenge that are evoked by the conventional image of overcommitment.

This image, in effect, adds up all the commitments and vital interests in one column and all the resources and elements of power in another and finds, inevitably, that the latter is inadequate to support the former. This procedure is misleading because it fails to differentiate the elements of power and their relevance to supporting vital interests. It is also misleading as applied to the adequacy of military power, since it seldom takes into account the nature and intensity of the threats to commitments, the kinds of contingencies in which these threats could and must be opposed with armed force, or the risk that any such contingencies would occur simultaneously.

Not that the danger of overcommitment is an illusion; it has played a central role in the decline of empires. But, to respond intelligently to the danger, one must come to grips with the complexity of the real nature and sources of the disparity between vital interests and the nation's capacity to support them. Without undertaking this monumental task here, it may be sufficient to suggest, on the basis of the preceding analysis, that the United States, in strict semantic construction, is not dangerously overcommitted. Its principal commitments serve as deterrents. They represent vital security interests. Therefore, it is unnecessary as well as unwise to try to diminish these commitments. In some respects, particularly with respect to conventional military strength in Europe and foreign assistance to the Third World, the United States is underpowered, rather than overcommitted. In operational military strategy, tactics, and weapons, the United States does not make the best use of military resources, but this is not the result of a geographical misallocation. There is no need, and it would be unwise, to substantially draw down forces in Europe in order to support Third World interests. The most serious problem is not overcommitment or either inadequate or misallocated power; it is too little of the right kind of power. That is, some elements of U.S. armed power are not sufficiently developed and directed to support the more challenging requirements of containment, especially those pertaining to grey-area situations in the Third World. This is primarily a matter of quality, not quantity. The deficiency is rooted in the American approach to the use of force. It is embedded in the hyperconservatism of the U.S. military establishment.

THE REAGAN ADMINISTRATIONS:
FIRST AND SECOND TERMS

Whatever else it may be known for in the sweep of postwar American foreign policy, the Reagan administration will be known for the revitalization of containment after the nation's deepest retrenchment. Actually, neither the American economy nor the American defense posture is so strengthened as to amount to a transformation. Arguably, the deficit, the low growth rate, and the high rate of unemployment now endanger the economy no less than inflation (or "stagflation") did before. The results of the defense buildup, which President Carter started, are notable chiefly for the extraordinary input of expenditures in return for only marginal increases in outputs relevant to coherent strategic objectives. Yet, undoubtedly, the nation's feeling of restored strength and confidence following the doubt and guilt induced by Vietnam, personified by the patriotic optimism and forceful manner of President Reagan in contrast to the anguished indecisiveness of President Carter, warrants the impression of revitalization. The question is whether the change of mood and perception is accompanied by the kinds of changes of substance that will lead to the effective support of containment on a steady basis or whether they are merely an interlude of euphoria preceding a lapse into complacency before the next alarm.

This point of speculation is quite different from the kind of worry that the Reagan administration has almost universally evoked among its critics, especially during its first term: the worry that President Reagan is a bellicose ideologue leading the country into a dangerous global confrontation with international communism. A number of American observers, unlike anxious European politicians and journalists, have by now come to the conclusion that the bellicosity was purely or mostly rhetorical. But even this judgment is questionable, because it is never based on a comparison with the cold-war rhetoric of other administrations and it always relies on only two or three of Reagan's phrases lifted out of context. It takes no account of some carefully prepared statements by the president and Secretary of State Shultz that were intended to reassure Soviet leaders, as well as Western nations, of American dedication to peaceful coexistence based on prudent reciprocal restraints and negotiated resolution of conflicting interests. Of course, the president's general style and manner in his effort to revive containment, the apparent but exaggerated influence of the Republican anti-Communist right-wing faction on his administration, and most important, the international context of his effort (the demise of the U.S.–Soviet détente) do lend credence to the popular characterization of his militant rhetoric. But they also exaggerate reality. Washington observers have now concluded that the Reagan style and rhetoric are shifting toward moderation and that the initial disparity between rhetoric and substance conveyed a misleading impression of the substantive change between the first and second terms.

What is undeniable is that no administration has throughout its tenure shown a greater disparity between the popular impression of intentions it conveyed and the actual means it employed, although critics of President Kennedy have emphasized the contrast between the expansively bold promise of his inaugural address and the bland performance of his remaining term of office. The continuity and the moderation of the administration's operational policies and actions, from the outset, have been in marked contrast to its image of reckless militancy. Consider the evidence:

- Immediate renunciation of the punitive grain embargo against the USSR
- Early resumption of arms negotiations as the centerpiece of U.S.–Soviet relations and as an indispensable concession to West European opinion during the INF deployment crisis
- Continued adherence to the ABM treaty and the SALT I Interim Agreement, as well as to the unratified SALT II agreement, despite evidence of Soviet noncompliance
- Explicit de-linkage of arms negotiations from Soviet behavior in the Third World
- Marked deference to European allied opinion and sensitivities as compared to the public hectoring by some previous administrations
- Continuing emphasis on foreign economic assistance as a crucial instrument of policy in the Third World
- Strong and consistent opposition to trade protectionism
- Continued commitment to the "peace process" in the Middle East, combined with reluctance to take initiatives that put Washington ahead of the willingness of regional states and movements to resolve their own differences
- Reliance upon patient, low-profile diplomacy to counter Soviet and Cuban influence in Africa, with a flexibility extending even to a congressionally blocked move to provide military assistance to the Marxist–Leninist regime in Mozambique
- Restrained, covert assistance to Afghan rebels and reliance on ASEAN to assist non-Communist supporters of anti-Vietnam forces in Cambodia
- Rejection of retaliation against the USSR for the Korean Airlines shoot-down (KAL 007 in 1983) or for the Beirut hijacking of an American airliner

Against this evidence there is Secretary Haig's expressed desire to go to the Cuban "source" of Central American troubles. But he was dissuaded from this course by his own department. There is also the Soviet pipeline and economic sanctions controversy, one of the very few instances of right-wing influence on foreign relations (the influence of Richard Perle on arms control positions being the most notable). But Secretary Shultz finessed this issue, and it remains an anomaly in the general disposition to put good relations with allies ahead of punishing the Soviet Union. The decision to put U.S. Marines into Lebanon to help resolve the disorder created by the Israeli invasion may have been ill-advised, but their withdrawal by President Reagan after the terrorist bombing of their Beirut headquarters is a unique example of the prompt voluntary extrication of American armed forces from an unsuccessful operation. In the aftermath of the aborted Lebanese interposition, the brief rescue operation in Grenada was widely welcomed in the United States as an action restoring the credibility of American will to use force against Communist incursions in America's backyard, although it was made easier to accept by the rescue of American citizens and a regional Caribbean appeal; but, considering the trivial opposition or risk of counterintervention, it came about as close to immaculate intervention as any president could hope for.

If there is an important exception to the disparity between tough pronouncements and moderate action, it would be in Central America. Yet even this case is hard to make, considering the limits on American military personnel in El Salvador to help a government fighting Marxist–Leninist insurgents, and considering the eschewing of direct intervention or a "military solution" in Nicaragua, in which Soviet and Cuban agents pervade the government. Wise or unwise, successful or unsuccessful, the nature and extent of American involvement in containing Communist influence in Central America is no more than any administration would have undertaken and considerably less than the Eisenhower, Kennedy, and Johnson administrations did undertake in Guatemala, Cuba, and the Dominican Republic, respectively.

Some see in second-term official statements of support to "freedom fighters," that is, to insurgencies fighting Marxist or Communist regimes aligned with the USSR, a sweeping new Reagan Doctrine. Although these statements do evince a reaffirmation of America's pre-Vietnam opposition to actual or prospective Soviet clients in the Third World, made more acceptable by the existing rather than contrived initiatives of armed anti-Communist forces, they do not mark a global innovation in containment strategy. Indeed, what is notable is the enhanced constraints on the direct and open use of force under which the implementation of this reaffirmation operates. Equally notable is the pragmatic, differentiated approach to dealing with actual insurgencies, judging from the Reagan administration's long-suffering efforts to secure a diplomatic resolution of the war in Angola, its diplomatic and military assistance to the avowed Marxist–Leninist regime in Portugal against anti-Communist insurgents, and its reluctance to provide tangible support to forces that oppose the pro-Vietnam, pro-Soviet regime imposed on Kampuchea (formerly Cambodia).

In the entire record of Reagan's foreign policy there is one, but only one, instance of an adventurous departure from the norm: the Strategic Defense Initiative, which the president proclaimed in March 1983. But this initiative, preeminently a personal one, amounted to endorsement of an ultimate goal more radically pacific (some have said pacifist) than any of Reagan's predecessors ever dreamed of: defensive systems that would make nuclear weapons "impotent and obsolete" by protecting the national populations of the United States, its allies, and the Soviet Union from nuclear attack.

Those who have focused their concern about Reagan's foreign policy on its alleged bellicosity and trigger-happiness have worried about the wrong thing. A more plausible worry, which conservatives (not just ideological right-wingers) are now beginning to voice, is that tough talk has become a surrogate for expedient action; that President Reagan's popularity reflects the public's inclination to savor the impression of national forcefulness without incurring any risks or costs to back it up; and that there will come a day of reckoning for which neither the government nor the public is prepared. Furthermore, now that the president has presumably become the champion of peace, they worry that he will let revitalized containment erode under the cover of futile pacifist gestures. Might not the old style and rhetoric, they might well wonder, be better suited to maintaining consistent support for the harsh requirements of containment?

Probably this latter concern is no more warranted than the former, if only because the realities of international politics are as uncongenial to a revival of the mid-1970s détente as to a recapitulation of the late-1970s arc of crisis. At the November 1985 Geneva summit meeting of Reagan and Gorbachev, President Reagan once again refuted his belittlers by managing to strike an appropriate stance of hopeful, pragmatic *modus vivendi*, while keeping expectations of a revived 1970s-style détente suitably low. One must doubt that this achievement foreshadowed a comprehensive arms agreement or a resolution of Third World conflicts. If regional differences are resolved, it will not be by formal agreements but by tacit mutual constraints that lead to their erosion over time. An arms agreement, based on a partial, time-phased limitation of strategic defense and antisatellite weapons in return for a reduction of strategic offensive weapons, coupled with traded limitations among asymmetrical advantages, may eventually result from protracted negotiations, although probably not in Reagan's term of office. But the technical complexities and practical difficulties of achieving such an agreement have never been greater, and the experience of SALT I and II portends a minimal prospect that an actual agreement will produce a lasting stabilization of the strategic balance in the face of the rapid pace of inexorable technological innovation.

This means that the management of containment will depend heavily on coping with the domestic and international politics of an East–West *modus vivendi* that lacks the gratification of formal accommodations. Reagan, in his second term, shows promise of mastering this task, with the help of a national outlook chastened by the harsh experiences of a lost war and a failed détente. But even Reagan's achievement, if the promise is fulfilled, will not fully answer the questions this paper poses: Has the Reagan administration, in its adjustment to the rather different international realities from the ones it expected when it came into office, reached a point at which it is ready and able to adapt the means and perhaps even the rhetoric of containment to the constraints on American, as well as on Soviet, power? Have the American people reached a point in their international experience in which they are prepared to support, despite further disappointments and even hardships, the kind of leadership that recognizes the limits of containment without neglecting its imperatives? On the answers to these questions rests the future pattern of containment: the repetition of erratic oscillations of national mood and effort, or their stabilization, in the ceaseless restraint of Soviet expansion without war.

3
The Second Enemy of the Alliance: Nationalist Ideology

Robert Rothschild

The creation of the Atlantic Alliance was conceived with two fundamental concepts in mind regarding the uses of political power. The first was born of a common perception of the Soviet threat and the urgent need to establish a collective security agreement for the West. The second was propelled by a patriotic desire to preserve the sovereignty of the nation-state. The creation brought together fifteen diverse and conflicting nation-states. One of them was a superpower that exercised influence over the global system; the others were ancient entities, reduced in power and uneasy in their sense of political destiny. It was not a simple or a painless creation. In the thirty-five years of its existence, the Alliance has yet to assuage the nationalist pride and the rivalries of its member nations. Their politics are inspired by differing ethics and historical memories, and their drive to secure collective benefits owes more to the sharing of common fears than to shared ideals and visions.

The American republic owed its origins to a human ideal that derived from the Old Testament, the rationalist beliefs of the Encyclopedists, and the dedication to the covenant that was voluntarily adopted by its free citizens. The nation-states of Europe derived their identity from many centuries of fighting their neighbors. They did not reject the humanist ideals adopted by the United States, but they clung to a political philosophy that contrived to justify their belligerent behavior. They cited the dictum of Machiavelli, that a prince must regard war as unique in thought and purpose. For Hegel, the *state* was a divine idea of human destiny; its vocation was to fulfill itself, to reach excellence by dominating its neighbors. International politics involved constant and legitimate struggle and relentless use of force. The interest of the state, not of mankind, was the supreme law.

God or Christian values were often invoked but, in reality, neglected. "My country, right or wrong" became the rallying cry of patriotic and warlike nationalism.

The emerging power of the nation-state came to destroy the relatively calm but static unity of the Christian Middle Ages. It led to the magnificent adventures of the European nation-states and to the building of wealthy empires. But the cult of force eventually resulted in two world wars and a scale of destruction that could no longer be brooked. By failing to shift its emphasis from martial ethics to a wiser form of humanism, by refusing to progress from the independent state to the supranational federation, it began to forfeit its historic strength. The European system of states lost its creativity, and it lagged behind the emerging superpowers that were inspired by universal creeds and by the growing power of nuclear and industrial technology.

France, Great Britain, Germany, Spain, Italy, and their neighbors no longer possess the capacity to mobilize enormous industries and financial resources, to exercise a world role, or to protect their citizens against the threat of nuclear annihilation. But defense is not the only sector in which the nation-state forfeited power and credibility. Economically, it is unable to create the mass production and mass consumption made possible by new technologies. Europe's growth and competition have dramatically weakened, especially in the most advanced sectors. Unemployment and national indebtedness have increased, and military might has relatively declined. Efforts to build a United States of Europe have faltered. The nation-state appears today as an anachronistic survival, somewhat like the independent Duchy of Brittany after Francis I had concentrated his power in Paris.

By and large, the electorates in Europe feel that the long history of the nation-state has finally run its course. What remains today of the fervor of bygone days? Very little indeed. Armies and navies, which were among its most adored idols, whose flags and parades used to fill eyes with tears on national holidays, can no longer define the existence of the body politic. They are no more than instruments of tactical maneuver, and they have lost their immense influence on daily life.

Numerous opinion polls, not always entirely clear, reflect the uncertainties of contemporary nationalism. They point to two disturbing trends:

- A *strong skepticism* about national defense: In polls taken in 1983, 58% of Frenchmen insisted that an invasion by the USSR should be answered only with negotiations; 65% of Germans considered themselves too weak to respond alone to any threat of aggression.
- A *new sense of reliance* on European and Atlantic systems of collective security alliance: cited by 57% of Frenchmen and 72% of Germans.

(The figures were given by *Allensbuch Archives*, August 1983, and *Le Figaro*, 1 December 1983).

In Great Britain, the situation is somewhat different. Victorious in World War II, the British do not feel as keenly as the French and the Germans about the decay of their political system. Even the loss of empire has not been as shattering as it was on the continent. The survival of the Commonwealth, mythical as it may be, sustains the illusion of inspiring, if not mastering, the many countries in which their sovereign nominally reigns. But among the many electors who urge unilateral disarmament, the decline of patriotic devotion has become pronounced. A comparable growth of nuclear neutralism has been seen in many smaller countries, whether in Scandinavia, the Mediterranean, or the Low Countries.

Electoral groups in Europe seem to be aware of the obsolescence of the political machinery, though governments have not matched their perception. It is not difficult to see why. Governments must bend every effort to preserve the apparatus of the state; they would not exist without it. Heads of state, ministers, ambassadors, senior civil servants, and soldiers have survived the century by clinging to the symbols of power. Their careers were built within the prestige framework of the nation, and they owe everything to it, whether it is real or not. Can one imagine the dreams of the president of France when he presides over his peers in the magnificent Galerie des Glaces at Versailles, using the Sun King's gilt plate? Or those of the sovereign of Great Britain, when the royal yacht is escorted by ships of the Royal Navy, as she sails to the lands that once belonged to the greatest empire of the nineteenth century? It cannot be easy to give it all up and to plunge into the threatening and unpredictable adventure of a uniting Europe, which itself must still shelter under the American nuclear guarantee.

On the morrow of World War II, a handful of statesmen endowed with exceptional vision was ready to accept the risks of the European adventure. Witnesses of the great massacres that took place during the war and conscious of the emergence of the two superpowers, they tried to create a partnership with the United States on one side of the Atlantic and a unification of Europe on the other. A humanist tradition linked their efforts together, rather than the martial philosophy that had inspired wars of ideological passion and conquest. But these men were in their prime just after 1945, and they are long gone. Their successors have forgotten the ideals that motivated Schumann, Spaak, de Gasperi, and Monet to build an integrated Europe.

In France, politicians are noisily debating how to renew the teaching of history in schools. Their aim is to emphasize not Western humanist traditions of civilization but how to "give back to the French their sense of identity," as President Mitterand put it in 1983. We must "fight the anti-national ideologies," added the former Gaullist prime minister, Michel Debré. M. Chévénement, the left-wing leader of the Socialists, urged "modern patriotism," and the Communists did not dissent. Clearly, opinion across the political spectrum is nationalistic, and long-term ideals or collective interests are rarely mentioned.

A similar attitude prevails in Britain. The Falklands War was the occasion for a powerful upsurge of nationalism, and patriotic feelings were dramatically revived. But, for political leaders on the left as much (if not more) as on the right, the myths of sovereignty cannot be dissolved. They "think British" and only turn to Europe when it appears to bring immediate benefits. As far as defense policy is concerned, London no more than Paris restrains the drive toward European integration. Both nations spend scarce resources to modernize their nuclear forces and to acquire expensive weapon systems. As they struggle to capture the interest of the superpowers, they also tend to become more insular in ambition and more fractious as members of the Alliance. Germany, the principal arena for East–West confrontation, has moved in a somewhat similar direction. The political leaders of the Federal Republic, who for thirty years were among the most dedicated of the Atlantic partners, are losing their sense of commitment. The illusions of *Ostpolitik* have dimmed their judgment and led them to forget the great Western perspectives of the Adenauer era. In the last year, East Germany has become the Mecca of their pilgrimages, even for Franz Joseph Strauss, Bavaria's arch-conservative leader. Chancellor Kohl speaks warmly of a rapprochement with the German Democratic Republic (GDR) and extends it important loans and trade privileges. On the left, the solid consensus of previous decades has been shaken. Helmut Schmidt speaks frequently and bitterly against the United States. Many of the Socialists question the commitment to NATO, and a significant number (together with the Greens) have suggested quitting the Alliance altogether. It seems that Ostpolitik could one day lead to a more nationalistic policy in West Germany.

To some American commentators the "malady of Germany" appears as an advanced case of schizophrenia, though the malady affects most European countries as well. Governments desperately cling to pretenses of national sovereignty and a supposed "historical heritage." In many cases, electors have lost confidence in the nation-state. They know that its power has gone and that a European Union might have eventually restored credibility and confidence, only it failed to materialize. A poll taken in France, Great Britain, the Federal Republic, and Italy confirmed that many citizens are now resigned to the fact that China, Japan, and the United States will "count more" in the next century than their own countries (*Newsweek*, 9 April 1984). Unfortunately, they have found no common agreement to reverse the trend or to secure a better destiny.

Schizophrenics are usually oversensitive, unstable, and difficult partners.

They do not know what they want, and they constantly try to create an identity despite the fog of their uncertainties. They bitterly disagree over ethical values, over assessments of adversaries, and over their own capabilities. They have contributed to the growing strains in transatlantic relations, and their refusal to cope with difficult problems has weakened the mechanism of the Alliance. The question must now be asked: Have these divisive tactics reached an order of magnitude that will jeopardize allied solidarity?

The answer must be an emphatic no. So long as the Soviet Union constitutes a threat to Europe, their joint efforts will prevail. The situation will probably not change in the foreseeable future, since West Germany, France, and Great Britain, for all their illusions, still depend on American military and nuclear protection. What else could they do? Align themselves with the USSR and surrender the vital linkages that they have established since 1945 both with each other and with the United States? Or opt out of the Alliance and become neutralists, pretending to safeguard their sovereignty against the colossal military might of the Warsaw Pact with totally inadequate national forces? Obviously, these alternatives are impossible.

For its own part, too, the United States has become a prisoner of its own position. If it were detached from Europe, with its magnificent cultural heritage and its still immense industrial resources, what would become of North America? Would it become an entrenched camp, a "Fortress America," concentrating its power on defending itself in isolationist detachment? A Spartan state, no more the country of Jefferson, Lincoln, and Roosevelt? In the future, it is likely that new power centers will appear in South America or the Pacific Basin, and the United States will have to turn more attention to them, as it has already done to Japan. The new power arenas will not reduce the importance of Europe. On the contrary, the division of East and West in the center of Europe will take on new significance in economic and security terms.

A people, as well as individuals, is sometimes tempted to commit suicide. No wish to die is evident in the West today, though one must expect that Europeans will continue to be morbidly dissatisfied and quarrelsome. That the Americans will be irritated, perhaps angered, by the antics of their partners is to be expected. It would not be rational, however, if members of the Alliance quarreled to the point of risking the destruction of a political system that has provided four decades of peace and unprecedented prosperity.

The present fascination of many Europeans lies not with their own shortcomings or with the combinations of threats and failures to be seen in Moscow. Europe's political perceptions and its changing concerns with power are focused largely on Washington. In the second term of President Reagan's administration there will be an ever greater attention paid to the conduct of American diplomacy. Will it pursue lines of change or of continuity in promoting the dual concepts of power that hold Europe in thrall? On the one side, there is a need to stabilize the collective defense of the Continent and, on the other, there is a need to dispel the rivalries and disputes of the European nation-states. The cause of the fascination is obvious. It is only the United States that can still furnish the authority to move the European members of the Alliance to undertake responsibilities they cannot separately fulfill. If one superpower is to help unify Europe with military threats, the other must do so through the exercise of political will. In the long run, it is hoped, the Europeans will learn to depend on their own good sense to unite their ancient civilizations.

4
American Foreign Policy and the Atlantic Alliance

Martin J. Hillenbrand

THE BURDEN OF HISTORY

My topic treads well-worn ground. From the inception of the Alliance, the role of the United States has provided both a source of essential strength and continuing anxiety for its European members. The experience of NATO during the past thirty-six years has been a mixture of unified effort and periodic crises of confidence; but the original purpose of the Alliance — to prevent Soviet expansionism and to preserve the peace in Europe — has consistently been achieved.

In the immediate postwar years, the United States and its Western European allies came to believe that an essential goal of the Soviet Union was to incorporate the potential economic and military power of Western Europe, particularly that of Germany, within its own sphere of influence, just as it had already done in Eastern Europe. Whether or not Stalin actually contemplated doing this by military action is a matter of controversy among historians. However, those Americans stationed in West Germany after the war can certify that there was genuine fear of Soviet aggression, shared by the British and the French occupiers, a fear generated by Soviet bullying in Berlin, the blockade of that city, and the overwhelming conventional military superiority of the USSR. That fear, after all, led to the creation of NATO. It is this fear that has provided the cement to hold the Alliance together over the years, although, as deterrence became an institutionalized and accepted reality, the rationale for the Alliance was essentially that, without it, the way would be open for the realization of the long-term Soviet objective, which is to master and use, in one way or another, the resources of Western Europe. The continuing presence of a large U.S. military force in Europe became the necessary symbolic representation of America's commitment to the defense of Europe.

These cogent realities tended to overshadow certain other facts of life that worked in an opposite direction. Although American involvement in two world wars had effectively disposed of classical isolationism, it was unable to exorcise the recurrent feeling among portions of the governing elite that there was something incongruous about an American military deployment in Europe on the scale that had seemingly become institutionalized. Even President Eisenhower expressed doubts about the durability and desirability of such a deployment, and what became known as Mansfieldism (after the Democratic Senate majority leader who, almost on an annual basis, presented resolutions that, if passed, would have required large-scale U.S. troop withdrawals from Europe) reflected broader unease. That successive American administrations were able to contain such pressures did not mean this could be accomplished without considerable expenditure of effort.

A segment of the American academic community contributed to this feeling of disjunction during the 1960s by questioning the accepted allocation of responsibility for the cold war. These revisionist historians and political scientists argued that the responsibility was primarily that of the United States. While the inevitable antirevisionist reaction was able to demonstrate the numerous factual errors and irresponsible interpretations in this approach, a whole generation of American students absorbed at least some of the revisionist doubts about the motives of Washington policymakers during the postwar years. The result was to undermine for them the moral claim of the Alliance to be a necessary response to threatened Soviet aggression. Such is the ephemeral nature of academic fads, however, that a new generation of students in the 1970s found revisionism either old hat or vanquished, except in those few bastions where aging professors teach in the old terms but with little impact on elite opinion.

A continuing problem was the inability of those Americans committed to the Alliance to develop and articulate any consistent intellectual framework for the relationship of the United States to Europe that went beyond the military and the expediential. The efforts during the 1950s of Undersecretary of State (later Secretary of State) Christian Herter and the group around him to promote the idea of an Atlantic Union never got off the ground. A few years later President Kennedy was to speak of a Grand Design binding Europe and the United States together, but it never went beyond the level of rhetoric. Since then there has been a paucity of attempts even to find a descriptive appellation for the relationship.

It is true, of course, that, during the formative years of the 1950s, American policymakers consistently and idealistically supported the movement toward European union. The formula used, which became almost a cliché, was that the potential benefits of such a union would inevitably outweigh any economic disadvantages that might result. The first Nixon administration accepted this evaluation of interest even at a time when it was becoming more and more evident that Europe was not going to unite in any truly supranational sense and that the European Economic Community would entail clear economic disadvantages for the United States. One of the early arguments made in the Herter group against supporting efforts at European union was that this would lead to anti-Atlantic tendencies within Europe. Little did they know that the return to power of De Gaulle would have precisely such consequences. In any event, the Atlanticists had already lost the battle in the U.S. government to the Europeanists.

The upshot of all this was that, in the absence of any coherent overall philosophy, the military arguments for the Alliance tended to dominate, and they were indeed strong. Article 2 of the NATO treaty became a dead letter, and the Harmel report of December 1967 (despite its obvious attraction to Western Europeans) never played a big role in American thinking. Ironically enough, a recurrent concern, particularly in Germany, was that, somehow or other, the two superpowers would get together and make a deal at the expense of Western Europe. Chancellor Adenauer was particularly concerned about this contingency, as were the French during certain phases of the Berlin crisis in the early 1960s, although in practice, even during the heyday of détente a decade later when both the chancellor and de Gaulle had left the scene, there was never any real possibility of this occurring.

It is true that during the 1950s the U.S. Department of State engaged in some creative thinking about a possible European settlement. Its thinking found expression in the Western peace plan put forward by the French, British, and American foreign ministers at the four-power Geneva Conference of 1959. Following its inevitable rejection by the Soviets, and their continued threat to the allied position in West Berlin, there was little further scope for proposals of this kind. By the time of the Harmel report, neither the Americans nor the Europeans had much specific content to give the report's statement that it sought "the search for progress . . . the promotion of détente and the strengthening of peace." Though they were discussed within the Alliance, the Nixon and Brandt initiatives that led to the détente of the early and middle 1970s did not result from any specific NATO action as such, although the organization supported progress, in its semiannual communiqués, toward the Quadripartite Agreement on Berlin and the opening of negotiations for multilateral and balanced forced reductions (MBFR) in Vienna.

Any official who has attended the semiannual meetings of NATO foreign ministers can attest to the frequent crisis atmosphere of such meetings. The atmosphere is partly generated, no doubt, by functionaries in various foreign ministries trying to prompt their respective ministers to say something significant at sessions that might otherwise seem too routine. As it was, NATO ministerial communiqués frequently tended to reflect the blandness of the discussions that preceded them, although the drafting of such com- muniqués often consumed a disproportionate amount of time, a complaint frequently made by successive U.S. secretaries of state. Other American complaints over the years involved the failure of Europeans to share the bur- den of defense equitably, the failure of the Alliance to move faster and far- ther toward weapons standardization, and the reluctance of Europeans to broaden discussion within the Alliance of geopolitical problems beyond the areas defined in the treaty itself.

On the other hand, the European members of the Alliance complained that American leadership was erratic, that it was inadequate or too heavy- handed, and that consultation by the United States came either too late (after unilateral action had already been taken) or amounted to little more than the sharing of information. Despite all these alleged failings, there was really no serious questioning of the survival of the Alliance either in Wash- ington or in the major European capitals. Even de Gaulle kept France in the Alliance when he pulled his country out of the military command struc- ture in 1966. The United States remained committed, and there seemed to be no prospect of any significant change in Soviet policy of a kind that might conceivably reduce the role of, and hence the necessity for, the Alliance. By any standard, NATO had successfully fulfilled its principal function, which was to deter Soviet adventurism and to preserve the peace in Europe.

THE PAST IS PROLOGUE, BUT TO WHAT?

To view everything against the background of history is to run the dan- ger of overlooking or misunderstanding distinctively new current develop- ments. In many respects the world has entered a transitional era that cannot leave the Alliance untouched. The relationship of the United States to the Alliance is bound to be affected by the broader problems presently emerg- ing or predictably on the horizon. These problem areas can conveniently be discussed under several general headings, but their interrelationship in many respects should be obvious.

Economics and the Will to Cohere

The postwar era was one of phenomenal economic growth in Western Europe and the United States. The institutional structures created at the end of the war and supplemented by the Marshall Plan worked well, providing both stability and the basis for release of dynamic and creative economic forces. World trade expanded on an unprecedented scale and, in a real sense, led the process of economic growth.

For a variety of reasons on which economists do not agree, that era has clearly come to an end. The old-line industrial countries of Europe and the United States have lost comparative advantage across a broad band of traditional industries to other parts of the world, and they have entered upon a period of painful structural change. The old assumed economic complementarities between Western Europe and the United States seem to have broken down, and the European Community and the United States find themselves involved in a growing series of trade disputes in both the industrial and the agricultural sectors. At the same time, the international monetary economy appears to be coming apart at the seams, with the possibility of Third World debt default threatening the stability of American banks and, to a lesser degree, European banks. But most incongruous has been the fact that in 1985, the United States became a net debtor country worldwide as a result of unmanageable deficits on trade and current accounts, the consequence in part of a greatly overvalued dollar.

What this all adds up to is far from clear, but it is difficult to believe that the implications for the Alliance will not be profound. One effect so far has been to turn the attention of some American policymakers away from Europe and toward the Pacific Basin. Robert McFarlane, President Reagan's former national security advisor, has already called for a redefinition of priorities precisely in this direction. One can establish statistically that this is nonsense, given the fact that Europe is likely to remain America's most important trading power in terms of overall balance of trade although the United States will, for the indefinite future, run a heavy deficit on trade account with the countries of East Asia. It also remains a reality that the other superpower, despite its eastern Siberian territories, is still essentially a European power.

The economic dimensions of America's relationship to Europe are in any event likely to assume increasing importance in the years ahead as part of the Alliance problem. A trade war between the European Community and the United States, not an inevitability if good sense prevails, could have a shattering effect on Western cohesion. Under the circumstances, one might be tempted to ask whether NATO, acting under a revived Article 2, could make any contribution. It could, of course, if governments wanted to use the organization as a forum for the discussion of economic problems other than those immediately concerned with defense expenditures. It is difficult to discern, however, what could be accomplished in NATO that could not be dealt with in the OECD or in direct American relations with the European Community. Even the problem of paying for defense procurement and maintenance within the Alliance will grow in difficulty, as all member governments face increasing financial stringencies and as the dynamics of procurement produce fewer weapons for ever greater outlays.

A predictable policy development, at least in the larger NATO countries, will be the growth of protectionism to preserve a portion of those old-line industries that are threatened today. No country that considers itself a military power can view with equanimity the disappearance of those industries,

such as steel, metals processing, shipbuilding and textiles, that have traditionally been associated with the production of arms or military supplies.
What the indispensable minimum will turn out to be each country will
decide for itself, but this additional pressure for protectionism will play
more than a negligible role.

The U.S. foreign debt situation raises unprecedented problems, too. No
one really knows what the international economic consequences will be or,
for that matter, the consequences for the internal American economy if the
inward flow of foreign capital on which the United States has come to
depend is no longer available to help finance both the budgetary deficits
of the federal government and the deficits on trade and current account.
Certainly the effects will be destabilizing, presenting the Federal Reserve
Board with a "Catch-22" situation. If the board moves to increase liquidity
and lower interest rates to stimulate the American economy, the flow of
foreign money into the country will dry up, creating a capital shortage,
which in turn, will put upward pressure on interest rates. On the other
hand, if the board contracts liquidity and raises interest rates, the economy
is likely to move into recession, so long as the dollar remains relatively
strong, exports continue to suffer, and the American payments balance is
unimproved. In either case, the results will put further strains on the Alliance relationship.

Can America and the Alliance Agree on Strategy?

There are two aspects to strategy: the military, with its concern for
weapons and their deployment, and what might be called "grand strategy"
or some theory of desirable conduct with respect to the Soviet Union. Cutting across both is the issue of arms reductions and negotiating postures in
Geneva and elsewhere.

An impartial observer of the European scene could not avoid conclud-
ing that some of the rhetorical pronouncements of the first Reagan administration about nuclear war had a profoundly unsettling effect on European
opinion. The fact that such views were not shared by many Americans,
including some in the U.S. government, did not serve as much of a pallia-
tive. The rhetoric out of Washington has improved somewhat in recent
years, and this has no doubt made some contribution to a shift of European
concern away from the nuclear threat. A recent poll conducted for the
Atlantic Institute for International Affairs in Paris led to the conclusion that,
whereas two years ago the proposed deployment in Europe of American
cruise missiles and Pershing II missiles had pushed nuclear issues into the
forefront of public attention, these had clearly been replaced in 1985 by
unemployment and related economic problems. Nevertheless, the potential
for divisive strife within the Alliance over strategic issues remains strong.

A few years ago there was much talk in Europe about a fundamental shift in the strategic balance having taken place between the United States and the Soviet Union. The assumed shift raised questions about the continuing credibility of the American nuclear deterrent. Ironically enough, the arguments by opponents of SALT II ratification in the United States fueled the impression that America had fallen behind the Soviet Union in strategic missiles and that a "window of vulnerability" had opened that might tempt the USSR to make a preemptive strike against U.S. land-based missiles in the event of a threatening confrontation in Europe or elsewhere. This unsettling prospect led some Europeans to conclude that the basic assumption of NATO strategy—that at each level of potential violence the Soviets would be deterred from initiating aggressive action by the prospect of adequate resistance or escalation—no longer had validity. Thus, the concept of flexible response or graduated deterrence was thought to be undermined.

A major contributor to this period of doubt about the credibility of the American deterrent was former U.S. Secretary of State Henry Kissinger. In a speech made in the fall of 1979 during an international conference in Brussels, he told his astonished audience that in effect they were foolish to believe that the U.S. government would risk the destruction of its own country to come to the aid of Europe. He quickly recognized the imprudence of his remarks and tried in a subsequent press conference to add some qualifications, but his original words were on the wires and the damage was done. Clearly, some things are better left unexpressed unless they can be put in a balanced historical and conceptual setting.

With the growing prominence of the INF deployment issue and early talk by some Reagan administration officials about fighting and winning a nuclear war, European concerns shifted. The conclusion in the Scowcroft Commission Report that the American deterrent was still credible, given our superior underwater nuclear capabilities, also helped to change the focus of attention. Because the numbers involved were not all that different from those of a few years earlier, one can only wonder at how quickly perceptions and the concerns based on them can change.

The INF problem provides a classic example of shifting objectives and short institutional memory. What started out as a well-meaning American response to a felt European psychological requirement, in the face of Soviet deployment of their SS-20 missiles, gradually became an American cause, while European acceptance of the proposed missile deployments became a test of loyalty to the Alliance. The parallels with the MLF experience of some twenty years ago were obvious to those few who could remember so far into the past. Heavy-handed Soviet attempts to block the proposed deployments, plus strenuous American pressures, combined to permit the initial stationing of cruise missiles and Pershing IIs in December 1983.

These deployments were preceded, however, by massive antinuclear demonstrations in the Federal Republic of Germany, the Netherlands, Great Britain, Belgium, Denmark, and Italy—demonstrations with strong anti-American overtones. Americans, including officials in Washington, were surprised and chagrined at the vehemence of the attacks on the United States. Certainly the U.S. record of consultation within the Alliance, in the special NATO bodies set up for that purpose, had been good, but there was a seeming lack of awareness in Washington of the deep emotions the nuclear issue had aroused, and of the distrust among many European intellectuals of American motives.

The Soviet walkout from the INF and START talks in Geneva just prior to the opening deployments of the Pershing II and cruise missiles evoked a new set of European concerns. The NATO decision of December 1979 to accept the new missiles had been conditional upon the failure of the Soviet–American INF talks to make progress. Of progress there was little, but reluctant Western European governments clearly would have preferred that the so-called dual-track decision take a different form. They hoped until nearly the end that, somehow or other, some agreement could be reached by the superpowers in Geneva. The current INF negotiations are now part of a linked triad of talks on weapons in space, strategic missiles, and intermediate range missiles. If they could move toward some agreement limiting further deployments, most European heads of governments would be greatly relieved.

Lurking behind all this has been a European suspicion that the Reagan administration is not deeply and sincerely committed to success in arms reduction talks with the Soviets. The American failure to ratify SALT II was the first of a series of developments that nourished this suspicion. Some of the rhetoric out of Washington, added to the known view of such officials as Secretary of Defense Caspar Weinberger, Assistant Secretary of Defense Richard Perle and Kenneth Adelman, director of the Arms Control and Disarmament Agency, did not bring much reassurance.

President Reagan's recent professions of dedication to arms reductions have helped to offset the early impression of indifference, if not downright antagonism, to any real negotiations on the subject with the Soviets. But his SDI has added a new and complicating factor, creating controversy in the United States as to its practicability and providing the Soviets with a propaganda theme and a possible pretext for lack of progress at Geneva. It has also revived in a new context the old European–American argument within the Alliance about what constitutes an equitable sharing of the defense burden and military technology. Efforts to rationalize and standardize arms production within the Alliance have generally failed to move forward, partly because of a European feeling that the arms business tended to be a one-way street in favor of the United States.

Yet common sense dictates that as modern weaponry becomes more expensive per unit, arms standardization should move ahead. Greater American willingness to share orders would make a significant contribution to the process, but the Europeans must also get their act in order. The record so far of the so-called Eurogroup has not been one of unmitigated success.

The problem of fair sharing has undoubtedly played a role in the discussion of SDI-related programs. Europeans have been divided on the question of SDI cooperation with the United States. President Mitterand has strongly opposed it, stressing the need for Europe to move ahead with its own programs of high technology, while Chancellor Kohl and Prime Minister Thatcher have favored some degree of cooperation. Whether the emerging arrangements between the United States, the Federal Republic, and Britain will prove satisfactory remains to be seen.

It is clear that SDI has considerable divisive potential within the Alliance if American diplomacy does not handle the various related issues with skill. The Soviets sense this, and their tactics in the revived Geneva arms talks indicate they will try to put the blame for stalemate on American obduracy on SDI. Their hope would be that European pressures on the United States to make concessions would build up, and anti-American sentiment in Europe would be further stimulated. There have recently been indications from Soviet sources, however, that the USSR might eventually accept continuing SDI research, since it is in any case unverifiable, and they know that we know they are engaged in a similar research program. Some observers already see the elements of an eventual deal emerging that would trade off testing and deployment of space weapons against sizable reductions in delivery systems and warheads, but it seems premature to count on a treaty settlement being reached.

One aspect of the SDI that is particularly troubling to America's European allies is its implications for NATO strategy if, contrary to the belief of many scientists, it should turn out to be feasible. One can already hear European expressions of concern about what might be called the "reverse decoupling" effect of SDI if the continental United States becomes relatively immune to Soviet intercontinental ballistic missiles (ICBMs) while the countries of Western Europe remain vulnerable to Soviet medium range missiles, specifically the SS-20s. American assurances that Europe, too, would be protected by SDI technology developed by the United States have only partially satisfied the skeptics. They point to the problems of interception of the shorter range missiles aimed at a relatively propinquant Western Europe.

It may seem premature to some to bother with all this fuss now within the Alliance about a defensive system that may ultimately prove impractical and that, even at best, will take many years to perfect. But both the high-technology and arms control aspects of President Reagan's initiative are of present concern. President Mitterrand's principal argument against European participation in SDI research has been that it would seriously detract from European research and development efforts within the so-called Eureka program. At the same time, apart from the way the Soviets may choose to use the SDI as an excuse for lack of progress in the Geneva arms talks, there are also the broader questions of whether it will lead to an arms race in space and to the dismantling of the ABM agreement of 1972. The concerns expressed by many Americans on these points have received considerable publicity in Europe, creating a receptive environment for Soviet propaganda.

Another divisive factor within NATO has been the feeling of some Americans, including prominent members of the U.S. Congress, that the Europeans have not borne a fair share of the financial and military burdens of the Alliance. Whether true or not, and there are cogent arguments to be made on both sides of the issue, this assumption has spawned such phenomena as Mansfieldism, offset arrangements, continuing U.S. pressures on the Europeans to spend more, and, most recently, the Nunn Resolution (defeated in the Senate by not too large a margin) requiring significant American troop withdrawals from Europe if our allies do not raise their expenditures on defense. There is no easy way, statistically or otherwise, to dispell, correct, or at least qualify such impressions. They will continue to stimulate attempts at action in the United States that, despite the good intentions of their proposers, basically tend to encourage a form of neoisolationism and an anti-Alliance mood.

The appreciation of the U.S. dollar in recent years has, however, helped to take care of one problem that had affected American troop morale in Germany and that led to horror stories in the media about the squalor and relative poverty imposed on soldiers and their dependents during the preceding period of dollar weakness. Our GIs can again afford to move out of their barracks and spend money in German bars and resorts. This may contribute to higher troop morale, and it may point to one of the marvels of forty years of American presence in Germany — the degree of institutionalization that presence has achieved. Whatever the unfortunate aspects of the Bitburg Cemetery fiasco in May 1985, one could only be impressed by the rapport between the townspeople and the heavy American presence in their community. If the overvalued dollar is now destined, as many international economists believe, to decline significantly against leading European currencies, we may hear a revival of the old complaints about GI sufferings that lead to arguments that it is high time to bring the boys back home.

A contradictory development to all this, in the sense that it would suggest a continuing and even greater U.S. involvement in Europe, is the growing difference between the American and European assessments of policy vis-à-vis the Soviet bloc. This difference stems from disparate views about the nature of Eastern European trends, including those in the Soviet Union, and what can best be done to achieve Western long-term goals. Despite the formidable Soviet military buildup in Eastern Europe, there is a declining belief in Western Europe that the Soviets are today contemplating military action. Proceeding from this assumption, the Europeans generally favor a more open trading relationship with the Soviets and their Eastern European allies than does the majority view in the United States. Moreover, Europeans tend to believe that there are greater possibilities of influencing Soviet behavior in desirable directions through the improvement of political relations than does the Reagan administration. The West Germans particularly, even with a relatively conservative government in power, continue to pursue the Eastern policy originated by former Chancellor Brandt more than fifteen years ago. They hope that, over time and through the extension of German political, economic, and cultural influence in Eastern Europe, a significant process of change can be achieved in Central Europe. The new and developing relationship between the two German states reflects this approach, as does the relatively more benign attitude of some Western European governments to the military dictatorship in Poland than is found in Washington.

It is far from clear where all this is leading. The natural gas pipeline embroglio of a few years ago may be only the first of a series of clashes within the Alliance stemming from real differences over what is the most desirable policy toward the Eastern bloc. On the other hand, since the Soviet Union is now led by a presumably more perceptive Gorbachev, it will do all it can to play on these differences and sow discord within the Alliance. Washington will have to take particular care that any repetition of the belligerent and simplistic rhetoric in which it sometimes indulged during the first Reagan administration does not play into the hands of the Soviets, because it could confirm the worst fears of the Europeans about American judgments and intentions.

Generational and Other Shifts within Alliance Countries

Concerned supporters of the Alliance in Europe and the United States have spent a great deal of time in recent years discussing what has come to be known as "the successor generation problem." It was obvious that the generation of officials and interested citizens that contributed personally to the development of the postwar institutional order, most notably the NATO Alliance, would find it difficult to pass on to a new generation of politicians, businesspeople, and even military officers the assessments of need and responses that they had shared so intensely and that their successors had not themselves encountered. The postwar world was in many important respects a different world from that in which we live today; there has been no automatic transmission either of institutional memory or personal involvement. For a variety of reasons, the image of America to many young Europeans is quite different today from what it was to the previous generation. Many young intellectuals, particularly in the Federal Republic of Germany and the Low Countries, have developed anti-American attitudes. They tend to allocate responsibility for the present state of affairs in Europe equally between the Soviet Union and the United States, even though they reject the former as either a political or an economic role model. While polls continue to show majority support in Western Europe for alliance with the United States, the proportion of those giving such support is considerably lower among younger than among older age groups.

Discussions of this problem serve a purpose if they do not end up in mere handwringing. There have been useful exchange programs for "young leaders" and attempts to bring young men and women into greater participation in Alliance support groups. But a frank appraisal will conclude that these activities only begin to scratch the surface. No one has yet come up with a formula that will significantly improve the outlook and attitude of the incoming generation as it takes over power.

One pitfall that the concerned older generation must avoid is to come across as patronizing or preachy. Perhaps the very term *successor generation* carries with it negative connotations and should be replaced. In chronological terms there have actually been several successor generations since the postwar era, and it is perhaps a tribute to the durability and continuing influence of the earliest generation that the issue has achieved the kind of definition that it has won. In any event, whatever the nomenclature, there is a real problem here, and we have yet to resolve it.

Another important change, only dimly, if at all, perceived by many Europeans, is the shift of political and economic power in the United States away from the northeast and central states to the southeast, southwest and far west. The old so-called Eastern Establishment, that for so long dominated the making of policy and the supplying of personnel to the foreign policy branches of government, no longer exerts the same influence. It was essentially Europe-oriented, whereas Western elite groups in the United States tended to look more toward the Pacific Basin. Americans are themselves only now beginning to comprehend the implications of these regional changes. Despite some successful efforts to revive industry in New England, the process appears irreversible, at least in the short term. It cannot help but complicate the efforts of those Americans who continue to stress the overriding importance of America's relationship to Western Europe within the Alliance.

LOOKING AHEAD

These then are the problems that have been plaguing the relationship of the United States with European members of the Alliance. Some are serious, some less so. Some will fade away merely through the passage of time, and others will remain. One cannot count on simply muddling through again, as we have done so frequently in the past; nor is it likely that the Soviets will accommodate us, as they have sometimes done, by creating a new unifying symbol by once again threatening West Berlin or some other vital allied interest.

Some reordering of NATO strategy will indubitably be necessary during the years ahead. The refinement of conventional weapons, and the new air–land scenarios and evolving strategic doctrines will require a rethinking of the role of tactical nuclear weapons in Europe. Given changing conditions and the greater potential of nonnuclear weapons, will a "no-first-use" doctrine become feasible? No one is sure, and few are comfortable with a strategic position that leaves the moral high ground on first-use of nuclear weapons to the Soviet Union.

At the present, any specific effort within the Alliance to move in the direction of no-first-use would be more disruptive than helpful. This was seen in the strong German reaction to the article advocating adoption by NATO of such a doctrine written jointly by McGeorge Bundy, George F. Kennan, Robert S. McNamara, and Gerard Smith and published in the Spring 1982 issue of *Foreign Affairs*. The appellation of "The Gang of Four" quickly became a popular reference to this group in the Federal Republic, and the next issue of *Foreign Affairs* contained a somewhat heated rejoinder by four prominent Germans: Karl Kaiser, Georg Leber, Alois Mertes and Franz-Josef Schulze. The strategy of flexible response may be unraveling at the margins, but the European allies of the United States are at this stage neither psychologically nor analytically prepared to consider moving beyond it. If and when the sophisticated conventional weapons associated with the incipient air–land strategy are ever deployed, the time may come to successfully rethink some of the long-standing assumptions held by NATO.

If the "nuclear winter" hypothesis should be verified, even to the point of being probable, this too would require a fundamental revision of Alliance strategy. A clear doomsday-weapon approach would be neither rational nor likely to retain the support of Western publics. We are not yet at that point, but it would be well to begin thinking about the implications for weaponry and deployments of such a radical transformation of current assumptions. There is some evidence that the Soviets are also aware of these implications.

It is difficult to foresee what developments will flow from the meetings between President Reagan and Chairman Gorbachev. Will they make a contribution to a real improvement of relations between the two superpowers or will they have been profitless encounters between leaders of the United States and the Soviet Union? Given current European misgivings about some aspects of American policy, the president must consider Alliance reactions with care. On one side, the European members of the Alliance can be gratified that the leaders met. But, on the other hand, they could become apprehensive that some arrangement between the Soviet Union and the United States might be reached over their heads. Chancellor Konrad Adenauer shared this concern on some occasions. The longer-term result will obviously affect America's relations with its allies in important ways if pressures build to achieve concrete progress in the Geneva arms talks and to improve East–West relations.

It is clear that the direction in which Gorbachev wishes to steer Soviet policy will play an important and determining role in the years ahead so far as the future of the Alliance is concerned. Despite the plethora of speculative articles about the new Soviet leadership, we really do not know enough at this point to predict the future with assurance. The surprises that Nikita Khrushchev sprang during his early years in power should warn against too confident a prognosis by the experts. Gorbachev and the supporters he has advanced in the party hierarchy will undoubtedly bring new vigor to the direction of the USSR. Barring accident or illness, he is likely to be around for a long time, dealing with a succession of Western leaders. The problems of internal economic and social reform that he must face are formidable, and he may well find that significant stimulation of economic growth and civilian morale is beyond his power. Eastern Europe will be a major source of difficulty for the Soviet Union; the trends there generally run contrary to any concept of a monolithic bloc, and, although the Red Army still has the brute power, any attempt to revert to a 1968 interpretation of the Brezhnev Doctrine would run directly counter to Soviet objectives in Western Europe. There were anxieties in the past that, if war were to break out in Central Europe, it would be in connection with an uprising in a Soviet bloc country, most notably in the GDR. This does not seem particularly relevant today since the standoff in the center of Europe is relatively stable.

We will discover during the next year or two whether rapprochement with the United States stands high on Gorbachev's list of priorities. It seems unlikely that he will be willing to pay a stiff price or to change behavior in order to restore détente, but one must always allow for the possibility of surprises. If American diplomacy is reasonably supple and imaginative, he will not find it easy to sow discord between the United States and Euro-

pean governments, or to influence younger Europeans who tend to be anti-American and who attribute responsibility for the present impasse equally between East and West.

It seems that the overriding purpose of the Alliance will survive in the indefinite future. Whatever the military intentions of the Soviet Union toward Western Europe, the United States will want to prevent Soviet political and economic dominance over the area, dissolution of NATO and American disengagement from Europe. Despite all the problems in their relationship with the United States, the Western Europeans have no interest in losing their political freedom and identity to the Eastern superpower. The Finnish model has little relevance to the larger situation; its preservation is at least in part a function of the crystallized postwar arrangements in Europe. Moreover, if all of Europe is once again, perhaps only at some distant point, to achieve its identity as a continent in peace and order, it will only be when the dissolution of the present alliance system in both East and West becomes compatible with the security of both superpowers.

Meanwhile, the Americans and the Europeans within the Alliance have no real option but to strive to deal with the problems that confront them. If Arnold Toynbee was right, great responses come only in the face of great challenges. No one is likely to claim that the challenges are not present and that great or at least imaginative responses are not required. When all is said and done, and despite the complexities that face the second Reagan administration, there is no call for unmitigated gloom. The challenge of the postwar years when the Alliance first came into existence, whether political, economic, or military, were indeed formidable. They were met and overcome by a high quality of leadership and diplomacy. It does not exceed the bounds of realism to think that this can happen again. The resilience and vitality of democratic economic and political institutions, including NATO, have been proven in the past, and they may well show surprising durability and adaptability in the future.

5
The Politics of the Atlantic Alliance: The Interplay of Internal and External Forces

Zygmunt Nagorski

It was in the mid-1950s that I began to reflect and write about the Alliance. Those were heady days. The Korean war was barely over, the Berlin blockade was still vivid in the minds of policymakers, and the Communist witch-hunt in the United States had come to an end. I went to Europe, looked around, talked to the people who mattered at the time, and came back with two distinct impressions. One was that it would take very little for Western Europe to move into the middle position, to become a third force between the two superpowers — independent, allied with the West, but resisting continuing American tutelage. The other impression grew out of my visit to Finland, where I had expected an almost iron curtain atmosphere. Instead, I found a fiercely proud and nationalistic people, engaged in heated political debates, spending a lot of energy and money on elections even while being acutely aware of the long shadow of power and influence cast by their next door neighbor. The Finnish neutrality appealed to me greatly. I was not sure whether the model would survive, whether the democratic passions would not be cooled by Soviet proximity, but at that time (the first decade after the end of the war) it was an impressive sight. The fact that Russia returned Karelia to the Finns was considered a victory of great dimension.

A voice casting doubts on the validity and strength of the Alliance was not especially welcome in America at the time. The firm conviction that the Marshall Plan and the North Atlantic Treaty Organization were pillars of stability and solidity was widely shared. There were no peace marches or anti-American demonstrations. The supposed peace slogans of the time were the monopoly of the Soviet-sponsored organizations that aimed at capturing the hearts and minds of the new generations as part of a fierce propaganda effort. The international youth festivals they set up, which survived the period of détente and which are once again in full swing, were created in that period. Some Western European groups sent representatives to the festivals, lending credence to their goals. But in Washington, where there were no illusions about how and for what purpose these events were staged, neither the Congress nor the executive branch viewed the Western European Alliance as being in any way undermined by the Soviet-organized activities. It took a couple of decades to even suspect that these events could make a dent on the face of the Alliance.

Today, thirty some years later, I still feel that Western Europe cannot be taken for granted. The possibility of a third-force movement lingers, and the changing pattern of our mutual relations depends heavily on circumstances that are often unpredictable and, even more, often unavoidable. The Alliance operates within the parameters of democratic principles, which puts it at a disadvantage in comparison with the Soviet block, where the centralized decision-making process holds sway. There is no party line within the Alliance. It is a conglomerate of fully independent nations whose diverse policies reflect the differing tensions, political uncertainties, and changing internal structures that each member nation faces. France is a good example, the Federal Republic of Germany another.

Clearly, internal and external forces directly affect the delicate fabric of the Western strategic component. It may be useful, therefore, to search for clues to the future by looking at these forces from the standpoint of the Western conceptual approach. The Marshall Plan is now history. NATO is approaching middle age, a time fraught with problems for organizations as well as for human beings. And the overall patterns of international interests, allegiances, and goals have changed drastically from the nerve-racking yet, in retrospect, relatively mild period of the immediate postwar years. While at that time both Western Europe and the United States were entering the age of nuclear adolescence, today we are passing through the years of full nuclear maturity, with all the implications clearly visible, clearly predictable, and clearly remaining on the top priority list of both superpowers.

The analysis can start with a look at the internal and external political forces, which have long provided the key to the continuity of the Alliance. Some may suggest that economic factors have replaced the political in the most influential role. Although there may be validity in that perception, politics both inside individual member countries and in the bilateral and multilateral relations within the Alliance cannot be ignored or considered minor.

The internal forces within the Alliance have undergone drastic changes over the last decade or so. Conservative trends eliminated the Labour Party from power in Britain, restored the Christian Democrats to the helm of the

Federal Republic, and swept Ronald Reagan to the White House. This common trend has created a far better mood for the Alliance. Philosophical affinities helped bridge certain differences: the pipeline dispute fizzled; the American armada of new missiles entered Europe with far less fuss than had initially been feared; and the rather unfortunate blunder of the American presidential visit to a cemetery with Nazi graves created only a temporary ripple on the otherwise smooth surface of American–European relations. The conservative forces in power in key capitals of the Alliance provided an ideological underpinning capable of glossing over temporary differences and floating freely in a seemingly undisturbed fashion.

But, within the inner strata of each of these countries, political protesters have been working their way up to the front row of political actors. It is in Germany that they have been the most vocal and the most visible. It is there that the Green Party, buttressed by fringe groups, emerged to challenge not only the purpose of the Alliance but also the basic socioeconomic structure of the republic. The peace movement, exclusively targeted against the American presence and conveniently omitting any criticism of the Soviet Union, gained ground in many circles. This is probably not surprising when one considers that Germany, forty years after the end of the war, is still garrisoned by a foreign army. I am not suggesting that the Federal Republic wishes the departure of American military contingents, but what I observed recently in Germany is a feeling of uneasiness regarding that presence. The post–World War II generations are entering key positions in government, industry, universities, and elsewhere. For them the American nuclear umbrella is almost a tradition, a historical continuity, even though there are doubts concerning its reliability. For many Germans, however, the physical presence of foreign soldiers on their soil is a sore subject.

Although Britain's protesters and the disenchanted have received less attention than their counterparts in Germany, a British peace movement does exist and indeed has deeper roots than any such movement anywhere else in Europe. After all, it was in the early thirties that the Oxford Union voted for peace at any price, that Oxford students swore never to fight for "King and Country." But, whereas this phenomenon a half century ago could be explained in traditional British isolationist terms, the situation today stems principally from opposition to nuclear rearmament. And, while the Oxford group, despite its impact, disappeared in the euphoria of the Battle of Britain, it is unlikely that a similarly clear-cut situation would emerge should there ever be a military confrontation between the two superpowers.

In the United States, on the other hand, challenges appear to be few and far between. It is true that the peace and antinuclear movements do gather momentum on occasion, that peaceful demonstrations occur here and there, and that the South African situation brings together people from various walks of life to demonstrate solidarity with the oppressed blacks. But the majority of the American people seem to be complacent, satisfied, and self-concerned. After the sense of drama that characterized the 1960s and 1970s, young Americans are once again thronging to business schools, large law firms, and investment banks and investing in venture capital. From time to time there is a flash of anger or compassion channeled into appropriate acts. The Solidarity movement in Poland ignited fires of tremendous sympathy; tons of food, clothing, and medicines were donated and assembled through the tireless efforts of volunteers. The Catholic Bishops' "Letter on Hunger in America" triggered a strong response. But these phenomena were like bright comets streaking across an otherwise dark and uniform sky.

This sense of complacency, of disinterest in political goals, this social apathy that John Kenneth Galbraith so aptly described in *The Affluent Society*, is probably the greatest danger for the future of the Alliance. For, a society preoccupied essentially with its economic well-being, unable or unwilling to eliminate hunger even in the midst of its own superabundance, a society that drifts back to simplistic slogans resurrecting the old sentiments of an America strong enough to go it alone, is a society bound to pull inward. There seems to be a prevailing sentiment among the majority of Americans that we are defending Europe with our money, arms, and manpower and that the Europeans are not doing their share. And this feeling is not directed at Europe alone. Even with so staunch an ally as Israel, very few Americans realize that the annual $3 billion in U.S. aid to the country is basically used to finance Israel's purchase of American military equipment, so the money does not actually leave our economy but provides jobs for America in our arms industries.

This growing sentiment affects the future of our relations with Europe. Some believe that we should withdraw our support, bring our troops home, and direct our resources to more pressing domestic or foreign needs such as Central America. We seem to be comfortable with the way the American dream is developing, and the huge fiscal problems clouding our future horizons seem so distant that we can simply ignore them. When the day of reckoning comes and the bills fall due, many of those who are today satisfied and complacent may raise their voices to clamor loudly for retrenchment and a return to fiscal sanity. Our commitments abroad, short of another Afghanistan or Poland, are bound to be high on their target list.

The political forces affecting the Alliance are without doubt linked to grave economic forces, the other component of the external factors we are examining. But before leaving the political aspect, it would perhaps be well to remind ourselves that the Alliance rests on two basic premises. One is common danger, fear of the Soviet Union and its traditional posture as a power-hungry empire. The other is mutual confidence and trust. While the fear element appears to be a constant, notwithstanding the tendency in certain circles in Europe to exonerate the Soviet Union and to castigate the United States as the guilty party, the confidence factor undergoes periodic fluctuations. For example, in 1984 a bitter dispute blew up when New Zealand objected to a visit to its ports by the U.S.S. *Buchanan*, a conventionally powered destroyer. The New Zealand government, responding to domestic public opinion, refused permission for the visit unless the United States would confirm or deny the presence of nuclear weapons on board the ship. The dispute itself created ill feelings among traditionally staunch friends of America, but what added to the resentment was Secretary of State Shultz's speech in 1985 castigating New Zealand for its stand. Ironically, the speech contained a stirring and apt description of the Alliance that contrasted sharply with the U.S. attempt to pressure New Zealand. After defining the Alliance as an agreement between free peoples, the secretary went on to say "Throughout history, there have been many alliances, but never before has there been so enduring a partnership between so many nations committed to democracy. Today our key alliances are democratic alliances; they are not agreements between rulers of governing elites but between peoples. The commitments made abroad must be approved and supported by our peoples through their elective representatives." Because it was precisely in the spirit of democracy outlined by Secretary Shultz that New Zealand had reacted to the destroyer's visit — asking for an American clarification because of the wishes of the electorate — his sermon appeared to many as hypocrisy itself.

The economic aspects of the Alliance have been aptly described elsewhere in this book. I would like to concentrate on one aspect alone, East–West trade. The very fact that the United States has become a debtor nation is an entirely unexpected, as well as negative, development. But within the framework of overall relations within the Alliance, it is the growing commercial ties between Western Europe and the Soviet bloc that are most likely to create stress and strain, as we saw in the notorious pipeline case. But that was just one element, one instance in the total equation. The Soviet Union needs Western European imports; they provide their best source of high-technology assistance. The economies of a number of Western European allies record an equal need for Soviet imports, particularly in energy-related transfers. The Soviet Union is still the leading oil producer in the world, followed by Saudi Arabia, and it is in the energy sector that a future conflict of interest between the allies may easily arise.

This particular aspect of East–West economic relations was addressed in the 27 June 1985 issue of the Brussels-based fortnightly bulletin *East–West*. It outlined in both statistical and analytical terms the great dilemma of the energy component of Soviet–Western European trade. According to the article, 85.2% of all Soviet imports from the West in 1984 were financed by income from the sale of oil, oil products, and natural gas, an increase of almost three percentage points over the previous year. These figures covered the advanced industrial countries, that is, the United States, Western Europe, Japan, Australia, and New Zealand. In the case of the European Community (EC) alone, the picture is even more disturbing. Soviet income from the sale of energy-related products in 1984 was 53.1% higher than the value of all Soviet imports from the EC. For certain individual countries, the numbers are worse: Soviet income from the sale of energy to Italy was more than double the value of all Soviet imports from that country.

A number of conclusions could be drawn from these cold statistics. One is that the Soviet Union's ability to earn hard currency depends heavily on the development of the energy market and on its ability to import modern energy-related equipment and machinery. Interestingly enough, while the current oil glut has negatively affected Soviet sales of refined products to the West, this decline has been entirely offset by the sale of crude oil and oil products and by exports of natural gas.

The other, and more disturbing, conclusion is that the West's dependence on Soviet energy imports seems to be growing. This could ultimately create problems in America's relations with its European allies when the question of export licensing with the Soviet Union comes up for such sensitive items as drilling equipment or the latest sensors used for oil prospecting. But there is still another curve to the rather bizarre relationship between East and West: the role of OPEC oil exports to the Soviet bloc countries.

In its report on the Soviet oil situation, the Brussels publication dealt with the Soviet resale of OPEC oil to offset the decline in its own oil output and to boost its hard currency earning. Although *East–West* conceded that its findings were not entirely based on hard evidence, it implied heavy reliance on Soviet statistical data. It estimated that a large share of OPEC sales to the Soviet Union was in payment for the supply of Soviet arms and munitions to such countries as Iraq. The irony of this piece of intelligence is that it is Saudi Arabia, America's closest ally in the Gulf area, that is one of the leading payees.

Libya, Iraq, Iran, and Saudi Arabia are the principal suppliers of oil to the Soviet Union. Within the last two years, according to statistical data compiled by *East–West*, the resale of OPEC oil doubled from such sources as Iraq and Saudi Arabia, increased slightly from Libya, and declined from Iran. But what comes out of the data is an extremely revealing fact: Without the resale of OPEC oil, Soviet trade with the developed countries of the West would show a trade deficit rather than the large surplus it currently reports. A footnote to this particular aspect of East–West relations, which illustrates the problem's complexity, comes from Czechoslovakia. A new cracking plant is to be built there involving a consortium of Western industrial firms from Austria (Voest Alpine), West Germany (Salzgitter

Lummus), and Italy (Snamprogetti). Once completed in 1988, the new cracking unit will considerably increase the Czech petrochemical industry and expand the range of its oil processing capacity. Given the role played by the Soviet bloc's energy sector in financing its hard currency deficit, not to mention its role in financing some of the existing conflicts in the Middle East, does Czechoslovakian–Western cooperation serve the interest of the Alliance? Or should it be considered harmful?

This leads to another item on the agenda, namely the security and military components, which remain, despite current political and economic differences, the underpinning factors of the Alliance. It is in the security and military domains that the Alliance premises of common danger and mutual confidence are absolutely crucial. It is here that the fringe groups and the "peace-at-any-price" activists are most in evidence and that the American nuclear dilemma, too often expressed in simplistic and unhelpful slogans about whether Washington would ever consider sacrificing New York to save Rome, enters the scene. Finally, it is here that the differing schools of thought concerning the Alliance itself collide. One of these schools attributes the well-being of the Western community to the existence of NATO and the EC. The other, more cynical perhaps and more pragmatically oriented, school suggests that the existence of NATO and other mechanisms surrounding the Alliance has been helpful but not decisive. In this view, it is Hiroshima and Nagasaki that gave the world a sense of impending global disaster and thus acted over the last forty years as the prime and principal deterrent.

The bumpy road along the highways and byways of strategic and conventional military thinking among the allied nations has been strewn with obstacles. The most important one, periodically encountered, is the credibility of the American nuclear deterrent. American statesmen from Henry Kissinger to Alexander Haig have aroused European fears concerning America's true intentions. Kissinger stated flatly that we would not risk a nuclear confrontation in defense of Western Europe. Haig, in his typical way, suggested using Europe as a testing ground for the newest and most devastating weapons to "scare the Russians out of their wits." Ronald Reagan, first with his total hostility toward any rapprochement with Moscow and more recently with his SDI (Star Wars) and his new flexibility toward arms control negotiations, gave rise to a mixture of bewilderment, respect, and fear. Western Europeans keep discussing the meaning of détente, which they hope will soon return, and keep wondering about their future.

Although far from being ready to assume the role of a third force, Europeans realize that, in point of fact, they already *are* a third force. Situated in the middle, facing the Soviet conventional armada on one side and relying on a distant nuclear American umbrella on the other, few are able to forget the realities of their situation. A 1985 issue of the *Bulletin of the*

Atomic Scientists asserted that since the Hiroshima bombing the United States has manufactured 60,000 nuclear warheads of 71 different types for use in 116 weapons systems. The Russians have manufactured almost as many. At the present, there is a total of about 50,000 nuclear warheads in existence in the world, carrying an explosive force more than one million times the power of the bomb that was unleashed on Hiroshima. In view of this, our allies keep asking, How much do we count? How far can we — Germans, Belgians, and others — consider ourselves nonexpendable in the event of a Soviet–American war? Is it not our role, our obligation, and our right to do our utmost to build bridges between East and West? Since we are not militarily considered the key players, should our role be that of a broker in the economic, cultural, and strategic negotiations, with arms control remaining the first priority item on our agenda?

This message came through in a subtle but forceful manner during the celebration of the thirtieth anniversary of the accession of Germany to NATO. Led by a Christian Democratic chancellor and considered to be the most valuable and the most reliable ally of the United States, the Federal Republic nevertheless clearly defined its position: "We remain as faithful and as close as we have always been, but we will continue to build bridges with the East." In his speech delivered for the occasion, Helmut Kohl, after reaffirming German faith and commitment to the solidarity and coherence of the Alliance, reminded his audience of other steps that Germany had taken in the past. The chancellor referred to the 1967 Harmel report, named for the Belgian foreign minister of that time, which "established a basis for relations with the Warsaw Pact countries which is valid to this day. It defined the two fundamental tasks of the alliance: a readiness for cooperation and for an improvement of relations, and a readiness for defense." Helmut Kohl then proceeded to list steps that the Federal Republic had initiated, including treaties signed with the Soviet Union, Poland, and Czechoslovakia and the "Basic Relations Treaty" with the GDR. "Reconciliation and the renunciation of force are the essence of these treaties. The people of our country support this unequivocal policy," the chancellor concluded.

It is significant that even while Kohl, representing the conservative current of the German political spectrum, was speaking, the Soviet Union was continuing its war in Afghanistan, the trials of Solidarity activists in Poland were going full swing, and the buildup of Soviet military might continued unabated. But Kohl, as a European and a realist, could not have spoken any differently regardless of his close ties with America. Nor could any other German political figure. He was reflecting the overall sentiments of his people.

Once again, the underlying theme that emerged from the chancellor's remarks was of Western Europe as a catalyst and bridge builder, in short, a third force. So we come full circle: from the 1950s and the first experience of Finland's successful experiment in neutrality to the present, when we are commemorating the anniversary of not only NATO but also the Hiroshima bombing and all that it demonstrated to the rest of the world. The internal and external forces affecting the Western Alliance have once again come into focus. They are difficult, sometimes painful and irritating, often strained but somehow surviving. There are, of course, other elements almost too numerous to mention, almost too complex to summarize in a short essay, such as the nature of the Soviet economy and the limits it places on attempts at economic reforms in the satellite countries, the limits being dictated by the dogma that central planning must be preserved, that the party must remain in full control of the economy, and that the main economic decisions must be coordinated with the Soviet Union. That spells the impossibility of the socialist countries' assuring dynamic economic development and technical progress, and it limits the impact of détente on East–West relations. Without détente, some political analysts maintain, the Solidarity movement in Poland would not have been born; so they question if détente is really on the Soviet strategic agenda. Furthermore, there is the relationship among China, the USSR, and the United States; the trade war between some of the members of the Alliance, particularly Japan; and the role of the European Community and its ability to survive inner tensions. All these questions must be answered, though not in this brief paper.

Enough has been said, however, to ascertain that the Western system of alliances is an extremely fragile edifice. It is vulnerable to political winds, economic hurricanes, and strategic blunders. But, as Secretary of State Shultz said, it is an edifice built upon the principle of free choice and the ideals of Jeffersonian democracy. The price to pay for its fragility often appears high. But it has survived years of crisis, as well as years of euphoria. Above the Alliance, as indeed above the heads of all those who make the Alliance a political reality, hangs the nuclear threat. That threat, reduced to human dimensions by the Hiroshima tragedy, has been a powerful factor in the continued success of the Alliance. Its effectiveness is clear from the most telling result: forty years of uneasy, but nevertheless unbroken and peaceful coexistence between two powers armed to the teeth, each obsessed with its own security and distrustful of the motivations of the other. The next challenge to the Alliance will be to survive another half century of that unbroken peace, a period of time in human history when new generations, forgetful and perhaps less willing to learn the lessons of Hiroshima, will hold the levers of power.

6

The Leadership of Reagan and Gorbachev: The Soviet Perspective

Otto Pick

For many years the senility and weakness of the Soviet leadership created serious doubts in the West about finding credible negotiating partners in the Kremlin who would not only be able to conclude agreements on matters of important concern, but would also live long enough to guarantee their implementation. This situation has now been reversed, for the Soviet Union has acquired in Mikhail Gorbachev a new, relatively young, and energetic leader, who has already given evidence of his ability to consolidate his position in record time and who, given the nature of the Soviet system, is likely to stay in power for many years to come. As a leading Spanish Communist wrote, perhaps optimistically, soon after his appointment as general secretary of the Soviet Communist party, Gorbachev symbolizes "the desire for change that exists within the Soviet Union's most dynamic sectors."[1] Continuity in the conduct of Soviet foreign policy seems to be assured.

In the past, continuity had been embodied in the person of Andrei Gromyko. He had held the post of foreign minister for over a quarter of a century. However, until the declining years of Brezhnev's life, Gromyko acted simply as the Politburo's chief executive in foreign affairs, without having many opportunities to develop and apply his own policies. More recently, as the central decision-making process became increasingly affected by sickness and debility, Gromyko's personal impact on East–West relations made itself felt in the shape of hard-line rejections of Western positions on arms control and other issues. Now that Gromyko has assumed the largely ceremonial post of chairman of the Supreme Soviet, it would appear that the new general secretary intends to pursue his own policies. It seems that a new style has emerged, though the basic content of foreign policy will probably remain the same.

Discontinuity presents a problem in Washington rather than in Moscow. This has nothing to do with President Reagan's age or any illness. It stems from the American Constitution, for in his second term, an American president inevitably tends to become a lame duck. Whatever the outcome of the 1988 presidential election, it is certain that the United States will acquire new leaders. It is by no means clear who the candidates will be and what policies they would apply if elected. From the Soviet point of view, the best attitude to East–West relations for the next two or three years would be to mark time, to wait for 1988, and in the meantime, to utilize any opportunities that might present themselves for adjusting the correlation of forces. Above all, they will try to delay progress on the Strategic Defense Initiative for as long as possible.

ASSESSING SOVIET PRIORITIES

This approach makes even more sense in the context of the grim range of domestic problems that Gorbachev has to face. He needs time, not only to solidify his personal position, but also to try to reorganize the Soviet economy. He seems to be determined to continue the campaign against corruption begun by Andropov; but that in itself will not suffice to create an economic base that would enable the USSR to enter the next century with any degree of confidence. In August 1985 a decree providing for a measure of decentralization of industrial management was published, but this was only a necessary first step. In a speech made before his predecessor's death, on 10 December 1984 Gorbachev claimed that "socialism has created and continues to exert its main influence on world development through its economic policy and through its success in the socio-economic field." Given the present state of the Soviet economy, this is little more than wishful thinking. However, Gorbachev may be determined to turn the wish into reality, and therefore the repair and restructuring of the Soviet economy must be his first priority. If he were to succeed, the USSR would then be in a position to conduct a more effective and even more threatening foreign policy.

In the meantime, foreign policy initiatives would have to be reduced for some time, and waiting for the next American president could logically be regarded as part of this relative lull. It is, however, obvious that a superpower cannot simply withdraw from the international arena; a return to Stalin's "socialism in one country" is quite out of the question today.

Gorbachev himself has tended to emphasize the theme of continuity in foreign policy and certainly has given no indication of wishing to deviate from the basic ideological premises formulated by Marx and Lenin. In his speech to mark the fortieth anniversary of the end of the war, he trotted out all the tired, stereotyped statements about "imperialism" and the "Munich conspiracy," without, of course, mentioning the Hitler–Stalin pact. His public statements, both before and after his elevation to supreme office, contained the customary quota of attacks on "U.S. imperialism" and its plans to "militarize outer space." In making his proposals for a nuclear freeze and, more recently, for a five-month moratorium on nuclear testing, Gorbachev did little more than repeat previous propaganda ploys, although the USSR observed a unilateral moratorium on tests until the end of 1985. In his press conference on the occasion of the Hiroshima anniversary, President Reagan said the idea of a moratorium was worth considering after the conclusion of the present series of U.S. tests. Subsequent official comment in Washington concentrated on the problem of verification procedures. In fact, Soviet opposition to the SDI has continued unabated since Gorbachev came to power, and Soviet support for Nicaragua has increased.

Yet there have been signs that the new Soviet leadership might want to develop a slightly revised order of priorities in the pursuit of its foreign policy goals. The U.S.–Soviet involvement, although central to East–West relations, could possibly be left to simmer for the time being. The Soviet Union will continue to utilize opportunities for increasing its influence in the Third World and will certainly try to maintain and improve its position there. Efforts to divide the West will not be abandoned, and it is likely that Western Europe will be given special attention, to differentiate it from the United States. In an interview published in *Pravda* on 8 April 1985, Gorbachev stressed that "we do not look at the world solely through the prism of U.S.-Soviet relations. . . . [We] realize the weight of other countries in international affairs." Paradoxically, past European fears of a Soviet–American agreement concluded over the heads of the European allies may give way to fresh American concerns about dealings between Western Europe and the USSR. They could lead to a strengthening of Mansfield-like tendencies in Congress, and Gorbachev is not unaware of this. He has, for example, supported moves for economic cooperation between the East European bloc (COMECON) and the European Community. Talks between the two organizations were broken off after the invasion of Afghanistan, but in June 1985 COMECON issued a formal invitation for EC representatives to come to Moscow for exploratory talks. In this context, the concern of West European governments about changing American strategic doctrines, implied by SDI, and the dissatisfaction of some sections of West European opinion with the Reagan administration's style, will certainly be fully exploited.

Special attention is being given to courting West European Social Democrats. The fiftieth anniversary of the Seventh World Congress of the Comintern and the proclamation of the Popular Front policy was marked by a feature article in *Pravda* on 25 July 1985. It drew an analogy between the common struggle of Socialists and Communists against Hitler and the "present global threat of nuclear cataclysm," which "demands a global response: united action by all those who speak out against the militarists." The Soviet Party paper concluded "A major role in the defense of peace belongs to the joint actions of Communists and Social Democrats."

In May 1985, after Willy Brandt's and Bettino Craxi's visits to Moscow, *Pravda* argued that "the continued development of contacts between the Soviet Communist Party and the Socialist International, and Social Democratic and Socialist Parties, in particular with the SPD, is taking on considerable significance."[2] In October a high-level Soviet delegation even attended a conference on disarmament organized by the Socialist International in Vienna.

In its attempts to split Western opinion, the Soviet Union will be firing at a variety of targets, and, in the short term, it will look to the controversy about SDI for most of its ammunition. The crude appeal to West European Social Democrats may not have much effect, but it is all part of a general campaign against the United States and its present administration.[3] Moscow seems to be pursuing a two-track policy of trying to isolate the United States on one hand, while hoping to win concessions on the other. Firmness, based on agreed positions arrived at after thorough and careful discussion, would appear to be the Alliance's proper response.

In his speech to the Soviet Communist party's Central Committee immediately after his appointment as general secretary, and again in his oration at Chernenko's funeral, Gorbachev went out of his way to affirm his determination "to preserve and strengthen in every way the fraternal friendship of our closest friends and allies — the countries of the great socialist community." However, it is by no means clear that a decision on the ways and means of achieving this goal had been reached in Moscow when Gorbachev met President Reagan in Geneva. The Soviet press has carried articles calling for more centralized control over Eastern Europe, but other commentators have publicly spoken of the merits of diversity. Thus on 21 June 1985, *Pravda* asked

> What question can there be of any mediation by particular socialist countries in resolving disagreements between the USA and the USSR if on key international questions the foreign policy of the USSR and of the Marxist–Leninist nucleus of world socialism is identical?"

This was a clear reference to Hungarian, East German, and Rumanian claims that smaller states in Europe had a special role to play in easing East–West tensions.

On the other hand, the party theoretical journal *Komunist* came out with two articles in July 1985 that acknowledged the importance of recognizing the national interests of the member states of the "socialist community." This debate could continue for some time, as other more urgent priorities have to be faced in the Kremlin. But a really major breakthrough in international relations would be achieved if Gorbachev were to succeed in really improving relations with China. The demonstratively cordial welcome he gave to the Chinese vice premier, Li Peng, who came to Moscow to attend Chernenko's funeral, and his call for "a serious improvement of relations with the Chinese People's Republic" would indicate that a new effort will be made in this direction.[4]

RETURN TO DÉTENTE?

The achievement of at least some of these goals over the next two years would certainly tilt the global correlation of forces in the Soviet Union's favor, and it could then approach the basic problem of East–West relations from a more advantageous position. The nature and outcome of Gorbachev's domestic policies will, of course, be closely affected by the state of East–West relations, and a return to détente would give him the time to think and to pursue his economic reforms. It would probably also confuse the West and cloud the real issues. During the ten years after the signing of the Helsinki Final Act, it became obvious that détente meant different things to different people. The USSR looked for the ratification of the post-1945 status quo in Europe, perhaps playing for time to press on with its armaments programs and hoping to reap some benefit from increased trading links with the West. The West Europeans, regarding themselves as the principal consumers of détente, expected to derive some advantage from a liberalization of East–West trade. They wished for a lowering of the barriers between the two halves of Europe and for an improvement in the human rights policies in the East. The East European regimes simply sought to obtain a greater degree of autonomy. The neutrals saw an opportunity to enhance their security by supporting a general relaxation of East–West tensions.

The United States regarded the Helsinki process as a means of persuading the USSR to behave like a "normal" state in the international system. It is not surprising that this confusion of goals led to renewed confrontation between East and West; there was a tough impasse when the foreign ministers of the Helsinki signatories assembled on the tenth anniversary of the Final Act but could not even agree on the wording of a communiqué. A new détente after 1988 could be forged by a well-established Soviet leadership from a position of strength or by a newly elected American president. It might, alternatively, serve as a prelude to yet another period of confrontation unless the Western alliance succeeds in defining its own goals, and the perceived purposes of the Soviet bloc, well in advance. Nothing is likely to happen until the United States completes its presidential election campaign.

ARMS CONTROL

It is usually agreed by arms control theorists that failure to achieve progress in this vital area generally reflects the degree of tension between East and West at any given time. Thus the Soviet invasion of Afghanistan prevented the ratification of SALT II by the U.S. Senate. Only an overall improvement in East–West relations could bring the two sides closer to an agreement. Yet the terrible potential and sheer size of the nuclear arsenal held by both the superpowers affects the international environment in general, and the climate of U.S.–Soviet relations in particular. In other words, the likelihood of a rapprochement between Moscow and Washington is diminished as the nuclear arms race accelerates. Similarly, the prospects for progress toward an arms control agreement will remain unpromising as long as there is no improvement in East–West relations. This is the key issue between the United States and the USSR.

The U.S.–Soviet arms control talks in Geneva have been deadlocked because the negotiating goals of the two sides seem to be incompatible. The Soviet Union's concern is to prevent the implementation of SDI, while the United States aims to achieve a reduction in the USSR's land-based offensive missile capability. At the time of writing, there were no signs of a breakthrough.[5] The inflexible positions both sides have adopted, for political rather than strategic reasons, have so far prevented them from exploring the possibility of a trade-off. The almost last hope for some kind of an agreement rested with the meetings scheduled between Reagan and Gorbachev.

It is unlikely that the USSR will be prepared to scale down its offensive missile capability to any marked extent. In the Soviet view, the USSR's status as a global superpower hinges on the primacy of its rocket forces. Furthermore, the Soviet Union wishes to preserve the ABM treaty. This has a bearing on Soviet attitudes to SDI, but it also extends to less exotic forms of antiballistic missile defense. According to the Soviet Chief of Staff, Marshal Akhromeyev, writing in *Pravda* on 4 June 1985: "Preserving the treaty between the USSR and the US on the limitation of anti-ballistic systems from destruction is of enormous importance." The Soviet Union has no desire to plunge into a costly arms race in space, especially as technologically it could not match the United States.

The Soviet Union was ready to negotiate about strategic arms limitations in SALT I only after it had achieved virtual strategic parity with the United States. There is no reason to suppose that it would be prepared to abandon the advantage it has gained except in exchange for a major and substantial concession by the other side. It is more than doubtful that such concessions would be made by the Reagan administration. Furthermore, Gorbachev's recent elevation to supreme office does place him under the handicap of not being able to show any signs of weakness, and meeting the United States more than half way could be interpreted in this way.

In view of the distaste for the SDI evinced in many quarters in Western Europe, the Soviets must know that this is one of the potentially weaker links in the Atlantic Alliance. Gorbachev aims to procrastinate and play for time in the hope that the outcome of the next U.S. presidential election will bury SDI, at least temporarily, giving the USSR an opportunity to carry on with its own long-standing research in space weaponry. He can then pillory the Americans for their intransigence on an issue that, it is claimed, might enhance their own security at the expense of their European allies.

The Soviets could also play upon the argument that any advance in the military utilization of space would reduce the effectiveness of the French, British, and Chinese nuclear deterrents. They could even turn to the Europeans with arms control proposals specifically addressed to these fears; for example, in the context of INF deployments, by driving an even deeper wedge into the Alliance. By 1988 the Kohl and Thatcher administrations may have been replaced by more left-leaning governments in the Federal Republic of Germany and the United Kingdom, and they might be more inclined to deal directly with the USSR on arms control and related questions. It is therefore imperative that NATO be in a position to respond to such diplomatic developments. However, given the virtual American monopoly over the arms control talks and East–West relations, provision within NATO for political contingency planning may be very difficult, if not impossible, to establish.

THE SPECIAL RELATIONSHIP

The meeting between Reagan and Gorbachev in 1985 symbolized an enduring trend in Soviet foreign policy. It put the "special relationship" with the United States at the very top of Soviet priorities. This concern to reach agreements on spheres of influence with the perceived major adversary lies within a well-established Russian and Soviet tradition, which has manifested itself in the eighteenth-century partitions of Poland, Alexander I and his bargain with Napoleon at Tilsit, a number of agreements with Prussia and later imperial Germany at the time of Bismarck, the 1907 Convention with Britain and, last but not least, Stalin's pact with Hitler in 1939. Perhaps Gorbachev had this in mind when he told *Pravda* on 8 April 1985 that the "confrontation" between the United States and the USSR should not be regarded as an "inborn defect," but only as an "anomaly."

In the 1970s the special relationship with the United States reached its apogee; the two superpowers were the providers of détente, which both the West and East Europeans received from their hands with varying degrees of gratitude. The invasion of Afghanistan and the arrival of Ronald Reagan in the White House put an end to this state of affairs, creating a vacuum at the very top of the Soviet order of policies. Gorbachev must now attempt to restore the superpower dialogue, and he may try to force the pace by concentrating on improving relations with China and according greater importance to Western Europe.

Failure to make progress with the United States on arms control could provide both the rationale and the excuse for recasting the Soviet order of foreign policy priorities. If successful, this approach could bring about the isolation of the United States within the international system in general and the Atlantic Alliance in particular. This, in turn, could reinforce both isolationist and Pacific-oriented trends in the United States. The hiatus in American policy caused by the final stages of Reagan's second term could thus be utilized to some advantage. Of course, a scenario of this kind is purely speculative. It assumes that Washington would be incapable of developing suitable responses and that the Atlantic Alliance would be politically as ineffective as the Russians would like to imagine.

THE 1985 GENEVA MEETING

More than any preceding superpower summit meetings, Geneva suffered from all the disadvantages inherent in this kind of public diplomacy. For months before the meeting, both sides indulged in concentrated propaganda campaigns that merely served to harden their positions in advance and to reduce their negotiating options. Most of the time they appeared to be addressing their domestic constituencies rather than one another. This opened the way for attempts by various pressure groups and vested interests to influence the principal negotiators in advance of their meeting. The leaked Weinberger letter, in which the secretary of defense tried to remind his president that the U.S. military buildup must continue, was a notorious instance of an all too open diplomacy. In the event, it was surprising that the Geneva meeting went as well as it did. The positive atmosphere generated was largely due to the personal interaction of two men. They seemed to be fully aware of their responsibilities, and they spent much more time together than had been originally planned. The news blackout imposed during the meeting also helped. It might have been even more useful had it been in force for several weeks before the summit.

Yet the immediate practical results of Geneva were meager. On the critical question of arms control, the two sides seem to have merely agreed to disagree. Ronald Reagan steadfastly maintained his position that SDI was nonnegotiable. Gorbachev simply went on repeating his demand that it be abandoned, choosing virtually to ignore the president's offer to share the results of American research with the USSR in due course. Before the meeting, Soviet spokesmen had indicated that the USSR might agree to a formula that would allow "pure" research to continue but that it would oppose development and testing. In view of the Soviet Union's own long-standing research on the use of lasers and particle beams in space, they could hardly do less. The Soviet leader acknowledged the president's sincerity in regarding SDI as a way of ridding humanity of the threat of nuclear war, but he appeared to dismiss Reagan's attitude as emotional. He still held to the Soviet position that SDI could never become 100 percent effective, but that it could give the Americans an opportunity to launch a first strike against the USSR while devising some sort of defense against a ragged Soviet response.

The United States and the USSR had gone to Geneva with the intention of reducing their offensive nuclear weapons systems by 50%, but they disagreed on which systems to scale back. The Soviets wish to include gravity bombs and all air-launched missiles, whereas the United States wants to count only air-launched cruise missiles, ground-based missiles, and submarine-launched ballistic missiles (SLBMs). The two sides agreed to accelerate only their negotiations on strategic arms control. In one respect, however, the improved climate resulting from Geneva has borne some fruit. Both sides have come forward with new proposals for reducing INF levels of weapons deployed in Europe though their proposals stand in total conflict in purpose.

Reagan and Gorbachev also agreed that the nuclear nonproliferation treaty should be extended and that discussions on the banning of chemical weapons should be intensified. The opening of consulates in Kiev and New York; the resumption of cultural, academic, and other exchanges; and the consideration of a jointly manned crisis center were highly welcome. But they cannot be regarded as major moves toward a new era of détente. More importantly, Gorbachev accepted an invitation to come to the United States in 1986, and President Reagan agreed to return the visit in 1987, thus accepting the responsibility to progress with summit negotiations.

On the key issue of arms control there was no progress at all. Although regional conflicts were on the U.S. agenda for Geneva, there was no agreement on controlling the crisis situations in Afghanistan, Ethiopia, Angola, Nicaragua, or Kampuchea. On human rights the meeting just produced the anodyne statement that they agreed on the "importance of resolving humanitarian cases in the spirit of cooperation."[6] In some respects, Gorbachev did make a minor concession by agreeing to speed up strategic arms control negotiations even though Reagan did not give way at all on SDI. Previously, the Soviets had refused to discuss the chances of cutting back nuclear weapons systems so long as the Americans maintained their position on SDI. On the question of chemical weapons, the USSR now agrees that intensified talks could lead to the destruction of *all* existing stockpiles, while previously it had only considered making partial reductions.

AFTER THE SUMMIT

The initial Soviet reactions to Geneva were favorable. Gorbachev went off to Prague to brief the leaders of his Warsaw Pact allies on his talks with Reagan, and they all seemed to welcome the outcome of the summit as an indication of an improving international environment. However, soon after Gorbachev's return to Moscow, caution and a return to the Soviet position adopted before the summit seemed to gain the upper hand. On 20 November, while the summit was still in progress, the weekly *Literaturnaya Gazeta*, in an article headlined "Days of Hope," spoke of "laying the foundations for the necessary though long and difficult process of improving the international climate." On 23 November, the party daily *Pravda*, though welcoming a new psychological climate, warned that "no miracles" could be expected. On 24 November, *Izvestia* said that "regrettably" there had been no progress on arms control and reiterated the hard-line Soviet position on SDI. On the same day, the Army daily *Krasnaya Zvezda* argued in a fairly harsh commentary that "the US is not yet ready for decision. That is the situation today."

Yet Gorbachev seemed determined to present the summit in a favorable light. During the Supreme Soviet debate on the defense budget at the end of November, he stressed that the USSR would not tolerate an American arms monopoly in space and it would, if necessary, develop its own responses. He added on 27 November: "We value the personal contact established with the U.S. President. It is important that the dialogue did take place; it is itself a stabilizing factor in our difficult time."[7] The Soviet Politburo assessment of Geneva said that it "marked the beginning of a dialogue with a view toward achieving changes for the better in Soviet–American relations and the world as a whole."

At the beginning of December, Gorbachev tried a new way of projecting well-worn arguments. Speaking to a group of 150 American businessmen that included the U.S. secretary of commerce, in a televised broadcast of a Kremlin dinner, the general secretary complained of "political obstacles" to Soviet–U.S. trade stemming from Washington's policies of linking most-favored-nation status to human rights issues, of supporting embargoes on strategic goods, and of indulging in trade sanctions for political reasons.[8] After stressing that the USSR would welcome economic links with the West in the development of its economy, and deploring that Soviet trade with the United States was less than with Finland, Belgium or Austria, he emphasized the stabilizing role that good trading relations should play.[9]

Gorbachev received the customary reply from the Americans when Secretary Baldridge made it clear that the Jackson–Vanik Amendment would not be repealed. A few days later Secretary of State George Shultz pointed out that the normalization of U.S.–Soviet trade relations could not be divorced from the human rights issue. At the December meeting of the NATO foreign ministers in Brussels, Shultz seemed determined to defuse some of the euphoria generated by Geneva on both sides of the Atlantic. He warned against excessive optimism and emphasized that the United States would not negotiate under the pressure of time and certainly would not agree to any measures that might compromise Western security. It now remains to be seen if the personal contacts between Reagan and Gorbachev, and the alleged improvement in the international climate, can ultimately produce concrete results.

The East European reactions to the summit provide an interesting footnote to the proceedings. They suggest that little has changed in the increasingly complex relationships between the USSR and its Warsaw Pact partners.[10] The Rumanian comments predictably played down the significance of the summit, probably because a true and lasting rapprochement between the superpowers would make Ceauşescu's quasi-autonomous foreign policy less interesting. The Hungarians, on the other hand, welcomed Geneva with considerable enthusiasm. Gyula Horn, state secretary in the Ministry of Foreign Affairs, repeated on Budapest television the established Hungarian line that any improvement in East–West tensions was "favorable for small and medium-sized countries in Europe," arguing that "more had been accomplished than anyone could have expected." The East Germans, insisting upon the significance of intra-German relations, talked again about the special responsibility of both German states for peace in Europe."[11] Czechoslovak comments ranged from initial optimism to caution;[12] but, in a communiqué, issued after President Husak's visit to East Berlin on 27 November, it was agreed to regard the outcome of Geneva as positive. In this context, it is interesting that, according to a parliamentary statement by the Foreign Ministry in Bonn, the German Democratic Republic (GDR) had agreed to take part in Soviet SDI research after the Soviet defense minister, Marshal Sokolov, had asked all the Warsaw Pact members in April 1985 to participate in relevant research and development.[13]

THE LIMITS OF SOVIET POLICY

In considering possible Soviet policies during what is left of President Reagan's term of office and beyond, it is dangerous to ascribe views of Soviet behavior from uncertain perceptions of the personalities involved. Soviet foreign policy, despite its theoretical reliance on Marxist–Leninist doctrine, is subject to contending and interacting elements within Soviet society, to developments elsewhere in the international system, and to the impact of advancing military technologies. In this respect, the Soviet Union has to behave like any other state.

The Soviet leadership faces fearsome problems at home, especially in the economic sector. The new men in the Kremlin will no doubt try their hand at economic reform, but, to be effective, they have to dislodge and turn around a well-entrenched bureaucracy that has acquired a vested interest in the status quo, and they must divert resources from the vastly inflated military expenditure budgets of recent years. The conflicts of interest among the East European regimes will also have to be resolved. Furthermore, if the USSR intends to present a more acceptable face to the West, it will have to resist the temptation to pursue overtly activist policies in the Third World, whether in Afghanistan, Africa, or Central America.

The freedom of action available to the Soviet leadership will continue to be subject to severe constraints stemming from objective causes, and Gorbachev may well be unable to pursue the policies that might appeal to the USSR. The Soviet Union is not exempt from the validity of Thucydides' axiom that a state does what it can and suffers what it must.

THE WESTERN RESPONSE

The task of U.S. policy and, indeed, of the Atlantic Alliance as a whole, will be to exploit this situation. It will require a high degree of political judgment and diplomatic skill. To pile on pressure and to indulge in the rhetoric of force would be a serious mistake, especially if it reduced the Soviet leadership to a suppliant role without leaving it any option, except intransigence, for the protection of legitimate Soviet interests.

The West must also strive to close some of the windows of opportunity that in the past have encouraged the USSR to expand its influence. The social and economic conditions of the Third World create revolutionary situations; the Soviet Union does not cause them, but it naturally tends to exploit them where possible. The West could certainly do more to assist the Third World and thus reduce Soviet opportunities. At home, in Western society, too, there are many defects that undermine its cohesion and weaken its efficiency. It is cruel to reproach the younger generation for their apparent inability to understand the threat from the East, when, in many Western countries, considerable numbers of young people face a future of almost permanent unemployment.

The Atlantic Alliance has always been in a state of crisis, a situation that cannot be avoided in a peacetime coalition of free societies. But as it approaches its fourth decade, it faces new problems and challenges that cannot be met by the usual policy of muddling through, hoping for the best, and relying in the final analysis on American protection and leadership.

Pious phrases about consultation should at long last be translated into reality, if only to avoid detrimental discussion in public about surprise initiatives such as SDI or the invasion of Grenada. There is no room for unilateral actions that are prompted by delusions of hegemony. If it is true that America's global capacity to project power has been declining in relative terms, then the European allies must be more forthcoming in supporting the United States. Although a renegotiation of the North Atlantic treaty lies outside the realm of practical politics today, the Alliance should be more specific about its readiness to act together outside the NATO area. While it is more comfortable to proceed by informal discussion behind the scenes, this approach fails to demonstrate the allies' clarity of purpose, both to adversaries and to themselves. To arrive at a common purpose is, of course, the precondition of all successful alliance policies.

Gorbachev may fail in his gigantic task of reform and consolidation. On the other hand, even partial success would present the West with a much more formidable adversary. It is unfortunate that, in the twilight of the Reagan era, it may be almost impossible for the Alliance to restructure its approach to East–West relations and to prepare for the testing time to come.

NOTES

1. A. Claret, in the Barcelona paper *Lan Vanguardia*, 13 March 1985.
2. *Pravda*, 31 May 1985.
3. Shortly before the summit, *Pravda* printed an article headlined *Europe Is Our Common Home*, 13 November 1985. It spoke of the special European responsibility to put an end to the arms race: "For Washington it is foreign ground, a battlefield on the maps of the strategists."
4. In his speech to the Central Committee of the Soviet Communist Party in March 1985. In contrast, China sees three principal obstacles to a normalization of Sino–Soviet relations: Soviet support for Vietnam in Kampuchea, the Afghanistan war, and Soviet troop concentrations along the Sino–Soviet border. But there has been some positive movement. Gorbachev repeated that the "the negative period in Soviet–Chinese relations, which has produced quite a few artificial overlayers," could soon be ended (*TASS*, 26 June 1985).

    In 1985 it was agreed that Sino–Soviet trade should be doubled to \$3 billion a year by 1990, including Soviet assistance in China's industrial modernization, together with Soviet shipments of machinery, raw materials, transportation equipment, building materials and chemicals to be exchanged for Chinese raw materials and consumer goods. An agreement on border trading was also concluded, and China contracted to purchase seventeen TU-15 airliners.
5. Czechoslovak News Agency, 12 November 1985.
6. Andrei Sakharov's wife Yelena Bonner was allowed to leave for medical treatment in the West shortly afterward.
7. *TASS*, 27 November 1985.
8. *TASS*, 11 December 1985.
9. In 1984 Soviet exports to the United States amounted to no more than \$600

million, and imports from the United States, consisting largely of grain, to $3.2 billion.
10. Since March 1984, the Hungarians have not hesitated, despite Czechoslovak and Polish criticism, to speak of the special interest of small states in relaxing East–West tensions. The East Germans have tried, too, to keep their special relationship with the Federal Republic alive in the teeth of Soviet, Polish, and Czechoslovak opposition. (See Pick, O. 1985. "Eastern Europe: A Divergence of Conflicting Interests," in *The World Today*. London: Royal Institute of International Affairs.)
11. *Neues Deutschland*, 23 November 1985.
12. Prague Radio, on 24 November 1985, claimed "it would not be wise to nourish too many illusions."
13. *CDU/CSU Pressediensst*, 25 October 1985.

7

Two Views from West Germany: What Can We Expect from the New Leaders in the Kremlin?

Stephan G. Thomas

My point of view is necessarily subjective. I managed to survive the Hitler regime, though I was a marked member of the opposition. After the war I became a committed Atlanticist, seeing the Alliance as an indispensable guarantee to the defense of Western Europe. Nearly forty years later I am still convinced that the principles of containment are vital to Western security and Alliance unity.

The advocacy of containment was first heard from George Kennan in 1947, and every American administration since then has adhered to the wisdom of vigilantly containing Russia's expansive tendencies. It is obvious that President Reagan will not depart from the pattern in his second term. It has become, along with the Harmel principles, the basic strategic doctrine of the Alliance.

Today the questions to be answered are, How far will it be possible to reduce the tensions between East and West? In the forthcoming rounds of summit meetings and arms control negotiations, can U.S. strategy be harmonized with Gorbachev's aims in central Europe? Can a genuine *modus vivendi* between East and West be agreed upon? Is it feasible to negotiate over reductions in the development and deployment of strategic, tactical, and defensive systems? More important, can the negotiations succeed unless there is a fundamental change in the political climate of the East–West relationship?

These are difficult questions to answer. In doing so I must again cite Kennan's dictum that armaments are a function and not a cause of political tension. Limitations of armaments on a multilateral scale cannot be effected as long as basic political problems remain unresolved, he warned.

What remains to be seen is whether change will come in the ideological doctrines of the ruling elite in the USSR. Several indications of changes in Soviet policy have been signaled, first by Andropov and then by Gorbachev. But do they indicate a new appraisal of power realities in the nuclear age, and will a new leadership in the Kremlin at last dislodge the sterile dogmatism of Soviet thought? Optimists allege that a turnover among the elite in the Andropov–Gorbachev era might produce a fresh approach to domestic and foreign policy issues. The pessimists are less convinced. They agree that changes started with Andropov's ascent to power after Brezhnev's death in 1982. As a former head of the KGB, he was in the best position to know how sclerotic the Soviet economy had become. He knew about the managerial inefficiency, the chronic inflexibility, the poor distribution system, and the deplorable service sector. Andropov entertained few doubts about "the inherent horror harbored by the established bureaucracy against innovation and change." The judgment came from the former British ambassador to Moscow in 1978–1982 (see Curtis Keeble, *International Affairs*, Autumn 1984). But Andropov also remembered the fate of the "reformer" Khrushchev. He emphasized the need for caution in starting the process of change, but he nevertheless tried to reform the power-encrusted elites and their rigid doctrines.

It is revealing that Andropov justified the need for drastic changes by referring to "the advice of Lenin" on how the victory of socialism was to be achieved. Raising productivity, according to Lenin, would be "decisive for the victory of our social order and for capitalism's defeat." This visionary forecast by Lenin in 1919 was quoted by Andropov in 1983 as a jolt to an apprehensive bureaucracy. Andropov and his crew of younger technocrats determined to initiate a far-reaching set of structural reforms in the Soviet economy, but without endangering the absolute power of the ruling Communist party and without changing the received ideology of Leninism. He was determined to start the corrective process, and Gorbachev will apparently continue in the spirit of his mentor. He is the heir and legitimate successor to Andropov, but it may be that he will find as little success in moving the Soviet system to modernize its economic and political structure.

Significantly, both Andropov and Gorbachev insisted on restating one vital point: "The question of preserving peace is the central problem of foreign policy." They called for a reevaluation of the dangers of nuclear war, proclaiming that "Communists should fight for the rights of man to live in peace." The revised party program adopted by the Central Committee in June 1983 emphasized their serious call to peaceful coexistence.

Gorbachev said in a *Time* interview of 9 September 1985, when asked about the future of Soviet–American relations,

> Whether we like one another or not, we can either survive or perish only together. . . . Are we at last ready to recognize that there is no other way

to live at peace with each other? . . . And are we prepared to switch our mentality and our mode of acting from a warlike to a peaceful track? As you say, live and let live. We call it peaceful coexistence.

No doubt that is the Soviet position President Reagan faces in his second term as he tries to define the policy of the United States toward the Atlantic Alliance.

In an article in *Foreign Affairs*, James Schlesinger, the former secretary of defense, commented on the changing relations between the United States and the USSR and on the different approaches that had been adopted by Truman, Eisenhower, Nixon, Carter, and Reagan toward the Soviet Union. Referring to Nixon's pragmatism, he identified its central feature as "the quest for an era of negotiations, not of confrontation."[1] This led in due course to the Moscow agreement of May 1972 and the SALT treaties, the goodwilled spirit of détente, and the serious effort to reduce tensions between the two nuclear superpowers. It was obvious that many of Reagan's followers came to question or reject the goodwill and the negotiations that were generated by détente. They insisted that the Russians must be met only with an armaments drive and implacable opposition. Their enthusiasms and certainties were not widely shared in Western Europe.

One of the strongest contributions to the era of détente came from the government of Willy Brandt, and it was later continued by Helmut Schmidt. Their aim was to reduce tensions between East and West and to establish normal relations between the Federal Republic and the GDR and Poland. To this end, treaties were signed with the USSR and Poland in 1970 and the GDR in 1972, and the Berlin treaty was signed in 1971. This network of international treaties in Europe became possible after Washington and Moscow had started the era of détente. If the mood of trust had not been strengthened, tensions in central Europe today would still be highly strained.

In the first years of the Reagan administration, in Schlesinger's opinion, Reagan believed that his predecessors had failed to convey to the Soviets how tough America could be. He talked about "the empire of evil" and pointed to the Soviet Union as the source of all conflicts in the world. His bellicose rhetoric was highly irritating to the European allies and sometimes difficult to comprehend. They were also offended by his moral sermons to the Russians and their allies. When his first period in office ended, his ideological style of confrontation softened, but his insistence on SDI hardened. During his first term the president reflected the popular hard-line mood in the United States and the distrust of Soviet movements in Africa, Asia, and Latin America. With a war starting in Afghanistan and a rising militancy in Soviet domestic positions, too, propagandists at the 24th and 25th Congresses of the Communist party of the Soviet Union (CPSU) proclaimed more aggressive aims in the Third World. They also justified the faster pace of the nuclear armaments drive and the deployment of SS-20s in Europe.

Brezhnev's record during and after the period of détente is fascinating to inspect. One can compare his policy with the global blunders made by Stalin after 1945 that led to the containment policies of the United States and the creation of the Atlantic Alliance. The serious blunders of Brezhnev and his Politburo were apparently based on their inability to recall the painful lesson that Khrushchev had had to learn after the Cuban crisis of 1962. Khruschchev had later confessed that, in the nuclear epoch, "a dogmatic approach without a sober assessment can only lead to fatal mistakes." Doctrines of Marxist–Leninism cannot subsist on abstract truth. Strategic conflict is always concrete, but Brezhnev never recognized the need to define realistic goals. There is some indication that Andropov knew and that Gorbachev knows better.

In his second term Reagan will discover whether Gorbachev is willing to be a subtle realist or not, and if he can initiate a thrust of domestic reform at home together with a change in Soviet foreign policy towards the United States and the Alliance. Forecasting is always a precarious activity, and prophecies about Soviet behavior must be doubly guarded. Some proof will soon be available of the basic aims and perceptions that will move Gorbachev's foreign policy over the next decade. The 27th Party Congress of the CPSU started on the historical date of 25 February 1986, exactly thirty years after Khruschchev destroyed the Stalin legend in 1956. A new program will be published, and Gorbachev will announce the lines to guide future foreign policy. President Reagan will be able to test whether his offer of a dialogue and a negotiated agreement will be accepted with a constructive response. The summit meeting in November 1985 provided the first opportunity to determine if the pronouncements of the new Soviet leadership will lead to a better *modus vivendi* in East–West relations.

Perhaps Reagan will succeed in convincing Gorbachev that his desire for arms control agreements and a more secure peace will lead to a less belligerent attitude on his own part. The position of President Reagan is strong, and it enjoys considerable support among the European allies. In his first term President Reagan restored the self-esteem of the American people after the disasters of Watergate and Vietnam. He was able to project in the Atlantic Alliance a renewed cohesion and a revived sense of security in facing the military might of the Warsaw Pact. At the Geneva summit the two great "communicators," armed with a deep awareness of their responsibility for maintaining peace, met for the first time. There is a danger that too much is expected of the first summit conference to have been held for ten years. There is also a possibility that positive developments will result.

In the past, great personalities have been able to shape the destiny of nations. Reagan will be able, in theory, to use his second term to win his place in history as the president who created the conditions for peace in the nuclear age. It is clearly his ambition to do so, and he may succeed if he reads the new leadership in the Kremlin correctly. To this end, one can paraphrase the wise warning once given by Raymond Aron:

> We should not necessarily see our enemy as the devil, but should not consider him our friend either, at least until he proves his friendship.

There is no doubt that there is still a long way to go before mutual friendship and trust can be reached. One can hope that Reagan, in completing his last term, and Gorbachev, at the beginning of a long term in power, will start to move toward each other's position. History will show whether they used subtlety and determination to advance their own stated aims of securing a more durable peace in our nuclear epoch.

NOTE

1. James Schlesinger, "The Eagle and the Bear," *Foreign Affairs* 63 (1985): 937–961.

8
Two Views from West Germany: What Do We Need Changed in NATO?

Peter Corterier

THE STRATEGIC DEFENSE INITIATIVE

It is useful to try to identify the issues that may present difficulties, from a European point of view, in transatlantic relations during Reagan's second term. Obviously, President Reagan's SDI stands out as the issue that is most likely to disturb Alliance discussions in the coming years, but three others must be noted as well: the burden-sharing of NATO's costs, the divisive issues of trade protectionism, and the multilateral controls over East–West trade.

In March 1983 President Reagan first announced a research program to develop a defense against nuclear weapons, a program that soon became known as the Star Wars project. The Soviet Union criticized the United States for starting an arms race in space, even though it had been secretly experimenting with space weapons for some years. The Soviets had built an operational system capable of destroying satellites (killer satellites), and, according to Pentagon sources, they were equal or superior to the United States in laser technology. Rival groups of experts claimed, or denied, that, in an all-out race, Soviets would be the first to build a rudimentary BMD. The core of their defense would be the BMD system around Moscow, the only one of its kind now in operation, and it could be supplemented by more than 10,000 surface-to-air missiles. In addition, the Soviets are constructing a radar site in Central Siberia, in Krasnoyarsk, that could one day coordinate a nationwide defense, thus violating the ABM treaty signed between the superpowers in 1972.

In view of the Soviets' ambitious research program in BMD, it is logical for the United States to continue its own research on strategic defense. However, there is danger that the research will develop a momentum of its own.

If the United States and its NATO partners should choose to develop a full-scale defense against nuclear weapons, they must take into account a wide range of risks and not stumble heedlessly into a new arms race. The ABM treaty provided an important turning point in arms control. Once it is violated, it may be difficult, if not impossible, to return to a mode of international security that has remained stable for many years.

Many difficult questions will be raised if the BMD race goes unchecked and if the SDI program moves from a research to a development stage. Geoffrey Howe, the British foreign secretary, suggested during the course of 1985 some of the questions that will have to be asked: How can we enhance deterrence? How can we curb the arms race? We have to base our answers on strategic concerns as well as technological potential. Strategic policy cannot be dictated by technological predictions. Will we have time to wait for five, ten, or fifteen years for the answers to these questions, and until the scientists and military experts deliver their results?

The questions involved are critical and complex. But, if the Europeans want to have any impact in the decision-making process in Washington, they need to work out a common position on SDI as quickly as possible. On one important point there already seems to be a European consensus. Bettino Craxi, Helmut Kohl, and Geoffrey Howe have said that the SDI would become superfluous if both sides in Geneva agreed to radical reductions in offensive weapons. What are the chances that this philosophy will be accepted in Washington? At present there are two conflicting schools of thought in the Reagan administration.

One strongly believes in the possibility of creating a comprehensive SDI and refuses to make it a negotiable issue in Geneva. SDI will be pursued no matter how the negotiations proceed. I fear that this push will end up like all other attempts in history that sought to replace offensive with defensive capabilities. It could prompt a new arms race, hamper agreements on arms control, and lead to greater instability. This thrust would also make it easier for the Soviet Union to use SDI as a propaganda weapon against the West. If the Soviets could demonstrate to the West Europeans that deep cuts could no longer be made in INF systems, which are the Europeans' major concern, the Soviets could put the blame on the Americans for refusing to negotiate over SDI. This would give them a dangerous opportunity to drive a wedge between the United States and its European allies and to disrupt Alliance unity. The SDI could then become a Soviet dream weapon in terms of its propaganda value.

But there is a second thrust to be seen in Washington today. It reflects the concerns of the Europeans that, in the absence of an agreement in Geneva, SDI could lead to an enormously costly arms race and that dangerous confrontations between the two superpowers would ensue. It is also concerned about losing support for SDI, not just among the allies, but also in the Congress. This would occur if the Soviet Union should demonstrate that it was seriously prepared to trade off deep cuts in its offensive systems if the SDI were suspended. A more flexible approach on SDI would give the West the moral high ground in further negotiations with the Soviet Union and in the ongoing propaganda war Gorbachev started with his proposal for an INF moratorium. This would clearly benefit Alliance unity, and it could frustrate Soviet attempts to drive another wedge between allied governments and electorates. This could be of critical importance to NATO. Mikhail Gorbachev claims to represent a new generation of Soviet leadership. He claims, too, to seek a halt in the escalation of the arms race and to preserve the balance in East–West relations. The dangers that lie ahead are grave. They should convince both sides to pursue controls on new areas of weapons competition and to make drastic reductions in existing strategic and intermediate range nuclear systems. If this opportunity is wasted, the future will become increasingly uncertain and insecure.

BURDEN-SHARING

The issue of burden-sharing involves allocation of the proportionate defense costs that each member should pay. It has been a source of irritation since the founding of the Alliance. The problem will become increasingly acute in the coming years if the U.S. Congress begins to reduce the U.S. defense budget and if resources for defense become more scarce in Europe. Arguments over contributions to the common defense will then raise the level of anger in the debate. The accusation has been heard in recent years in the United States that Europe is not contributing a fair share toward its own defense. The seriousness of the criticism was reflected in the Nunn–Roth amendment proposed to the U.S. Senate in 1984. It called for a reduction of up to 90,000 American troops over a period of three years unless certain conditions were met to strengthen NATO conventional defense contributions. The amendment was not adopted, in the end, but a signal had clearly been sent by the Senate.

According to 1985 NATO figures that are generally cited in the European press, Europeans supply 90% of ground forces, 80% of combat aircraft, 80% of tanks, 90% of armored divisions, and 70% of combat naval forces directly under Alliance commands. Western European armed forces currently comprise 3 million men in uniform and 2 million in the reserves. In comparison, the United States maintains 2 million men in uniform and 1 million reservists. These statistics are seldom cited in either the American press releases or statements by the administration, even though a Department of Defense report in June 1984 concluded that Europeans were contributing "roughly their fair share." The argument is heated, because attention focuses on the percentage of real *increase* in defense spending relative to gross domestic product (GDP). This is often singled out as the sole or the best indicator of burden-sharing. According to this index most European members of NATO failed in 1983 to meet the minimum increase of 3% that had been commonly agreed upon, while the real increase in defense spending claimed by the United States was 7.6%.

These figures fail to reflect, however, the "hidden" defense costs of the European members of NATO. European draftees, unlike highly paid American volunteers, receive little financial compensation during their term of conscription. A paper published by the Royal Institute of International Affairs suggested that, if European manpower costs for the year 1979 were computed at American pay rates, non-U.S. contributions to NATO would increase by 20 percent. This revision alone would make European defense expenditures approximately equal to those of the United States. Conversely, the United States could significantly reduce its own defense expenditures by reinstating the draft, though it would surely lead to protests from vocal segments of the American public. Europeans are intimately acquainted with that kind of protest.

Another point must be made with regard to burden-sharing. According to a former U.S. assistant secretary of state, Robert D. Hormats, transatlantic arms sales ratios in 1984 ran 7 to 1 in favor of the United States. This trend cannot continue. There must be a "two-way street" between the United States and Europe in military research and development (R&D) procurement, and sales, because military contracts can be an important factor in creating jobs. The higher rate of unemployment in Europe lends emphasis to the Europeans' demand for a larger share of these contracts. For example, the recent decision to order an electronic identification system for NATO airplanes provided a step in the wrong direction. The system is badly needed, for without it, NATO would probably shoot down one-fifth of its own aircraft in the heat of battle. Both German and American firms invested heavily in competing for the contract. Though experts agreed that the German identification system was superior, the Pentagon decided to purchase the American model. Examples of this order do little to foster a spirit of cooperation or weapons standardization, and they painfully remind Europeans of the extensive benefits that are won by the high-technology industries in the United States that rely on costly defense contracts.

To cite another problem, there is a dispute, not over armaments, but over land. As the Federal Republic is a densely populated country, real estate prices are on the average much higher than in the United States. The land it puts at the disposal of allied garrisons and maneuvers is extremely expensive, and it is worth many billions of dollars. This valuable contribution never appears in burden-sharing statistics, and the damage done to property during NATO training exercises is never mentioned in American assessments. A statement regarding the European contribution to the common infrastructure program was adopted by NATO defense ministers in December 1984. It goes a long way toward meeting U.S. complaints about burden-sharing, but it is likely that the issue will become even more divisive over the next few years. A number of Europeans fear that the Nunn-Roth amendment will be reintroduced, or something like it, unless the Reagan administration chooses to put to rest the acerbic arguments over the division of defense expenditures.

THE DECLINE OF ATLANTICISM?

A number of political analysts insist today that the dynamism of Asia constitutes a long-term challenge to the Atlantic Alliance. They argue that U.S. foreign policy during the first Reagan term has been characterized by a gradual shift away from Europe toward the countries of the Pacific rim. There is reason to be skeptical about such theories, but they are worth examining.

Asia has recorded a far more rapid rate of economic growth than Europe. Japan has become the world's second largest trading economy, and the total volume of trade between the nations that border the Pacific Ocean now exceeds the trade flow that crosses the Atlantic. Yet it would be mistake to underestimate the continuing economic importance of Europe. In GDP in 1982, NATO Europe recorded an output worth more than 3 trillion dollars—three times that of Japan or of the rest of Asia and slightly larger than that of the United States itself.

In terms of security interests, the United States obviously cannot afford to turn its back on Western Europe; we cannot afford to lose Europe's human and industrial resources to any opponent. This truth is plainly perceived within the Alliance.

Much of the discussion about an "Asia-first" strategy and American frustrations with Europe can be attributed to disputes over burden-sharing, even though the complaints are unjustified. It is likely that there would be a similar problem for the United States if its Pacific allies were more active. Japan, the cornerstone of American security policy in Asia, has claimed constitutional reasons for spending less than 1% of its GNP on defense, while the average defense spending of the European allies is three or four times greater. Obviously, the United States must safeguard important security interests in the Pacific, even though it has no alliance arrangements like NATO to share its costs in the Pacific. However, since Western Europe will continue to be a top priority for Soviet foreign and security policies, the

Pacific nations will be of economic rather than military importance to the United States. It is possible that less will be heard about a shift from Europe to the Pacific during the second Reagan term, especially if the Reagan–Gorbachev talks begin to clarify issues involved in INF reductions and East–West relations. Anxieties over the U.S. trade gap will keep attention focused on economic and protectionist disagreements with Asia. But the resolution of security matters within the Alliance, and with the Warsaw Pact, will not diminish in importance.

THE DANGER OF PROTECTIONISM

The high standards of living enjoyed in the West today are due in large part to the free movement of goods across national borders. Since the end of World War II, international trade has expanded at an average rate of 6.7% a year; in 1984 it reached 8.4%. This would not have been possible if the General Agreement on Trade and Tariffs (GATT) had not been generally, though not fully, observed. The last round of GATT negotiations, in Tokyo in 1979, succeeded in reducing a range of trade barriers, tariff charges, and import quotas. Today we desperately need a new GATT round to combat protectionist measures that appear in disguised forms, in quota levels, export subsidies, import restrictions, and orderly marketing arrangements. If countermeasures are not legislated by multilateral agreement, leading powers will be tempted to resort to unilateral action, to protect either their balance of payments or the domestic industries that are threatened by foreign competition. That would provoke a retaliation by trading partners and a vicious circle of restrictions that could prompt economic decline and an eventual financial collapse.

It is time for the United States to initiate significant trade reforms. The American trade deficit reached a record-breaking $150 billion in 1985 and the deficit on current account will again exceed $100 billion. The Reagan administration has largely resisted pressures to protect domestic employment by stemming the flood of cheap imports, but it may one day have to reduce its resistance. The present American position is that, so long as there is a possibility of starting a new GATT round, protectionist forces can be held in check. Since agreement has yet to be reached on the agenda and the timing for new GATT talks, the threat remains that the Congress will extend trade restrictions and thus choke off the prospects for a global economic recovery.

Japan bears special responsibility in preventing the rise of American protectionism. The U.S. trade deficit with Japan alone was $37 billion in 1984, or almost one-third of the total of $123 billion, and it will probably reach $50 billion in 1985. The Japanese trade surplus with the Federal Republic and the EEC also reached a record high in 1984 and will exceed it in 1985. On the strength of its aggressive export policy, Japan has amassed a greater trade surplus and a faster growth rate than any other industrialized nation in the last decade. Its success has provoked resentment in the United States, and 300 bills were introduced in the Congress to condemn Japan for unfair trade practices or to impose retaliatory measures. So far, few have been adopted, though rumblings of protest are often heard. Prime Minister Nakasone appealed to Japanese consumers to buy more Western goods, but his commendable gesture does not amount to a sufficient policy change. Japan must open up its markets, reduce its quotas, and eliminate barriers to importing foreign goods if it is to fulfill the "fair trade" rules for which President Reagan has called.

Of course, it cannot be forgotten that the American administration must share considerable blame for the trade crisis. Its failure to reduce the federal budget deficit, running at $200 billion a year, has drained money from private capital markets to finance government debt. This, in turn, has raised interest rates in the United States and boosted the dollar to artificially high values, thus intensifying America's trade deficits. So long as U.S. interest rates remain high, the capital that needs to be invested in Europe to create jobs and growth will be drained away. Moreover, the too-strong dollar threatens the world banking system by aggravating the debt repayment difficulties of countries in the Third World. Most economists agree that the United States must reduce its budget deficit by applying financial self-discipline. If the stability of the world financial and trading system is to be preserved, a strong and immediate initiative from the United States is imperative. If it is not forthcoming, the remaining accomplishments of Reagan's second term will be viewed in a critical, if not disparaging, manner.

EAST–WEST TRADE

Disagreements have flourished in recent years between Europe and America over the controls to be exercised over East–West trade. No one could fault the formula adopted at the Williamsburg summit in 1983: "East–West trade must be compatible with security interests." Problems necessarily arise in trying to define the list of prohibited products and to implement enforcement measures because disagreement waxes over the content and significance of the list. The greatest problem concerns the "dual-use" technology that has both civilian and military applications. Given the increasing importance of microelectronics, it is estimated that fully 50% of all Western products falls into "dual-use" categories. There would be a drastic cutback in East–West trade if all relevant items were included on the Coordinating Committee (COCOM) list.

Excessive restrictions are not in the best interests of Western Europe. Trade with the USSR and Eastern Europe has strengthened détente by expanding the "web of interests" that binds us together. Furthermore, European firms are much more dependent on East–West trade than their American rivals and have more to lose from tighter COCOM restrictions. Nor does it escape notice that the sale of American wheat to the Soviet Union has survived the trade freeze, suggesting that the United States is not willing to make the sacrifices that it demands of its European allies. The idea of burden-sharing can be applied to the defense costs of the Alliance partners as well as to the burden of restricting East–West trade. What is needed, for a start, is a better definition of two issues:

- Narrower definitions of "sensitive" technologies, with sharper enforcements of inspection, customs controls, and illegal transfers.
- Closer cooperation between Western Europe, Japan, and the United States in developing new technologies to improve their science-based production.

If the West is to maintain its technological edge over the Soviet Union, attention must be paid to the classifying of "dual-use" technology in order to segregate innocent civilian products from those bearing military applications. Even under the strictest controls, the Soviets will find ways to steal or purchase Western technology. Thus the transfer of militarily relevant technology must be policed as effectively as joint marketing and customs procedures allow. If the Reagan administration becomes excessively stringent or restrictive, however, it might irritate governments and commercial enterprises in Europe and even drive them toward the practice of subterfuge.

West Germany suffers from an unjustifiably bad reputation in the regulation of East–West trade. German newspapers reported that a CIA study in 1984 accused the Federal Republic of regularly circumventing COCOM rules, though the study's findings were later questioned. The FRG supposedly sold unauthorized lathes, computers, and ball bearings to the Soviets, though the reports proved to be unfounded. These false alarms are now so frequent that there is a risk of losing the cooperation of German industry, since firms cannot be too hamstrung in extending research and development or the marketing base of sophisticated technologies. European industry has to cope with an enormous increase in the costs of research and development and to compete in the division of labor among the United States, Western Europe, and Japan.

Many fear that the United States will one day resort to unilateral action. In a number of well-documented cases, Europeans have been restricted in attending American scientific conferences; U.S. export licenses have become difficult to acquire; and European firms have found difficulties in licensing the technology they themselves need. In the last resort, wasteful duplication could slow the pace of industrial innovation and make it easier for the Soviets to catch up. Or, alternatively, the United States could antagonize its closest allies, as it did in trying to embargo the pipeline technology sold in 1982 to build the Siberian gas pipe. America's attempts to impose its view of East–West trade on its own European partners can only be destructive to the Alliance. A more cooperative and understanding view must be taken by President Reagan's second administration if it is to avoid the arguments over extraterritorial controls and COCOM licensing that raged during his first term in office.

9
Changing French Perspectives: The Atlantic Alliance and the United States

Guy de Carmoy

The conduct of French defense policy is entrusted by the 1958 Constitution, and even more so by practice, to the president, as the main initiator, guide, and executor of policy. In geopolitical terms, the key partners of France are the United States, as protector of Western Europe, and West Germany, as the country separating France from the zone of Soviet military and political domination. It is within these geographic constraints that diplomatic action and the military buildup have developed in the 1980s. More pressing, however, have been the constraints of history. General de Gaulle put so strong a mark on French defense and foreign policy in the 1960s that, years after his resignation, the effects are still vivid. His name is a compulsory reference, even if contemporary events have basically changed, and his legacy is in no way forgotten. Critical and important adjustments have had to be made in recent decades, and under the presidency of François Mitterrand the adjustments have become more pressing and visible.

In 1960 de Gaulle proclaimed the autonomous use of French nuclear power, which France had developed without external help. As early as May 1962, he stressed that the United States and the Soviet Union were now able to strike directly at each other, and so, in 1966 he decided to withdraw French forces from NATO's integrated command. He cited two reasons. First, that France should assume responsibility for its own destiny; and second, that it must not become engaged in an unwanted war. He insisted that the rigid confrontation of the two alliance blocs was unsatisfactory. Though he favored a policy of détente and cooperation with the Soviet Union, he was careful to maintain ties with the Atlantic Alliance. He arranged for France to sign bilateral agreements with NATO, but he rejected the participation of French troops in a forward deployment strategy in West Germany. A French contingent remained in the FRG, but it was close to the French border and required no German financial contribution. Security issues in Western Europe were basically considered in a national perspective, and they were divorced from economic integration issues following the rejection of the Fouchet Plan in 1962. The plan had called for an interstate system of cooperation, to cover both economic and military matters, with a view to restricting the role of the European Economic Community (EC). In 1963 de Gaulle moved forward a bilateral agreement with the Federal Republic in the form of the Franco–German Treaty of Cooperation. The German commitment to NATO was strongly underlined in the preamble to the treaty where it was submitted for ratification to the Bundestag. However, the clause on defense cooperation was not implemented.

French public opinion was initially divided on the nuclear option, but it gradually began to take pride in French membership in the restricted club of nuclear powers. A significant change in the position of the parties of the left regarding nuclear weapons took place in the 1970s. Socialists and Communists had opted for unilateral nuclear disarmament in the 1972 "Common Program of the Left," but the Communist party unilaterally reversed its position in 1977. This helped the Socialist party reverse its own stand, and, from 1978 on, the striking force was backed by all political parties. The striking force was (and still is) based on the strategy of "proportional deterrence" from the weak to the strong. Its technical limits impose a first-strike, countercity intervention; that implies a massive retaliation against the enemy in case of a major military action against the French homeland, or the "national sanctuary," as it is called.

When the Socialists gave their support to the *force de frappe*, the international geopolitical balance had already undergone considerable change. Détente between the superpowers and détente in Europe had run a parallel course between 1969 and 1975, and France had benefited from both. France was a signatory to the 1971 four-power agreement on Berlin and to the 1975 Helsinki Conference on Security and Co-operation in Europe (CSCE). These moves led to a recognition of the postwar borders of the European states, including those of the two Germanies. But by 1975 the central military balance was slipping in favor of the Soviet Union, and by 1977 Chancellor Helmut Schmidt warned of the threat to the Alliance that came from the deployment of the Soviet SS-20s aimed at Western Europe. Was the premise still valid, it was asked, that the security of the French "national sanctuary" could be separated from the security of its European allies, especially West Germany?

In 1976 President Valéry Giscard d'Estaing envisaged an enlarged sanctuary, one that extended to West Germany the protection of French nuclear forces. The concept was criticized in French political circles and soon discarded. Doctrine held that nuclear deterrence applied only to the vital interests of the French territory and its approaches. Giscard remained silent after the NATO decision of December 1979, which he tacitly approved, to request several West European countries to deploy Pershing II or cruise missiles. In that same year, Henry Kissinger, speaking at Brussels, stressed the far-reaching consequences that nuclear parity had brought to the two superpowers. He said that it was now "absurd to base the strategy of the West on the credibility of the threat of a mutual suicide." In short, the United States could not expose its territories to destruction for the sake of Europeans who did not want to be exposed to the same risk themselves.

The uncertainties regarding France's two key alliance partners came to worry François Mitterrand. A few months before his election as president of the republic, he summarized his views on French defense policy: "There is today an antinomy between the strategy based on the role of defense of the national sanctuary and the strategy based on the Alliance." He recommended a mix of policies to harmonize the three instruments of modern defense, conventional, nuclear, and in outer space, and that each should be examined in turn.

President Mitterrand's first choice was to strengthen conventional ties with both NATO and the Federal Republic. In 1981 his government created a Rapid Action Force to be used either in overseas operations or at the earliest signs of a crisis in Europe. From the first moment that the government made the decision to intervene, the Rapid Action Force would operate in close contact with the NATO command. It was a clear sign of renewed concern with the Alliance, since France would require wide air support from either its own air force or its allies.

To this end, the president revived the dormant Franco–German treaty of cooperation of 1963, and he began regular meetings with the FRG on issues of military cooperation and arms procurement. Bilateral projects for a combat helicopter and a military transport plane were started, and it was decided to study a multilateral project for a new combat aircraft to be built by five countries — France, West Germany, Britain, Italy, and Spain. This envisaged an unprecedented operation, the construction of 1,000 aircraft, and a sales volume of $30 billion. After two years of negotiations, France finally quit the project in 1985, citing technical disagreements about the type of plane to be built. The French had wanted a land-support plane, while the Germans, the British, and the Italians had wanted a long-range fighter plane. The political clash reflected a conflict between the two major West European aircraft industries, the British and the French. The German industry had cooperated earlier with the British on the Tornado land-support plane, but the French industry had claimed the leader's role in the new venture. The two governments were unable to arbitrate, and France will now have to build its own aircraft at a high unit cost.

Should the French striking force extend its protection to the Federal Republic of Germany? This is the question that was brought out into open debate because of French fears that neutralist attitudes would intensify in West Germany; but no clear answer has ever been given. President Mitterrand frequently asserted that France would use its nuclear capability to enhance its deterrence strategy and that the decision to ever use it could not be shared. But there were indications that France had become more interested in the nuclear protection afforded to its neighbors. The first came upon the acceptance by the West German government of the deployment on German soil of the American intermediate range nuclear weapons, in the wake of the "dual-track" decision taken by NATO in 1979. Mitterrand took the unusual step in February 1983 of addressing the Bundestag, urging it to accept the intermediate range ballistic missiles (IRBMs) to secure the balance of power in Central Europe and to safeguard the solidarity of the Atlantic Alliance. A second sign appeared in the formal recognition by the French defense minister in June 1985 that France and West Germany must recognize "common security interests." The remark led his German counterpart to thank Charles Hernu for admitting that France now considered its neighbor an important ally and that it was no longer committed to "la France seule."

The third indication was that French public opinion was moving toward a multinational defense position. A nationwide poll in June 1985 showed that 57% of those who responded were in favor of going to the aid of West Germany if it were ever threatened. And then, in July 1985, the Socialist party made a statement on European security. It declared that France had an essential interest in global deterrence and in the defense of Western Europe, and that it included the most forward and vulnerable territory, that of the FRG, in the French zone of security. Each of these signals suggested that a great change had occurred in French strategic thinking.

Determined to advance the development of the *force de frappe* in the 1980s, Mitterrand pursued the broad lines of his predecessors' armament policies. French nuclear submarines were equipped with strategic-range missiles with multiple warheads, and new tactical missiles were designed to replace the present systems in the early 1990s. He strongly objected to the Soviet proposal at the Geneva negotiations between the two superpowers regarding the counting of INFs. The Soviets had suggested reducing the number of their SS-20s to the total number of British and French strategic missiles, but neither Britain nor France (nor the United States) agreed to the Soviet plan.

The future of the *force de frappe* had to be reconsidered when the two superpowers turned their attention to military plans for outer space. A first reaction by France to President Reagan's call for an SDI was to propose that the United Nations hold disarmament talks to head off the development of

ABMs. The proposal was unacceptable to both superpowers. The Soviets had already started building ABM systems and the Reagan administration aimed to build a space defense capability to protect U.S. territory against Soviet ballistic missiles, especially SS-18s. President Reagan invited the Western scientific community to engage in a massive research program to "eliminate nuclear war." The SDI gained further attention in Western Europe when Defense Secretary Caspar Weinberger urged European companies to participate in the $26 billion research project. This aroused a stormy debate among the member states of the Western European Union. In the end they were unable to agree on a common position, and they decided to negotiate with the United States on separate terms for each nation's participation in industrial research funding.

Initially, France had attempted to respond to America's SDI challenge by proposing the creation of a European Research Coordination Agency, in short, EUREKA. Its goal was to promote research in lasers and other emergent technologies, and to reduce the growing gap in research and development between the United States and Western Europe. At the economic summit meeting in June 1985 in Bonn, Mitterrand hardened his arguments against President Reagan, claiming that France would not participate as a subcontractor in SDI and appealing for support for EUREKA from the other European leaders. No allusion to SDI was made in the communiqué following the Bonn summit meeting, and the outcome is still uncertain. West Germany and Britain have accepted some of the American terms for SDI despite their doubts and reservations, though the FRG was also sympathetic to EUREKA and Britain expressed guarded interest. Splitting along party lines, the conservatives gave their support to SDI, notably Jacques Chirac in France, while the Socialists in France and West Germany argued that SDI would lead to a strategic "decoupling" of Western Europe from the United States.

Clearly, political and industrial leaders are interested in both the SDI and the EUREKA programs because of the promise of lavish research spending. But there is a marked difference of emphasis between them, largely because SDI is defense oriented and EUREKA has civil purposes in mind. Both seek to accelerate military and civil programs in order to develop vital technologies in information sciences and aeronautics. France has already made a good start in the space industry, assuming technical and financial leadership in the first European satellite launcher, Ariane. It tried to utilize the European space research program to compete with the Challenger space shuttle launchers in the United States and to deny to the Americans a monopoly of outer space technologies. It remains to be seen whether the Ariane will be as successful as the Airbus project in competing with an American rival that is better organized and financed.

François Mitterrand has made a laudable effort to reduce the antinomy that he rightly diagnosed in 1980 between a strategy based on the defense of the national sanctuary and a strategy based on alliance unity. The Socialist party came out in favor of extending French deterrence to include the FRG, and a new consensus in public opinion is moving in this direction. The creation of the Rapid Action Force is a step toward closer French cooperation with the FRG and NATO in conventional defense planning. But it is misleading to exaggerate the opposition between SDI and EUREKA simply because Mitterrand's negative attitude to SDI has been pronounced. No one knows today what will be the outcome of the SDI project, and a national presence in the American project is certainly preferable to abstention. EUREKA has met with a positive response from some European companies, notably in electrical engineering and electronic components, but prospects for a European "defense identity" will remain dim if no progress is made in joint arms production ventures. The lack of agreement to build a new European combat aircraft does not bode well for the cooperation across frontiers that Europe's defense industries so urgently need.

The financing of sophisticated and fast-moving weapons technologies is now too burdensome to be handled on a purely national basis. This is especially true for France. The country has been condemned for several years to slow economic growth, as it has tried to cope with its long-standing inflationary problems, and it may have to choose between cutting its conventional defense budget or reducing the development costs of its nuclear forces. It does not command the financial means to fulfill its ambitious goals on land, sea, air, and outer space simultaneously. The same limits were recognized long ago by Britain, though it did little to resolve its dilemmas. The fact remains that no European nation can move alone, without full-scale cooperation, in financing modern arms industries and weapons developments. Though the French have taken an obdurate stand on SDI, and have not reentered the integrated command arrangements of NATO, France has begun to reinforce its strategic relationship with members of the Atlantic Alliance and, first and foremost, with West Germany and the United States. It might conceivably move more rapidly in this direction if sensitive encouragement were to come from the second term of the Reagan administration.

10

The Northern Flank: Scandinavian Relations with the Superpowers

Ellmann Ellingsen

To most foreign observers it was the Soviet submarine 137, *Whiskey on the Rocks*, that helped revive the debate on Soviet–Nordic relations. The official Swedish submarine commission revealed in April 1983 that a foreign midget submarine had paid a bold visit to the most restricted parts of Stockholm harbor. This spurred anxious discussions about the Soviets' intentions and the response that should be made by the Nordic powers.

There are various reasons why both superpowers have paid the Nordic area renewed attention in recent years. Its northern ports are located on the shortest aeronautical routes between the most populated areas of the United States and the Soviet Union. The importance for the USSR is obvious. Airfields in the Kola Peninsula provide a forward base for early warning posts and defense against long-range bombers and ICBMs. The airfields in Kola and in the northern regions of the USSR can also extend the range of Soviet bombers operating against targets on the North American continent.

During the past few years a considerable expansion has taken place in the Kola base for the Northern Fleet. The fleet includes about forty Soviet strategic submarines, or nearly two-thirds of the fleet. The SLBMs of the Delta and Typhoon class enjoy sufficient range to reach targets anywhere in the United States and Canada (or China) from the Barents Sea or the Polar Basin. The Northern Fleet, including surface ships, aircraft, and submarines, serves as a key component of the Soviets' deterrent capability. Coordinated attacks by a large number of cruise missiles, launched from aircraft, surface vessels, and submarines, could present a serious threat to NATO aircraft carriers and other major surface ships. In addition, the capability to interdict NATO's Atlantic sea transports, the lifeline of the Alliance, has become an important asset to the Soviet Union. It is expected that a large number of the modern attack submarines of the Northern Fleet will go out into the Atlantic to cut the sea-lanes of NATO in time of international hostilities.

Although mainly a strategic and global force, the Northern Fleet and its air arm can also threaten the local balance of power and interdict, when necessary, the transportation of allied reinforcements to Norway and Denmark. The Northern Fleet could carry out landing operations, and it could, with presently available merchant ships, transport the marine infantry brigade and one of the motorized divisions at Kola to nearby war zones. Movement to the south and west for such operations will, however, depend on the provisions of air support and air cover against NATO forces. Control over the Norwegian coastline and air bases in Norway could be critical for the protection of the sea lines of communications to Europe as a whole, along which the reinforcements would have to be carried. An adequate and sustained defense effort from NATO is therefore essential to preserve stability in the Nordic area in the face of the Soviet military buildup.

The Kola complex is today one of the largest in the world, and its base provides a wide range of facilities. Its stockpile of nuclear weapons serves to remind NATO of the Soviets' formidable strength in the Far North.

Apart from strictly military interests in the area, the offshore oil resources in the North Sea and further north are of international significance. Norway has yet to solve key issues with the Soviet Union in the North. No progress has been made in negotiations on the delimitation of the continental shelf. Both parties are holding onto their positions, which for Norway is the median line and, for the Soviet Union, the sector line. In the absence of an agreement on the delimitation of the continental shelf, the two countries in the summer of 1978 agreed on a temporary regulation of fisheries in the disputed areas. This so-called "grey zone" agreement has since been renewed annually by mutual consent.

A few years ago the Soviets started drilling for petroleum near the disputed area, close to the median line. If they should find oil or gas in substantial amounts a new set of problems will have to be solved. Another issue is Svalbard, or Spitsbergen, because it is an integral part of the Kingdom of Norway. The 1920 treaty limits Norwegian sovereignty in the archipelago by prohibiting the building of military bases, but it is still legally a part of the Kingdom of Norway and therefore covered by the North Atlantic treaty. The Soviets have tried to take action on Svalbard, and in the North, generally in order to achieve a condominium rule. Norway has so far successfully withstood their claims. A privileged position for the USSR in the archipelago would be contrary to the equal-treatment clauses of the Spits-bergen treaty and it would extend Soviet influence.

The Soviet presence in the Baltic Sea has been built in a better geopolit-ical and military climate. About 40% of the value of Soviet trade goes through the Baltic. Before World War II the Soviet Union owned a shore-line in the Baltic of only a few kilometers, but the earlier vulnerability of Leningrad has been dramatically changed since 1940. Today the Soviet Union and other Warsaw Pact countries control shorelines that extend over 2000 km, including parts of Karelia, Estonia, Latvia, Lithuania, Poland, and the GDR. As seen from the Soviet Baltic fleet headquarters at Baltiisk, Denmark looks like a cork in the Baltic bottle. About 60% of Soviet ship construction and repair facilities are located in the Baltic, and the Baltic Fleet is the third largest of the four Soviet fleets. It includes major surface ships, amphibious ships, six Golf II class submarines armed with three medium-range SLBMs apiece, and a number of Juliet class cruise missile submarines. It seems that the Soviet navy feels comfortable in this closed sea. New submarine bunkers are being built at Liepaja to take the most modern nuclear classes.

Until twenty-five years ago Sweden was a significant naval power in the Baltic, but today it has a coastal navy that only strives to police its own coasts. The changing pattern of Soviet naval dominance has raised ques-tions about Swedish defense efforts. The submarine violations of the Soviet Union prompted strong Swedish protests. On the other hand, there was an uneasy Finnish reaction to the Swedish submarine debate. Leaders in Hel-sinki feared a Swedish overreaction that could influence Finnish–Soviet relations.

Most Scandinavian military analysts today assume that the Soviet and other Warsaw Pact forces in the Baltic Sea are meant to control the area and, if necessary, to take out the Danish cork. This could require taking control not only of the Danish islands and Jutland, but also of the south-ern part of the Norwegian coastline. The area is vital to the defense of the Baltic outlets and the Northern Fleet's repair and base facilities. However, one could think of a situation where Warsaw Pact forces preferred to *keep* the cork in the bottle to avoid allied operations in this sensitive area.

Submarine incidents and NATO surveillance patrols have revealed that there is an almost permanent presence of Soviet and Warsaw Pact picket vessels at the entrance to the Danish straits and the Kattegat. They moni-tor all traffic, military and civil, passing through the international water-ways. It has been suggested that the opening of the two-hundred mile-long canal connecting Leningrad to the White Sea will diminish the importance of the Danish and Swedish controlled outlet to the North Sea. However, the canal cannot take ships larger than 2500 tons. It is closed for many months of the year by ice, and its series of locks is vulnerable to interdiction attack.

SOVIET POLICIES

It is often thought that the Nordic countries, aside from the parts of Finland that Stalin seized during World War II, might be immune from Soviet expansion. This does not suggest that the Soviet Union will refrain from exerting pressure on its Nordic neighbors. The supposed objective of any Soviet policy toward these countries must be to impose a socialist system. With few gains won through peaceful measures, the second objective must be to weaken the ties of these countries with the West and to push them toward a neutral or nonaligned course. The Soviet Union has used threats, diplomatic pressure, persuasion, and propaganda to influence the political decisions of the Nordic countries. In late 1944 Soviet leaders demanded the revision of the Svalbard treaty into a Soviet–Norwegian condominium and the cession of Bear Island, which was a part of the treaty. Soviet troops had already "liberated" a part of the Norwegian province of Finmark, and they remained standing on Norwegian soil. Their diplomatic attempts collapsed, and the liberation forces withdrew.

In 1949 Norway joined the North Atlantic treaty parties, which resulted, despite Soviet objections, in a unilateral declaration that Norwegian territories would not be used for aggressive purposes. Norway wanted stable relations with the Soviets and low tension in the North. Therefore, in joining NATO, Norway insisted that there would be no obligation to provide bases for the military forces of foreign powers on Norwegian territory, so long as it was not attacked or exposed to threats of attack. Norway's declaration came in January 1949, and Denmark followed in 1953.

Predominantly domestic pressures, along with active Soviet political maneuvers, dissuaded the Norwegians and the Danes from stationing nuclear weapons in those two countries in peacetime. Premier Bulganin warned the Norwegians and the Danes that NATO bases in their countries would constitute "legitimate targets" for a Soviet nuclear attack. In recent years the Norwegians decided to ask West German forces to take no part as frontline troops in NATO's mobile force exercises in Norway. The request was made after Soviet and Finnish objections had been raised.

Finland, as one of the losing parties in World War II, is the Nordic country that is most influenced by Soviet political activities. In 1948 the Finns signed a pact with the Soviet Union for "Friendship, Co-operation and Mutual Assistance." It appears from Article 1 that, if Finland or the Soviet Union should be exposed to an armed attack through Finnish territory by Germany or a country allied with Germany, Finland would firmly repel the attack, if necessary with Soviet assistance. Article 2 establishes that Finland and the Soviet Union will consult each other in the event of a threat. However, as Soviet leaders come and go and the stability of the region remains untroubled, the Finns' situation is much improved. Finland is a Western democracy with a typical capitalistic system. The phrase "Finlandization" is easily misunderstood.

A NORDIC NUCLEAR WEAPONS FREE ZONE (NNWFZ)

Today few Scandinavians are eager to disturb the Nordic equilibrium or to change the anomalous position of Finland. But there are other policies that could force changes in Northern Europe. One would be the replacement of NATO guarantees with a policy of neutrality and an NNWFZ. A *unilateral* Norwegian — and Danish — declaration to this effect would take the two countries out of NATO's military defense zone and away from its nuclear options. Geographical vulnerability would endanger Norway more than Denmark, since it is more exposed to Soviet influence, while Denmark is tied directly to West Germany and the European Community. The Soviet position in the area would be strongly improved if Norway were forced to leave the military integration of NATO. There would also be serious effects on the balance of power in the region for Sweden and the Atlantic allies.

There is some popular support in 1985 in the Nordic countries, located largely outside the party structures, for a unilateral declaration for the NNWFZ. The "Treaty Now!" movement has been supported by leaders in the church, in the universities, and in various civic groups, though most of them at the same time support current defense arrangements and NATO. The question is asked, Is this the right signal to send from Scandinavia to Moscow at the present time? It could easily be interpreted as compliance with Soviet coercion, and, because strict verification would be needed, it could even give the Soviets inspection rights as a guarantee power. Nonetheless, it is argued that an NNWFZ could be part of a *European* settlement within a *NATO* framework of confidence-building measures and it has been broadly supported in Norway.

A book published by the Institute for World Economy and International Relations in Moscow, *A Non-Nuclear Status for Northern Europe* (1984), drew considerable comment in the debate among the Nordic countries on the NNWFZ. The author, Lev Voronkov, repudiated the Swedish claim that the Baltic Sea must be included in an NNWFZ. The claim, he wrote, cannot be recognized until nuclear arms reductions are agreed upon by the United States for the whole of Central Europe. The author praised Finland, and rebuked Norway and Denmark, for their defense policies. But to widespread surprise, Sweden was also criticized for its implicit cooperation with the United States and NATO. The author dismissed the claim of Swedish neutrality, expressing doubts about Sweden's nonalignment and criticizing its strong defense establishment.

With regard to Norway, the Soviet author concluded that its self-imposed restrictions are only cosmetic and that it cannot convince neighboring countries, such as the USSR, of the defensive character of Norwegian defense policy. Voronkov implied that for Norway and Denmark to do away with nuclear weapons is simply not enough. Their military installations, he claims, are a part of the U.S. and NATO design to use nuclear weapons against the Soviet Union, and they must be eliminated. In 1984 a general on the Soviet General Staff added not only that nuclear warheads and weapons launchers must be eliminated but also that infrastructure installations must go as well if the NNWFZ is to be negotiated.

While the Nordic governments and political parties continue to discuss Soviet strategic intentions, Soviet basing operations, and the campaign for the NNWFZ, it is likely that relations with the United States and the allied powers will be cordial and relatively smooth. Norway and Denmark refused to station Pershing II or cruise missiles on their soil in peacetime, but both countries continue to modernize their defense forces and to join in annual crisis-planning exercises. Sweden remains very friendly to the United States, even though critics of U.S. foreign policy in the Third World or in the conduct of arms control negotiations have been outspoken. By its own efforts, Sweden is capable of making the likely costs of an attack upon it exceed the likely gains. There is a high probability that its defense capabilities will be seriously regarded, by both NATO and its adversaries.

The conclusion is that Norway and Denmark, two of the founding members, look to NATO, especially to the United States, to protect their ultimate security interests. The balance of Baltic power hinges upon the stability of East–West relations in general, and of the Northern flank of the Alliance in particular. Because it is difficult to pressure Soviet behavior, considerable attention is paid to the development of policy in Washington. The pattern will surely continue in the second term of Reagan's administration.

American cultural and political values have exercised a significant influence on the politics of the northern countries. For good reasons, the statecraft of the United States draws more comment (and criticism) than that of any other country in the contemporary world order. Norway and Denmark have always been geographically exposed to Russia's military and political pressure. It is a testament to the strength of Nordic–American relations that such small countries can speak openly and candidly on Alliance issues. Their loyalty has never wavered at times of crisis, nor has their fundamental respect for American leadership declined. The development of their domestic and foreign policy is strongly influenced by the shifting priorities of American diplomacy, and this pattern will surely survive during President Reagan's last years in office.

11

Foreign Policy in the Second Reagan Administration: Alliance Interests, Ideology, and Domestic Pressures

John E. Rielly

I shall divide my analysis into the three subjects listed in the subtitle, examining each one in turn. First, I will give a brief summary of the interests of the Atlantic Alliance as seen from a European perspective. Second, I will review the Reagan administration's response to Alliance interests during its first four years. Third, I will ask how important and how confining has been the influence of both public and elite opinion in the United States, and how both are likely to operate in future years. The public opinion polls cited in this essay extend from January 1981 to July 1985, and in a number of cases there is evidence of change in opinion trends. The larger share of the paper is devoted to the third subject, which is the impact of public opinion in the United States on the foreign policy of the Reagan administration.

ALLIANCE INTERESTS

In any discussion of Alliance interests the first to be mentioned is that which brought NATO into existence, namely, the adherence to a policy of extended deterrence under which the nuclear power of the United States is pledged to defend the territory of Western Europe in case of a Soviet military attack. Despite the refinements of later years, this fundamental security objective of the Atlantic Alliance has not changed from Eisenhower to Reagan. What has changed is the Alliance interest in going beyond containment of the military might of the Soviet Union and involving the Soviet Union in a set of limited constructive relationships. The period of détente, following the signing of treaties between the Federal Republic of Germany and its neighbors and the Soviet Union and the implementation of the Helsinki Accords, did ease political tensions within Europe. The actual condition of thousands of Europeans, especially of the Federal Republic of Germany and of selected neighboring counties to the East, did improve. European determination to preserve the benefits of détente has continued through the 1980s, despite the criticism, if not outright opposition, of the Reagan administration.

Europeans throughout the past decade and a half have continued to develop commercial relations with Warsaw Pact nations, despite the Soviet deployment of medium range missiles and the Soviet invasion of Afghanistan. On the security side, Europeans coupled their support for deployment of U.S. Pershing and cruise missiles with a desire for arms control negotiations with the Soviet Union. Through such negotiations they hoped it would be unnecessary to actually deploy the missiles that the nations of the Alliance agreed to in 1979. From 1981 to 1983, therefore, most European governments strongly pressed the U.S. administration to proceed with arms control negotiations with the Soviet Union.

Although disputes on security issues often captured the headlines, it was on economic and monetary issues that more pervasive differences on policy persisted between Europe and the United States. Here competitiveness continued to be the dominant aspect of the relationship, rather than cooperation. Europeans welcomed the strong measures aimed at controlling American inflation initiated by the Federal Reserve Board in 1979 and accelerated by the new American administration in the period 1981–1983. Europeans welcomed the resurgence of the American economy after 1983, recognizing that the increased demand would have a strong positive impact on the European economy. They uniformly condemned both the continuation of high interest rates in the United States, which drained capital from Europe, and the massive U.S. federal budget deficit. The latter was blamed for both keeping interest rates high and contributing to the persistence of an overvalued dollar. Many soon came to believe that Europe was financing the American budget deficit, a view epitomized by former Chancellor Schmidt's remark: "To finance the deficit, you are not printing money, you are importing it."

Europeans soon learned that the massive trade deficits of $123 billion in 1984 and $150 billion in 1985 would accelerate protectionist pressures. Preserving access to the American market has taken on greater urgency among Europeans, especially for items such as steel, chemicals, and agricultural products.

Europeans have worried regularly about several other aspects of Reagan's foreign policy, including the aggressive confrontational style vis-à-vis the Soviet Union, U.S. policy in Central America and the Caribbean, and especially American intervention in Grenada. Today no major European government shares the Reagan administration's judgment that Nicaragua represents a threat to the security of the United States. All governments are sensitive to a public opinion in Europe that is largely opposed to not only American policy in Nicaragua but also the American posture in Central America as a whole.

Finally, following the November 1984 elections, the emergence of the SDI as a central issue provoked further strains between the two continents. European skepticism about both the feasibility and the desirability of SDI is pervasive. Some Europeans wonder whether the proposed defense strategy will inevitably undermine the overall rationale for deterrence, while others see in the SDI scheme an effort by the United States to maintain its overwhelming technological superiority, despite its offers to share in technological development. For other Europeans this is but another provocative move designed to arouse the Soviet Union and to insure that no real progress in the field of arms control is possible.

THE REAGAN ADMINISTRATION RESPONSE

The Reagan administration response to Alliance interests has combined conservative internationalism with nationalistic unilateralism. Conservative internationalism, to use the formulation of my colleague William Schneider, is interventionist, promilitary anti-Communist, and anti-Soviet. It supports the Atlantic Alliance but not only regards it as a security alliance of Atlantic nations but also views it heavily as an ideological challenge to the Soviet Union.[1] The nationalistic unilateralist strain, in contrast, emphasizes the national interests of the United States and its capability to protect itself, as well as the liabilities of abiding by the restraints of any alliance. In making decisions, whether on Grenada, or Nicaragua, or the SDI, it has favored unilateral action irrespective of allied responses. Proponents of nationalistic unilateralism are not explicitly opposed to the Western Alliance but undervalue it or ignore it.

Perhaps the most important manifestation of the conservative internationalist strain in the Reagan administration is the massive military buildup designed to offset the perceived superior military power of the Soviet Union. The military component of the U.S.–Soviet relationship is the decisive one. Until the alleged Soviet military advantage is erased and American military power restored, arms control agreements are either irrelevant or a positive hindrance to the restoration of military balance. Until 1984, a presidential campaign year, the Reagan administration continued to reject the policy of détente that had characterized the Nixon, Ford, and Carter administrations between the early 1970s and the Afghanistan invasion of 1979. Not only were arms control negotiations put on the shelf, but also a serious attempt was made to impose restraints upon Europeans on the sale of industrial goods to the Soviet Union such as the gas pipeline that became the focus of an acrimonious dispute in 1982.

On the most important security issue of the early 1980s, the deployment of medium range missiles in Europe, the Reagan administration adhered to the policy of its predecessor and applied consistent pressure on its European allies to adhere to the agreement to deploy that they had jointly entered into in 1979. On economic and military issues, the administration all but ignored complaints about the $200 billion federal deficit, the high dollar, and high interest rates. The president did resist some extreme aspects of congressional protectionist pressure, more so on steel and automobiles than on agriculture. On Grenada, the administration completely ignored European protests and proceeded with a unilateral invasion. In Nicaragua it gave some rhetorical attention to European pressure to involve the nations of the so-called Contadora group. Nevertheless it continued its military buildup in neighboring countries and continued to arm and finance counterinsurgent groups that sought to overthrow the Nicaraguan government.

In short, the Reagan administration's response on Atlantic Alliance issues pleased Europeans on some issues even if it appalled them on others. The strong military buildup had a favorable impact on the NATO forces in Europe, an impact that should have been reassuring to Europeans. At the same time the rhetorical suggestions about experimental nuclear "shots" terrified Europeans and suggested to many that careless United States leadership might provoke a war with the Soviet Union. The massive American military buildup for the first three years of the Reagan administration embarrassed the Europeans who, for the most part, failed to adhere to the 3% goal that they had previously agreed to. But the buildup also reassured those who had been apprehensive about the weakness of the United States vis-à-vis the Soviet Union at the end of the 1970s.

DOMESTIC PRESSURES ON THE REAGAN ADMINISTRATION: AMERICAN POPULAR AND ELITE OPINION

I will argue here that on most of the vexing issues that have come up during the past five years, the differences between the United States and Europe are not primarily the result of massive shifts in American popular or elite opinion. In many cases they result from the conviction of leaders in the current government, whether the president himself or his principal appointees, rather than being a direct response to the pressure of the public or the American leadership class.[2]

To cite several specific issues on the question of the massive military buildup during the Reagan years, public opinion polls show that the administration enjoyed no strong popular support for its objective of further increases. From 1974 to 1978, a 20% shift in favor of increased defense spending in the United States occurred. From the end of 1978 to the end of 1982, support for an expanded military dropped by 10%. On the question of expanding or curtailing government spending for defense, in November of 1982, 24% favored increased defense spending and 34% favored cutting back. This represents an exact reversal of the percentages of 1978. The number who favored maintaining defense spending at the current level remained the same, 34% in December 1978 and 36% in December 1982. Later polls taken by Gallup have indicated that this trend has continued. In September 1983, 37% thought we were spending too much on defense; 21%, too little; and 36%, about right.[3]

Independent surveys by the Gallup Organization, the National Opinion Research Center, and others taken in early 1981 indicated that popular support for increased defense spending reached its highest point in January of 1981, the month when Ronald Reagan took office, when about two-thirds of the public favored an increase. Support for increased defense spending has diminished steadily since then, in part because both the public and American leaders have expressed a greater sense of security than before. It is also related to a changed perception of the U.S.–Soviet balance, one of the most important reasons leading to a reversal of the trend on defense spending. At the end of 1982, about two-thirds of the public and four-fifths of American leaders believed the United States was equal to or stronger than the Soviet Union in the military field. This represents a substantial change from four years earlier, when 60% of the public and 29% of the leaders felt the United States had fallen behind the Soviet Union militarily.

In 1985 support for increased defense spending continued to decline. Following the sustained attention given to the budget deficit since the 1984 election, popular pressure has increased to curtail further increases. In the spring of 1985, two-thirds of the public favored cutting the defense budget in order to reduce the deficit, far higher than any other category such as welfare or other domestic programs.[4] On the question of change and continuity in public opinion, the biggest shift in popular opinion has occurred since 1981.

On another issue, after two years of the Reagan administration, Americans shared the concern of many Europeans about the increased possibility of war. In our study published in 1979, so few responses spontaneously mentioned nuclear war as a foreign policy concern that the response was not even separately reported. Four years later, in December 1982, 10% mentioned war as a major issue, and the proportion of those concerned about the nuclear arms race had doubled. This concern continued at least until the end of 1983, according to a study by the Atlantic Institute; and by November 1983, 45% of the U.S. public were concerned about the possibility of war.[5]

On the subject of arms control, at a time when the Reagan administration was largely ignoring it, during the first three years in office, both the American public and American leaders registered strong support for arms control measures. Three-fourths of the public favored arms control negotiations between the United States and the Soviet Union. Among foreign policy goals, arms control came out on top, with 64% of the public and 86% of the leadership considering it a very important goal in December of 1982.

Some European and American commentators have commented on the alleged shift in attitude on the part of the American public and its leaders in the priority given to Europe. Our public opinion studies between 1975 and 1985 do not support that conclusion. One way to gauge American popular sentiment on this issue is to ask where Europe fits into overall American foreign policy priorities. Which countries are considered of greatest interest to the United States and which are of lesser interest? In response to the question of which countries are of vital interest to the United States, we found once again that Great Britain and the Federal Republic of Germany ranked among the top four in the list, along with U.S. neighbors Canada and Mexico. When we asked the question in a different way (how warmly people felt about a country, as distinct from the vital interest aspect) again Great Britain, France, and West Germany were among the top five. Whether ranked on a vital interest chart or on a feeling thermometer, America's principal allies in Europe ranked with Canada, Mexico, and our principal Asian ally, Japan, as the countries most important to the United States. On the subject of where vital U.S. interests lie, American leaders are even stronger in their estimation of the importance of Europe. Germany and Great Britain came out on top of the list, even above Canada, with 98% and 97% of the leaders, respectively, considering them of vital interest. These rankings have varied little in the ten years of the studies.

Support for NATO

On the question of support for NATO, the American people and their leaders have been in tune with the Reagan administration. At the beginning of 1983, two-thirds of the American public (67%) felt that the United States should keep the commitment to NATO at the same level or increase it. Fifty-eight percent favored the same level, and 9% favored increasing it. Here there was no change from four years earlier.

On a related question, some commentators have suggested that the support evident in the Senate for the Nunn Amendment to reduce American forces stationed in Europe suggests some shift in popular opinion in that direction. Our own study did not specifically ask a question about reducing the number of Americans in Europe but it did ask how the American public and its leaders viewed the possible commitment of American troops in a crisis situation. We found that, despite the diminished support for a larger defense budget, Americans in general were more willing to support the use of troops in a crisis situation in 1983 than was the case four years earlier. What is significant here is that the willingness to support the use of American troops in the case of a Soviet invasion of Western Europe continues to be stronger and enjoy broader support than is the case in any other area of the world. A total of 65% of the American public and 92% of American leaders would support the use of American troops in such a situation. Significantly, this represents an increase of 11 percentage points on the popular scale in the period from 1978 to 1982. Leadership opinion remained unchanged at the very high level of 92%. Later surveys did not substantially modify this conclusion.

U.S.–Soviet Relations

On another issue on which Europeans have differed markedly from the Reagan administration, which is the relationship with the Soviet Union, opinion in the United States during the early years of the Reagan administration did not support the administration's confrontational approach. The public and the leadership both remained interested in cooperation with the Soviet Union in nonmilitary areas. A total of 77% of the public and 96% of the leaders favored negotiating arms control agreements; 64% of the public and 78% of the leaders favored support of joint solutions to energy problems; and 70% of the public and 81% of the leaders opposed imposing a grain embargo on the Soviet Union. On the other hand, on the issue of trade, both the public and the leaders are more supportive of the Reagan administration's position, with 47% of the public and 69% of the leaders favoring trade restrictions on the Soviet Union. Despite support for these restrictions, American opinion on the pipeline issue, which led to so much friction between the United States and Europe in 1982, was surprisingly cautious in criticizing Europe. When asked how we should respond to the Soviet–European natural gas pipeline deal, 87% of the public said we should let our allies pursue policies they think best — the largest single response. Only 27% favored putting diplomatic pressure on the Europeans, and a modest 15% favored economic sanctions if other methods did not work.

Although, as I will indicate later, American leadership opinion is today divided on some issues related to Europe, our studies have consistently shown over the period from 1975 to 1985 that American leaders tend to remain more strongly oriented toward Europe and more strongly committed to honoring America's commitments to Europe than does popular opinion. For example, in rating foreign policy goals, the goal of defending our allies' security was considered very important by 82% of American leaders, which is second on the list of goals only after worldwide arms control. As noted earlier, 92% of American leaders favored the use of American troops in the case of Soviet invasion of Western Europe. Ninety-eight percent of American leaders thought it best that the United States continue to take an active role in world affairs, 67% of American leaders favored eliminating tariffs and trade restrictions (as against 22% of the public) at large. On other issues of central importance to Europe, 69% of American leaders opposed restricting U.S.–Soviet trade and forbidding grain sales to the Soviet Union, and 94% favored cultural and educational exchanges with the Soviet Union. On many issues, American leadership was stronger in its support of current American commitments in Europe than popular opinion. At the same time, these attitudes are more similar to those of Europeans on a number of issues, especially those related to the Soviet Union.

Most of the foregoing analysis focuses on security and political issues between the United States and Europe. We should not conclude without mentioning the critical question of trade and commercial policy, on which there is also a sharp divergence between the public and the Reagan administration. Here the public continued to favor by a wide margin the preservation of tariffs, with 57% favoring tariffs and only 22% eliminating them, a figure that did not change at all from 1978 to 1982. The four-year period did see a slight change in the attitude of leaders who, for a decade, had always supported a free-trade system and opposed tariffs. In 1978, 78% of the leaders favored eliminating tariffs, and 23% felt they were necessary. Four years later, in 1982, 67% favored eliminating tariffs, and 28% thought they were necessary. There is some indication that selective support for temporary tariff barriers has continued to gain support among American businesspeople and was slightly higher in mid-1985 than in December 1982. In continuing its approach to the most extremist protectionist measures, the Reagan administration opposes popular sentiment, which, at the level of 60% for over a decade, favored protectionist legislation.

This brief summary indicates that, on many of the issues that are most important to the United States and Europe in the 1980s, the Reagan administration's position does not reflect either a strong popular or an elite sentiment. In a number of cases both are opposed to it. In no area is this more evident than on Central America, an issue that has become an important point of difference between the United States and Europe. On the question of U.S. support for sending troops "if Leftist guerillas were about to defeat the government of El Salvador," 80% of the public and 90% of the leaders were opposed to this in 1982. On a related question, when asked how much of a threat it would be to the United States if the Communists came to power in El Salvador, only 21% of the public and 10% of the leaders thought it would be a great threat. Later surveys indicated that the administration's position on Nicaragua has enjoyed a little more support. The strong and persistent opposition in the Congress to assisting the opposition forces seeking to overthrow the current government of Nicaragua reflects this lack of popular support.

This analysis suggests that, during the first four years of the Reagan administration, the increase in friction between Europe and the United States was not due principally to shifts in popular or elite opinion. Indeed, based on other studies, I would say that the problem of attitudinal change, especially with regard to the elite, is a much greater problem in Europe on issues related to the Atlantic Alliance than it is in the United States.

United States–European Prospects After 1985

Since the Reagan administration has only begun its second term, it is not possible to empirically measure substantial shifts from the first to the second term. My remarks in the final part of this paper therefore represent more speculation than empirical analysis. The biggest problem for the United States and Europe in mid-1985 is the same: how to come to grips with the massive American budget deficit that threatens to undermine both the economic and the social stability of the United States and Europe. Here a shift has emerged since the election of 1984, evidenced by the determination of selected congressional leaders, including Republican party leaders to do something to reduce the massive budget deficit. Under the leadership of people like Senator Dole, there is a far stronger attempt to address this issue than has come out of the White House or the Treasury Department, places from which one might expect leadership on this issue.

The overwhelming importance of economic and financial issues has also had an impact on the Reagan administration's policy toward the Soviet Union. At a time when frictions over trade, monetary, and financial issues are so important, it is more difficult for the Reagan administration to sustain a cold war policy focused primarily on security issues. For this, among other reasons, the administration policy toward the Soviet Union has undergone substantial evolution since the beginning of 1984. Presidential elections sometimes stimulate movement on such issues. It is clear that the Reagan administration, whether responding to current popular and leadership opinion or for other reasons, has modified the confrontational approach of the first three years in office. It has displayed a new willingness to enter into arms control negotiations in Geneva and it scheduled a meeting in Geneva between President Reagan and First Secretary Gorbachev for November 1985.

Among the various motivations for the change is the traditional desire of an American president to be remembered as a peacemaker. Some believe that President Reagan and his advisors concluded by the beginning of 1985 that there is no political constituency on the right for a hard-line anti-Soviet foreign policy. He and his advisors are more aware today, as Senator Richard Lugar, Chairman of the Senate Foreign Relations Committee emphasized in January 1985, that "in poll after poll, Americans display an overwhelming opposition to any course of action which might actually frustrate governments that are harmful to the United States."[6] Since January of 1985, foreign policy has become more centrist, while domestic policy, especially on social issues, has become tougher.

In modifying our posture toward the Soviet Union, there is no question that the departure from key foreign policy roles of original Reaganites like Richard Allen, Edwin Meese, William Clark, and Ambassador Kirkpatrick has made a difference. The ascendency of Secretary of State George Shultz to a position of dominance in the overall foreign policy field has strengthened this centrist tendency. Instead of ideologists like Allen or Clark, one finds a traditional foreign policy establishment type, Colonel MacFarlane, or Admiral Poindexter appointed as national security advisor. The appointment of a large number of senior foreign service officers and other centrist-oriented noncareer appointees to key foreign policy positions has further accented the centrist orientation of the current Reagan foreign policy. This has not gone unnoticed by defenders of the original "Reagan be Reagan" faith such as Senator Jesse Helms. Most of these recent appointees not only are less ideological and less anti-Soviet in their outlook, but they also tend to be multilateralists, opposed to the kind of unilateral decision making that characterized many of the early Reagan appointees and that is still characteristic of the Pentagon leadership.

When you see that Kissinger's chief protégé, Winston Lord, is being appointed by Ronald Reagan as Ambassador to China, and Richard Burt, Jesse Helms's least favorite journalist and bureaucrat, is being appointed Ambassador to the Federal Republic of Germany, you know that we have come a long way since the autumn of 1980, when George Shultz was rejected as the candidate for secretary of state by the Reagan inner circle on the grounds that his views were too close to those of Kissinger, that much-despised apostle of détente.

That does not mean that all sharply edged ideological currents that came in with the Reagan administration have run their course. Ronald Reagan himself retains a strong anti-Communist strain and on several occasions has reminded the American people that not one inch of territory has been lost to the Communists "on his watch." Defense Secretary Caspar Weinberger continues to defend sharply increased defense expenditures. We still have influential people like neoconservative Irving Kristol claiming that the very existence of NATO is at stake in the dispute between the Reagan administration and European governments on Central America. For Kristol, America's European allies are fast approaching a moment of decision. According to him, the United States is not going to remain committed to the defense of Europe at the risk of annihilation if Western Europe is not equally committed to defense of American interests. In his view it has always been assumed that the nations of Western Europe would be deferential toward American policy in such non-NATO areas as the Western Hemisphere. Today that means Central America. Because America's European allies today express not only unofficial but also official dissatisfaction with U.S. policy, U.S. enemies in Central America are aided. As a result, American popular opinion is entering a period of disillusionment with allies and of impatience with the restraints such allies exercise upon us.[7]

Although Kristol undoubtedly reflects the view of a small minority of elite opinion, especially that associated with the neoconservative movement in the United States, there is little empirical evidence that his view is widely shared among either the American leadership as a whole or the public. The one area where both American leadership and the public continue to be in sharpest disagreement with the Reagan administration is on Central America. The general skepticism and opposition that Europeans feel about Central America is mild compared to much of the organized opposition in the United States.

Generational Differences

Concern continues about the attitudes of American young people about Europe, a subject that has been with us for almost a decade now. As indicated in other writings, I believe that to be more of a problem in Europe than in the United States. On the central questions related to the Atlantic Alliance, one does not find differences in American opinion dividing along generational lines, as is characteristic of certain European countries. For example, on the question of direct support for NATO and foreign policy priorities, there was no sharp generational dividing line. The big differentiating factor was not age but level of education. This was considerably more important than age or geography.

But there is another troublesome concern that social scientists have identified as increasingly true of several generations in the United States, not only of the younger generation. There is an increasing self-centeredness that makes us less interested in common interests with the rest of the world. To the extent that Americans are increasingly interested exclusively in their own material well-being, to the extent that they consider themselves only as individuals, irrespective of the world around them, their feelings impact on their attitudes toward other parts of the world including Europe. If American social mores are diminished by an ethos and an ethic that emphasizes the self at the expense of others, rather than the self in relation to others, that will eventually have a grave bearing on relations with other societies. If individuals are not concerned about their families, their communities, their fellow citizens, why would they be concerned about what happens to Europeans? Today, among young Americans who are interested in common problems, the highest percentage continues to be interested in Europe. Although the data on the subject are incomplete, every general survey indicated that the highest percentage of American students abroad is studying in Europe.

CONCLUSION

This discussion of NATO-related issues focuses on American attitudes. But I would like to note one difference between American attitudes and those in Europe as I currently understand them. In Europe there appears to be a substantial change in political ideas and culture, a change that is more neutralist, more skeptical of association with the United States, less sympathetic to American society, and more favorable to developing a third position separate from alliance with the superpowers.

This is not the major problem in the United States in terms of its relationship with Western Europe. Although support for internationalism weakened between 1975 and 1985, the priority given to Europe and the willingness to defend Europe did not. There has not been a massive change in political ideas and culture among the American elite or the public. In the United States, the foremost obstacle to maintaining the Atlantic Alliance and retaining European confidence in American leadership is institutional, not ideological. The foremost problem for American participation in the Alliance is the weakening of American governmental institutions and the unraveling of the foreign policy process.

The Atomization of Politics

The United States has experienced a diffusion of political power in the wake of Watergate and Vietnam. This has been characterized by the rise of special interest groups, electoral reforms, the demise of political parties, a weaker executive branch of government, and a different balance between the executive branch and the Congress. The result has been a stalemated society whose political institutions face a two-edged crisis of governability and credibility. Leaders of intermediary groups that have traditionally structured public opinion and given it political effect can no longer be said to automatically represent the views of their groups. Constituency groups within the political parties can no longer be counted on to turn out the base vote for their views. Despite President Reagan's personal popularity, the United States has become a country without any center of popular confidence, a nation whose last two presidents have won elections with an "anti-

Washington" campaign directed against the very government they sought to lead. These problems of governability and credibility are combined with decentralizing tendencies that magnify the problem.

The Decentralization of the Foreign Policy Process

The consensus that prevailed in the United States from 1945 to 1970 on the role of America in the world was destroyed in the wake of American involvement in Vietnam and has not been replaced. There has also been a sharp change in the role and effectiveness of various institutions in the American foreign policy process. As recently as two decades ago, it was possible for the president and the secretary of state, with the concurrence of perhaps the majority and minority leaders of the House of Representatives and the Senate, to make a commitment in the foreign policy field and to see it honored. This is no longer true and not only because of the shift in the balance of power between the White House and the Congress. Given the atomization of power within all institutions, the leaders of the Senate and the House have far more limited influence with their colleagues on any issue. The Chairman of the Senate Foreign Relations Committee or Armed Services Committee or his counterpart in the House often has little influence over the final actions of the committee.

The change in character of official governmental institutions and the decline in their authority has been accompanied by a diffusion of elites active in the private foreign policy establishment and a broadening of the network of private individuals and institutions that interact with the official foreign policy network. The leaders of the Eastern foreign policy establishment no longer carry the same influence in the United States and can no longer successfully intervene to restore confidence and trust between America and Europe.

What is significant about these trends is that the American foreign policy process has changed a good deal, not primarily because a group of people from the West Coast are running it today, as distinct from people from the East, and not because of any great shift in political ideas and culture. The most significant thing is that the policy process itself has changed as American society has changed. A weaker national government is facing problems of governability and credibility. This is true, though to a lesser extent perhaps, even with a "strong" president backed by a massive electoral mandate, as in the case of Ronald Reagan. There is a different balance of power between the Executive and the Congress, a much broader role for individual senators and members of Congress in the foreign policy process, and a continued dominant role by the electronic media in the foreign policy process. All this has resulted in a high degree of uncertainty and inconsistency in American foreign policy, both in its formulation and its implementation.

It is this problem that is the greatest current American obstacle to harmonious relations between the two continents, not a shift in public opinion or elite attitudes on security questions.

To an American looking at Europe today, one disturbing note is that, in the last decade, we have begun to see some of the same institutional problems that have affected the United States for the last two decades, specifically the weakening of governmental authority and governmental institutions. Until recently in the European parliamentary system, if a government was elected with a strong majority, it generally had the power to govern. When it lost its majority, it was replaced by another government. Yet, increasingly, major countries of Europe like France and Germany have elected governments whose authority is being steadily weakened. Germany has enjoyed strong governments based on strong political party structures for the last three and a half decades. Yet the current government, which was elected by a decisive mandate only two and a half years ago, sees itself weakened by internal bickering of the coalition partners. In France there is a real prospect that the Socialists will continue to hold the presidency of France after 1986 with the opposition running the government. If, in addition to changes in political culture that are occurring in Europe, there is an emergence of the kinds of institutional problems confronting the United States, a serious problem for U.S.-European cooperation could develop in the coming decades.

NOTES

1. William Schneider, "Elite and Public Opinion: The Alliance's New Fissure," *Public Opinion* (February/March 1983): 561.
2. In discussing both popular and elite opinion in the United States, I will draw principally on the study published by the Chicago Council on Foreign Relations in March 1983, entitled "American Public Opinion and U.S. Foreign Policy, 1983," editor, John E. Rielly. The conclusions and analysis in this study are based on data collected for the Chicago Council on Foreign Relations by the Gallup Organization in November and December of 1982. If other trends have emerged in the last two and a half years that diverge significantly from the conclusions in this study, they are noted.
3. Gallup Poll, 16 September 1983.
4. Gallup Poll, April 1985.
5. Atlantic Institute of International Affairs, Harris Poll Report released 28 November 1983. The citation here is from the summary issued by the Atlantic Institute and cited in the *International Tribune*, 29 November 1983.
6. Quoted in S.M. Lipsett, "The Economy, Elections and Public Opinion," *Tocqueville Review* 5 (Fall–Winter 1983): 431–71.
7. Irving Kristol, "A Transatlantic Misunderstanding," *Encounter* (March 1984): 8–21.

12
The Foreign Economic Policy of the Reagan Administration

Walter Goldstein

Two bitterly opposed arguments have been raised by economists in recent years about the leadership exercised by the United States in the world trade system. Those supporting the policies of Reaganomics have hailed the powerful recovery enjoyed by the United States economy since the recession of 1982 and the stimulus that the U.S. expansion brought to its many trading partners and rivals. The opponents have been sharply critical. They point to the phenomenal deficits in the federal budget and in the balance of payments, and to the great lag in American export earnings. When the dollar appreciated steeply in the 1980s, they attributed its rise to the manipulation of U.S. interest rates and not to the prowess of the United States in competing in world trade.

Critics of U.S. policy, especially in Europe, have argued that the tight monetary and loose fiscal policies of the Reagan administration might have benefited business at home, but they could eventually wreak havoc in the worldwide trading and credit markets. As the largest actor in the international order, the United States has run up perilous deficits in its merchandise balance and in its external accounts. It is living well beyond its means and the critics warn that a sharp correction will have to be made one day in the American standard of living. The impact of the correction, they add, could force the world order back to the recession and inflation that beset the early 1980s.[1]

The arguments between the rival schools of analysis tend to focus on two issues. First, has the Reagan administration acted in a short-sighted and irresponsible manner in boosting the nation's recovery? Did it secure high growth by borrowing too heavily overseas and by disregarding the needs of its allies, neighbors, and trade rivals? And, second, if there is a correction in the U.S. balance of payments, will it lead to a soft or a hard landing for the dollar? The issues are complex and politically dangerous. If it can be shown that the import boom in the United States did, indeed, bring a valuable stimulus to worldwide trade and output, then the United States cannot be accused of abusing its superior monetary strength to promote its own welfare at the expense of others. Alternatively, if the United States expects to finance its astronomical deficits, both at home and in its external accounts, by siphoning off foreign funds and domestic savings to support its endless borrowing, then its policies might prove to be as myopic and destructive as many of the critics have claimed. [2]

The second issue is closely related to the first. Even if it is granted that the U.S. import boom has been helpful to the exports of Western Europe and East Asia, how will the United States extricate itself from its present financial crisis? Its growth in GNP cannot generate a surplus large enough to repay its borrowing of capital or to comfortably handle the servicing of interest on the debt. But something will eventually have to be done to balance the outstanding accounts. Foreign funds have flooded into the United States at an unprecedented rate to sustain consumption and investment; the United States was the leading creditor nation until 1982, but by 1985 it had become the largest debtor, spending overseas 50 percent more than it managed to earn. Were foreign funds ever to start emigrating from the United States, in fear of a severe devaluation, the dollar could plummet into a hard landing. If that occurred, the Federal Reserve would have to immediately raise interest rates, the political clamor for trade protectionism would intensify, and the U.S. economic recovery program would grind inexorably downward. This would create acute hardship throughout the trade and money markets of the world, prompting a sharp recession in business activity and acute instability in the banking system and among Third World debtors. [3]

Criticism of U.S. economic leadership has run rife at Western summit meetings, especially at the meeting in Bonn in May 1985. The administration countered the attacks of its critics at home and in Europe by insisting that the U.S. economy could "grow its way" out of the deficit crisis and that, in doing so, it would enhance the currencies and the trading strength of its Atlantic allies. Most of the allies were not convinced, though they cooperated in the efforts mounted in 1985 to bring down the value of the dollar. By intervening collectively in the exchanges, they succeeded in lowering the dollar's standing by 25%, though they doubted that their action would help the United States achieve either financial retrenchment or a balance in its payments. If economic balance is to be secured in the long term, it might be necessary to devalue the dollar by another 25%, and that might lead to high-risk consequences. [4]

For the time being, neither the critics nor the supporters of Reagan's economic initiatives feel secure about the course of future development. Both sides agree that the success of the U.S. economic recovery will depend upon the ability in the late 1980s to expand industrial output and the volume of international trade. If the rate of expansion should flag, however, U.S. leadership efforts will be severely censured and a major crisis might spread through the world markets. Though the American dollar is supported by borrowed assets and borrowed time, it still serves as the base for global trade and currency stability. Were that base to lose its solidity, the Reagan administration would be criticized for its stubborn assurance that it can rely on short-term growth curves to cure long-term ills.

The administration tends to scoff at the doom and gloom projections of its allies and critics. It insists that U.S. economic policy has been neither irresponsible nor short-sighted; and that the global recovery would be better assured if its richer trading partners, especially in Japan and West Germany, were to follow the U.S. lead in boosting GNP growth at home and enforcing free-trade principles overseas. But it admits that there is reason to fear a deterioration on two vital fronts. First, the awesome debt crisis facing the Third World is moving toward a dangerous point. Second, threats to resort to trade protection have come from many countries, rich and poor; they could rapidly lead to an economic recession and a full-scale trade war. To cite just one example: the U.S. steel industry has lost 25% of its home market to cheap imports, and it wants President Reagan to replace voluntary import restrictions with mandated quotas and price supports. If he bent to their pressure, many EEC steel mills would have to close, and several steel exporters in the Third World, such as Mexico and Brazil, might have to enter into default on their towering debt payments. Were he to give in to the steel lobby, he would have to make concessions to many other industries that have priced their exports out of effective competition.

Fortunately, the economic growth forecasts prepared by OECD and the International Monetary Fund (IMF) look fairly promising for the near future. Though an overall growth rate of nearly 3% is projected for global output, some economies will fare well and the laggards will continue to coast into decline. Japan and several of the newly industrializing countries (NICs) will grow at a faster rate than the West German and the U.S. economies, but the sluggish pace of most members of the European Community, which *The Economist* calls "Euro-sclerosis," is likely to drag onward at a depressing rate. Their resentment against U.S. economic policy will probably become more shrill. As the most powerful agent in changing market conditions, the United States is called upon to fulfill contradictory expectations. On one side, it is expected to import vast quantities of primary commodities and manufactured goods, to the benefit of its trading partners in Europe and the Third World. But on the other, it is expected to devalue the dollar, to lower its interest rates, and to stop living off the capital transfers entering the United States for speculative and short-term profits. So far, a compromise has been struck between these policy contradictions, assuring steady growth in U.S. trade and debt, but the assurances of long-run growth are far from secure.[5]

Underlying the good tidings projected by the forecasts of the OECD and the IMF, unfortunately, signs of serious troubles can be seen ahead. They can be briefly listed.

First, *unemployment* is likely to stick in some of the OECD countries at 11% or more; in many of the less developed countries (LDCs) it will persist at 40 or 50% of the potential work force. Second, *deficits on current account* pose a grave threat to many trading nations. The annual deficit in the United States alone is now $100 billion and it could feasibly rise to a total of $1 trillion by 1990. To this alarming figure must be added the deficits racked up by several members of the OPEC cartel and the EEC. It has been questioned whether the trading system can long survive when deficits continue to accumulate year after year. Nation-states can afford to run up a vast national debt but the international order cannot operate in a state of permanent deficit.[6]

Third, *the LDCs' external debt* gives cause for anxiety. The current total stands at $950 billion, and it is increasing at a rate of 12 or 15% a year. Much of the debt is poorly secured and subject to default, and obligations could conceivably double by 1990. There is a realistic threat that several of the debtors will either default on interest arrears or declare a moratorium on further debt-servicing payment if there should be another downturn in the global business cycle.[7]

Fourth, *trade protection and nontariff barriers* have been increasingly adopted by nations that have lost their competitive edge in selling manufacturing and agricultural exports. The clamor for protectionist measures has become strident in the U.S. Congress and in the EEC. Protests against the unfair trading practices of Japan, and of other aggressive exporters, have provoked demands to impose countervailing duties and import quotas. President Reagan's proposal to initiate a new GATT round of trade negotiations has not been eagerly taken up, and the maintenance of free-trade flows will remain uncertain in the next few years.[8]

Fifth, *the regulation of currency exchange rates* poses a great difficulty. Nations with strong currencies have argued that there is no reason to return to the fixed rates of a gold standard or of the Bretton Woods standard that prevailed between 1946 and 1971. Nations saddled with declining currencies have angrily dissented. They point in particular to the appreciation in value of the American dollar of nearly 70% in the decade following the early 1970s. They insist that its recovery was due not to the strengthening of the U.S. economy but to the mix of tight monetary and loose fiscal policies that had been adopted by the Reagan administration. That policy mix spurred flights of capital from the weakest of the LDC and European economies to the American money market, leading the *Financial Times* to remark that the United States had bought its economic recovery by "running a raid on the world's savings." The United States has relied on high interest rates and capital inflows to boost the value of the dollar and to finance nearly one-third of its public and private investment capital. Its enormous deficits on domestic and external accounts have been funded by inflows of $500 million a day from affluent trade rivals and from poor debtor countries. In one sense, U.S. trade deficits have provided a formidable stimulus to exporters in Europe, East Asia, and the Third World; in another, U.S. reliance on deficit financing threatens to overwhelm the financial resources of global credit institutions.[9]

SHORT-TERM CHANGE:
THE CHALLENGE TO ECONOMIC LEADERSHIP

In the United States and the market-driven societies of Western Europe and Japan, government leaders and corporate managers tend to worry about short- rather than long-term anxieties. Regrettably, they have good reasons to do so since governments more frequently think about the political cycle, of election timetables and party contests, than about the business cycle. Industrial democracies operate today on the assumption that productive employment and adequate income will ultimately be made available to all citizens. This has become a grave error. In an era obsessed with inflation spirals and recession, trade gaps and financial deficits, expectations of full employment are no longer justified. Industrial obsolescence and structural unemployment pose a fundamental threat to the high standards of living that are enjoyed by most economies, if not people, within the Alliance. It is conceivable today, even in the richest nations, that the fragile mechanism of democratic regimes will be strained if a large sector of the work force is condemned to lifelong unemployment or to a decline in mass consumption standards and credit card affluence.[10]

It is in this somber context that the economic leadership of the United States has been forced to confront a historic dilemma. In the 1980s it managed to suppress the spiral of inflation by hiking interest rates and exchange rates, though U.S. manufacturing and agricultural producers lost much of their competitive place in overseas markets. As much as Reagan rejects the notion, it seems that one day the United States will have to choose between protecting the nation's failing industries and severely cutting back its standard of living. It cannot build a high dollar and "jobless prosperity" on an ever widening trade gap.

Basically, the United States has failed to preserve its export industries, its economic autonomy, or its comparative advantage in global trade. The deficit on its merchandise account rose from $35 billion in 1980 to $150 billion in 1985. As the value of the dollar soared, the United States lost much of its commanding lead in high-technology industries, and many other industries were badly hurt.[11] The question now has to be asked: How long can the United States subsist on foreign savings, trade credits, and short-term capital transfers from its trading partners? And at what point will its dependency on overseas funding, to balance the federal and the current account deficits, leave it hostage to panic movements in the world money market? These questions will be anxiously raised if the business cycle of world trade should swing into another downturn in the second half of the 1980s, and if the high-flying dollar should head toward a hard landing. Unwelcome as they are, these are realistic possibilities that deserve to be carefully considered.

U.S. prospects of change must be viewed in a global perspective. The startling growth of U.S. imports in the 1980s was welcomed by exporting nations in the OECD bloc and the Third World. However, if the decline in the U.S. trade balance continued, and the dollar weakened as the world's reserve currency, an emergency operation would have to be mounted by the stronger and the weaker nations to secure the mechanism of world credit. Their intervention would be needed to shore up the market, because it is not as strong or as autonomous as the idealists suppose. The trading system could be fractured if strains appeared in the U.S. fiscal structure or in the handling of Third World borrowing arrangements. Industrial nations have come to rely on sustained borrowing and on export revenues to fuel their economic growth. But one-quarter to one-third of their prized export earnings come from sales to the debt-laden LDCs; in the case of the United States they account for 41% and, of Japan, 61% of export revenues. The weak link in the chain is clearly visible.[12]

The financially weak countries in the Third World owe Western banks and government agencies nearly $1 trillion in poorly secured debt. Were the economic recovery in the OECD bloc to flag, primary commodity imports from the LDCs would continue to fall and their currency reserves could soon be exhausted. The severe consequences of a decline in commodity prices have already been experienced by the OPEC cartel; its oil sales shrank from 31 to 16 million barrels a day, and prices on the spot market fell by 65%. Were the falling off in other commodity trade to be prolonged, Third World governments would be sorely tempted to default on debt service payments; and Western banks would then have to cope with loan losses that far surpassed the $4.5 billion shortfall of one bank, Continental Illinois Bank, that rocked the financial community in 1983.[13]

The short-term dangers faced by the world trading system can be better understood if the trends established since World War II are contrasted with those observed today. During the golden years of growth, in the 1950s and 1960s, the creation of wealth doubled in many countries, and world trade increased by 8% a year, a rate that matched the rise of Japan's GNP. A sharp setback occurred in the 1970s. Oil prices escalated by 1300%, from $3 to $39 a barrel, and double-digit inflation brought growth to a halt. In the recession that followed, nations ran up towering deficits on current account, and Third World debt rapidly swelled. A gradual recovery began in 1982, but its progress is still uncertain. If it should prematurely peter out, the world trading cycle could begin to move sharply downward. This could lead to a renewed spiraling of inflation, an alarming volatility in currency exchange rates, an overloading of the credit market, and a system-wide crisis as debtors began to enter into default. There could also be an aggressive resort to protectionism and trade warfare as nations tried to shore up export earnings and to stifle imports or capital flows.[14]

Realistically, any of these developments could burst into the newspaper headlines as abruptly as the explosion of the first of the "oil shocks" in 1973, and they could do considerably more damage. The international credit market is already overstretched, and there is no effective mechanism to enforce GATT rules or to curb the rampages of trade warfare. The depressing prospect must be envisaged that the upturn in trade will be halted in the 1980s and that many nations will have to cut back their consumption patterns and public expenditures before the decade comes to its end.

Without question, a more optimistic course of events might appear, and it is hoped that the projection of pessimistic outcomes will prove to be false. But there is a chance that it could be correct and that a breakdown in the control mechanisms of the economic order could eventually appear. The machinery of the international economy is difficult to adjust, or to fine-tune, and powerful nations have shied away from taking joint action to stimulate the money supply and trade expansion. Trading nations usually act as solitary agents, blindly hoping that the strength of the system will help them survive from one year's crisis to the next, but their confidence might be misplaced. It is likely that the first sign of a breakdown will be seen in a failure to reschedule Third World debt; a second might appear in a growing resort to measures of trade protection, exchange control, import quotas, and other limits on free trade; both forces together could move the business cycle into a sharp downward turn.

On the other hand, it is possible that action can still be taken to safeguard the global system against excessive strain and disrepair. If action is firmly decided and crisis management is implemented, we can begin to ask what patterns of long-term change are likely to develop if the system should manage to survive the 1980s. Will it be feasible to harmonize measures of financial planning and trade cooperation among national economies that bitterly compete in the world market? And will the rapid development of industrial technology force major policy modifications to be made in the conduct of international business in the following decade?

The optimistic assumption today is that system changes can be made through multilateral agencies, such as GATT, the IMF, and the European Monetary System. Though they presently lack the institutional authority to discipline national trade policies or to correct swings in the global money supply, they could be reformed. As professional pessimists, economists have warned that revolutionary changes could sweep through the global economy, but few governments are ready to pay heed to multilateral forms of contingency planning. Changes in the "rules of the game," to restrict the flow of hot money and competitive trade, will sooner or later have to be designed and enforced through collective action. But little has been done to prepare for the long-term changes that are likely to appear in the 1990s, and practically no attention has been given to the subject by the Reagan administration.

ANTICIPATING LONG-TERM CHANGE

There is an extensive literature in "futurology" that tries to predict fundamental patterns of change in social values, economic competition, or nuclear war.[15] If the excesses of its popular "scenario building" can be shunned, three empirical trends of behavior can be projected for the world trading system in the 1990s. A selection of economic data can illustrate the magnitude of the three change factors that need to be examined.

First, *trade and investment flows* are changing rapidly. The flows in 1979 across the Atlantic were twice as great as those crossing the Pacific; by 1985 U.S. imports from both sources were roughly equal, and Japan enjoyed a trade surplus with the United States of nearly $50 billion and with the EEC of $11 billion. Japan has overtaken West Germany as the leading exporter of manufactured goods; in 1984 alone it raised its export sales to the United States by 40%. Nineteen percent of worldwide export growth in 1984 came from Japan and 14 percent from Southeast Asia, while Western European and U.S. export sales proportionately declined. As a result, the unsuccessful trading nations racked up deficits on current account of dangerous proportions. Total foreign debt exceeded export earnings in the United States and in seven countries in Western Europe. Were the economy of the debtors not so powerful they would now be subjected to disciplinary action, along with Portugal, Turkey, and several dozen LDCs, and they would have to submit their budgets to the "conditionality" requirements for fiscal retrenchment dictated by the IMF.[16]

The imbalance in trade accounts has generated protests against "unfair trading practices" and a demand for retaliatory measures of protection. The EEC countries have tightly limited the import of Japanese cars and electronic equipment, while the United States and the EEC have strenuously contested each others' farm price subsidies and steel quotas; both of them have haggled over multifiber agreements and commodity price stabilization schemes with the developing countries.

It appears that all governments have raised import charges or nontariff barriers to deter foreign competition. The most serious threat to take further action has come from the U.S. Congress. It has talked about imposing steep import duties on Japanese goods in order to protest against Japan's resistance to American exports. Last year the House actually approved a "domestic content" requirement, though the Senate killed it. Its aim was to require major foreign firms to include a value-added tax on finished goods sold in the United States. Japanese automobile and European manufacturing companies have anticipated that further constraints will be imposed and they have bought nearly $1,000 million worth of production facilities in the United States.[17]

These measures are seen today as opening shots in what could become an intense and prolonged trade war. President Reagan urged the OECD nations to cooperate in resisting the tide of protection and import restrictions. His proposal to stage a new GATT round of trade talks was greeted with considerable sympathy, but not by all of the European allies. President Mitterrand saw the proposal as a renewed attack against the collective subsidizing of European agriculture and as an attempt to consolidate the present range of U.S. import quotas. He insisted that the first priority was to cope with the realignment of world currencies and to halt the manipulation of interest rates that had falsely inflated the value of the dollar. He urged that "targeted zones" of exchange be established, so that governments could forcefully intervene in the currency markets. His campaign eventually succeeded. A meeting of the Group of Five (G-5) finance ministers of the OECD convened twice in 1985. They decided to abandon their free-market principles and to bring down the value of the dollar, especially against the yen, by 25%. They set a precedent for future intervention and for a coordinated realignment of national currencies. Their action was seen as a sharp reversal of Reagan's laissez faire theories of economic adjustment, though they failed to agree about procedures to reduce interest rates across national boundaries.[18]

Belated promises were also offered by Prime Minister Nakasone to modify Japan's use of trade and exchange controls. No one was sure, however, if his promises would at long last change the nation's allergy to foreign imports or its powerful craving to export savings and investment funds to the U.S. market. Even if Nakasone eventually succeeds in changing policy priorities, Japan will still command a staggering surplus on current and capital account, and this will incense U.S. protectionist forces. Moreover, along with West Germany, Japan has refused to help its trading partners by expanding its own domestic money supply. Both countries have resisted any move to reflate their money supply, to reduce government tax revenues, or to enlarge the international reserve role of their currencies. It appears that neither country aims to follow the Reaganomics model proposed by the United States or to join it in promoting a controlled risk experiment in global reflation.[19]

Second, *the migration of employment* is likely to impose painful changes on many national economies. The geographical location of work has shifted remarkably in recent years. Argument rages today over the push versus pull theories that are used to explain the high and persistent rate of unemployment in the OECD bloc. The first theory suggests that a mistaken "push" of monetary or fiscal policy has deterred the modernizing of industrial plants and the creation of new jobs. Structural obstacles were raised as a result of errors in macroeconomic planning, and high-wage economies too often discouraged capital formation and the expansion of employment. The second theory focuses on the "pull" of dispersing routinized and semiskilled work to the NICs. Labor in these countries is not collectively organized, strikes are forbidden, and wages (plus compensation) cost $10 per week rather than the $10 to $20 an hour paid in Detroit or Dusseldorf. Criticism has been leveled against the multinational corporations that relocated labor-intensive work, component production, or assembly line investments from their home countries to the NICs. Their "pull" of labor to cheap-wage economies has helped reinforce the structural unemployment and the obsolescence of the work force in the home country, leaving behind a residue of political distrust and labor unrest. It is often suggested that the United States adjusted more easily to these shifts than the EEC countries because the American economy is less regulated and the work force is not strongly unionized. As a consequence, real wages fell more sharply in the United States than in Europe but the rate of job creation was far more rapid.[20]

Each of the OECD governments urgently needs to improve labor productivity, but few of them know how to do so. Though employment in high-technology sectors and service industries can be profitably expanded, because of the surprisingly low wages paid, it is the millions of jobs in intermediate manufacturing that can be neither protected nor multiplied. The production of cars, televisions and VCRs, rolled steel, ships, wearing apparel, and consumer durables is already threatened with bankruptcy and possibly extinction in many parts of the United States and Europe. It cannot be revived with public subsidies or import tariffs. Nor, for that matter, can the elimination of blue-collar jobs in Western society easily be accepted by political parties or their electors.

The calculus of labor as a factor cost presents daunting challenges to governments concerned with maintaining welfare standards and a high level of consumer spending. The NICs will obviously undercut the cost calculations of OECD countries in the years to come, leaving a work force that is increasingly priced out of manufacturing competition. The only logical solution is to stimulate capital formation and consumer demand, to upgrade workers' training, and to finance the machinery needed to raise per capita productivity. This sounds like a simple remedy, but if the swelling of the money supply were too abrupt there would be a renewed surge of double-digit inflation, while if the money supply remained inadequate, growth would be choked off. The strategic choices facing elected governments and the central banks are perilous. On one side, they worry about the revival of inflation and the chaos that it could generate. On the other, they need to provide ample sources of consumer spending and capital investment, at manageable rates of interest. How best to stimulate GNP growth and employment in an era of inflation and international competition is not really known. The unilateral policies of the United States in the world economy have secured great benefits, but this has done little to advance the cause of multinational planning.[21]

Third, *the momentum of technological change* can be neither halted nor artificially imitated. Industrial production has been revolutionized by new technologies in data processing, numerical machine tools, assembly line controls, and development of robot applications. Significant economies of scale have been realized in such high value-added industries as component engineering, automobile production, telecommunications, computer hardware and microchip manufacture. Technological advances have led to sharp changes in productivity ratios for both labor and capital, prompting the rise of Silicon Valley complexes in some regions and the burnout of depressed areas in others. While new industries have sprouted, often as a result of investment funding by multinational firms in such countries as Singapore and Hong Kong, industrial decay has spread blight through the Rhone and the Ruhr valleys, the Midlands, and the aging plants of the American Midwest.

It has been suggested that a "third wave of the industrial revolution" is about to shake up the manufacturing and service economies of the old world and the new. Plans to build a "world car" are now being developed by American and Japanese firms, and the manufacture of tools, appliances, and microchips is becoming highly robotized. Efforts to catch up with the thrust of change will require massive outlays on the part of world companies and nation-states, but the consequences of inaction will be even more costly. No government can sit idly by, regardless of its free-market ideology, while rival economies sweep forward into a new era of modernizing plant and work skills.[22]

It is possible that governments and multinational corporations will determine to catch up with the achievements of their rivals, but they will succeed only if the total volume of world trade continues to expand. If trade levels should contract during a subsequent downturn in the global business cycle, a significant number of nations will find it too expensive to stay in the race. Were that to occur, governments would be sorely tempted to raise protectionist barriers and to step up *dirigiste* efforts to protect their failing economic assets. It will not help them, in fact, if they resort to measures of economic nationalism, and they might severely impair the functioning of the world trade system. The argument is frequently heard today that if the collective mechanisms of world trade were to falter, the only defense available to the losing and the declining nations would be *sauve qui peut*. Economic autarky and a "siege economy" provide attractive but illusory models to nations that cannot keep up with the rigorous challenges of technological competition and market risk. The models may be built on mirages, but they can have a highly destructive effect.[23]

THE ROLE OF U.S. ECONOMIC LEADERSHIP

In the first term of the Reagan administration, the strong growth of the U.S. economy provoked surprise, applause, and severe criticism. The surprise stemmed largely from the Keynesian policies that President Reagan and his team of supply-side economists had first condemned and then put into practice. While a tight control was kept on the increase in the money supply, the federal deficit was pushed to unprecedented heights. The use of fiscal policy to stimulate GNP growth was welcomed by business, conservative, and labor interests, since it led to an expansion of industrial output, defense procurement, and civilian employment. Surprisingly, Reagan complained that it was the Congress that was responsible for the lavish level of public spending and therefore for the alarming size of the deficit. In fact, he had initiated the trouble by slashing $750 billion in tax revenues while running up defense expenditures to more than $1 trillion in his first term. Few critics at the time recognized that the tax cut would be financed in reality by the inflow of foreign funds. The borrowing of the U.S. government kept increasing, thus pegging real (as against nominal) interest rates at a high level, and foreign depositors were rewarded for helping to fund the $200 billion a year deficit, a sum equal to 5% of GNP and unprecedented in American peacetime history.[24]

If the loosening of fiscal policy to boost the GNP provoked surprise and applause at home, especially in the election year of 1984, it prompted a more critical response overseas. The Reagan administration had concocted an expansionary mix of deficit spending and lowered taxes on the treasury side, while there was a continued tightening of the money supply on the part of the Federal Reserve Bank. As government borrowing and foreign lending increased, the value of the dollar rose sharply. The United States was flooded with cheap imports, while U.S. exports declined, and American investments overseas were rapidly run down. It was estimated that the appreciation of the dollar had levied the equivalent of a 40% tax on U.S. exports. Factory employment and revenues fell significantly in the manufacturing industries that relied on foreign sales, and agriculture was badly hurt by the high cost of credit on the farm and the low volume of sales abroad. Admittedly, total civilian employment expanded and inflation was forcefully curbed, but the external obligations of the United States overtook those of Brazil or Mexico, and soon they will be larger than the debts of all the LDCs put together.[25]

There were surprisingly few leaders in the Reagan administration who shared the anxieties that spread across the world as U.S. deficits widened in the domestic and external accounts. Cabinet leaders admitted that the annual deficit of $200 billion a year was indeed worrying, but they noted that the debt amounted to a lower percentage of GNP than in many other industrial countries. Moreover, the merchandise deficit of $150 billion had brought cheap goods to benefit millions of U.S. consumers, though not many producers; and the spiraling of external debt obligations could be safely collateralized against America's rich asset worth. If short-term funds flowed into the United States, in response to high interest rates and an appreciating dollar, there was no cause for alarm. Foreign investors regarded the United States as a safe haven for their funds, and there was no better place in which to profitably park money.[26]

Protests against U.S. economic policies were raised at each of the Western summit meetings that convened during the first half of the 1980s. Alliance members complained that investment funds had been unfairly siphoned into the United States, retarding their own efforts at economic recovery and job creation. The complaint was not sympathetically received. American leaders pointed to the invaluable boost that the United States had provided to the export industries of Europe, the LDCs, and Japan. They insisted, too, that open flows in the capital market should not be deflected by government exchange controls or central bank interventions to manipulate currency exchange rates.

One issue created considerable anxiety, even in the United States. The LDC debtor countries had found it increasingly difficult to maintain their debt service payments as dollar values and global interest rates continued to rise. Though the administration resisted any easing of IMF "conditionality" requirements for Third World borrowing, it called for a gradual expansion of the reserve funds of the World Bank agencies, and it chose to overlook the trade restrictions that had been adopted by many of the LDCs. Indeed, it hailed the LDCs' success in blocking imports and subsidizing their own exports, many of which came to the United States. The expansion of the LDCs' commerce allowed them to double their currency reserves and to negotiate in several cases a favorable rescheduling of external borrowings. So the claim was made that "the ticking fuse in the debt time-bomb had been stopped." The judgment may prove to have been terribly premature.[27]

There was an undeniable sense of triumph in the economic claims advanced by Reagan's first administration. Though many worrying problems were left unresolved, and the incidence of domestic poverty had risen, the U.S. economy had enjoyed boom years of growth. It was asserted, though not with convincing proof, that the commitment to laissez faire politics and to industrial deregulation was largely responsible for stimulating the formidable rate of growth. President Reagan urged the EEC to follow the American example.

The only acknowledged grounds for criticism appeared in the growing resort to trade protection in the OECD markets and, to some extent, in the United States itself. Reagan called for a new GATT round of negotiations to control the numerous import tariffs, quotas, tax-driven subsidies, and market interventions that had begun to deflect the flow of trade. He was pushed from behind on many of these issues by the anger stirring in the Congress. Though 300 bills were introduced to curb the alleged use of "unfair trading procedures" by the Atlantic and Pacific partners, Reagan held firmly to the doctrines of "fair," if not free, trade. Angry charges were traded with the EEC and Japan over America's own trade controls, such as the steel trigger price system, the multifiber agreements on textiles, and the subsidizing of shipping or agricultural export sales. In most cases Reagan rejected the strident lobbying that called for retaliatory or protectionist measures to shelter America's declining industries. He gave way on a few issues, as in the voluntary limits to Japanese automobile imports, but he otherwise stood firm against adding to formal protectionist measures.[28]

In his second term the administration began to shift its position. Once the election of 1984 was decisively won, policy became more flexible and less aggressive. The new secretary of the treasury, James Baker, agreed to act with the five leading finance ministers of OECD (the G-5 group) to realign currency exchange rates and to reduce the value of the dollar by one-quarter. Many critics were surprised but not displeased by the G-5 decision to intervene in the global money markets and to "talk down" the dollar. They also welcomed Baker's proposal to stimulate international bank lending, to enlarge the funds of the World Bank agencies and the allocation of Special Drawing Rights.

These decisions were long overdue. They were prompted by growing doubts about the dollar and the even more dangerous accumulation of LDC debts. It is still far from certain that the debt crisis has been defused, because few of the commercial banks are willing to lend new money to their insecure borrowers, and real interests rates are still too high to encourage new borrowing. Bankers are uneasy about the overhang of debt and the potential volatility of exchange rates. Unlike Baker, they include the external debt of the United States in their inventory of potential anxieties, and they are not at all sure that the dollar can be gently brought down to a soft landing. [29]

The critical challenge to President Reagan's second administration is obviously that of coping with the deficits on external and domestic accounts. Reagan refuses to raise tax revenues, to lower defense spending, to protect American trade against international competition, or to subsidize industrial growth. He insistently blames the Congress for spending too much money on welfare assistance, social security, and a wide range of "entitlement" programs. A majority in the Congress has successfully deflected his criticism; first, because the spending projects are extraordinarily popular among farmers, pensioners, the unemployed, and millions of other recipients; and second, because the president has had to concede that the expenditures are now indispensable to large segments of American society. If President Reagan remains adamant, the national debt will be vastly swollen by the time he leaves office in 1989, and U.S. borrowings overseas will leave it vulnerable to panic movements on the world money exchanges.

The confidence of Ronald Reagan appears to be as unshakable as his personal popularity. He believes that the U.S. economy can "grow its way" out of debts at home and overseas. Defense spending is pegged at almost 7% of GNP and the deficit at 5 percent; but the equivalent of one-half of the deficit is funded by foreign capital inflows, and the domestic personal savings rate has fallen to such a low point that foreign fund transfers are invaluable.

Reagan's critics vehemently disagree with his optimistic expectations. They point to the short-term burden of debt servicing that today accounts for 15% of the federal budget and that could conceivably double, depending on the course of interest rates, within five to ten years. More serious are the long-term prospects of America's indebtedness. If foreign investors should begin to fear that their dollar assets were too heavily exposed, or if they lost confidence in the sustained growth of the U.S. economy, they might begin to pull out their funds. Were they to do so, the dollar could lose another 20 or 25% of its value. The consequences could be disastrous. Deficits could no longer be bridged with foreigners' funds, interest rates would immediately have to be hiked, the rate of capital formation would be halted, and the dollar would head for a crash landing. Should these terrible tidings materialize, a resurgence of inflation would be needed to preserve the U.S. economy and the rest of the world's business that it helps fuel. [30]

There is no intention in this essay to predict whether this worst-case scenario will develop, but it is sufficiently realistic to merit attention. The administration has prepared few defenses to stave off a slide toward recession or another debt crisis, should they ever occur. It still believes that GNP growth will be sufficiently strong to cure the nation's fundamental problems and to expand international commerce and liquidity. This sense of assurance might quickly be diluted in the next few years for reasons that were previously cited. Moreover, if the groundswell of criticisms advanced by bankers, labor, international forecasters, and Alliance governments should continue to gather force, there could be a serious loss of confidence in the resilience of America's debt-laden economy. It is a risky proposition of the Reagan team: If the next downturn of the business cycle can be delayed by a year or two, the U.S. economy will rapidly grow, and the international order will be appreciably strengthened.

The key issue facing Reagan's second term can be tersely questioned. Will it unilaterally rally U.S. economic efforts, despite the doubts and criticisms of its allies, to promote domestic growth and disregard the swelling indebtedness? Or will it utilize the powerful instruments of America's economic leadership, and the authority of multilateral institutions, to strengthen the market structures of world trade and global credit arrangements?

In its second term Reagan's administration can choose whether to encourage or discourage the building of multilateral trade and credit arrangements for the worldwide economy. To a great extent its choices will determine the courses of action that will be taken by the Atlantic allies, the LDC bloc, and America's trading rivals. There are many contradictory expressions, both of business anxiety and economic confidence, that are voiced today about American leadership in world affairs. The strongest factor in shaping a global consensus will be the decisions taken in U.S. foreign economic policy. Will it lean toward unilateral or collective action to shore up the structures of world order? Will President Reagan use his second term to practice laissez faire economics with a potent nationalist tinge, or will he emphasize the need for collective trade initiatives and an international realignment of exchange and interest rates? Whichever direction his leadership leans, the impact of U.S. foreign economic policy on holding together the Atlantic alliance will be powerful and lasting. Indeed his leadership choices will probably determine the course of economic development to be pursued for the rest of the century.

NOTES

1. See the excellent analysis of Stephen Marris, *Deficits and the Dollar: The World Economy at Risk* (Washington, DC: Institute for International Economics, 1985); and the tabulated data on GNP, debt, interest rates, and trade flows collected in the *World Economic Outlook, 1985* (Washington, DC: The IMF, 1985).
2. Two opposing points of view are ably set forward in C. Fred Bergsten and Henry R. Nau, "The State of the Debate on Reaganomics," *Foreign Policy 59* (Summer 1985): 132–53.

3. An exploration of possible crisis scenarios appears in Jeffrey E. Garten, "Gunboat Economics," *Foreign Affairs* 63(3), (1985): 538–59; and in Susan Strange, "Protectionism and World Politics," *International Organization* 39(2) (Spring 1985): 233–59.

4. A good historical analysis is given by Charles Pigott and Vincent Reinhart, "The Strong Dollar and U.S. Inflation," *Quarterly Review* of the Federal Reserve Bank of New York, 10(3) (Autumn 1985): 23–28; and W.M. Corden, *Inflation, Exchange Rates and the World Economy* (Chicago: University of Chicago Press, 1981).

5. A cautious but gloomy prognosis appears in Richard N. Cooper, "A Monetary System for the Future," *Foreign Policy* 63 (Fall 1984): 166–84.

6. A thorough analysis of the management of the economic order has been written by Joan E. Spero, *The Politics of International Economic Relations* (New York: St. Martin's Press, 1984).

7. For an extensive analysis, see Walter Goldstein, "The Continuing World Debt Crisis," *International Tax and Business Lawyer* 3(1) (Summer 1985): 119–53.

8. An assessment of current costs of trade protection appears in the *IMF Survey* 12 August 1985 and 23 September 1985.

9. See Guy Pfeffermann, "Overvalued Exchange Rates and Development," *Finance and Development* 22(1) (March 1985): 17–24.

10. On popular expectations of employment and affluence, compare Chalmers Johnson, ed., *The Industrial Policy Debate* (San Francisco: ICS Press, 1984) and Lester C. Thurow, *The Zero-Sum Solution* (New York: Simon and Schuster, 1985).

11. For a vivid though popular account of industrial change, see Bruce Nussbaum, *The World after Oil* (New York: Simon and Schuster, 1983); also see the essays in John Zysman, ed., *American Industry in International Competition* (Ithaca, NY: Cornell University Press, 1983).

12. A useful collection of essays on trade and finance issues appears in John Sewell, ed., *U.S. Foreign Policy and the Third World* (New Brunswick, NJ: Transaction Books, 1985).

13. A full listing of external debt liabilities was itemized in a special supplement on world debt in *Wall Street Journal*, 22 June 1984: 35–40.

14. The genesis of the debt and world trade crisis is lucidly evaluated in William R. Cline, *International Debt and the Stability of the World Economy* (Washington, DC: Institute for International Economics, 1983).

15. An outstanding and potent example of futurology analysis appears in Immanuel Wallerstein, *The Capitalist World-Economy* (Cambridge: Cambridge University Press, 1979).

16. The experience of the IMF in applying "conditionality" requirements is examined by five different authors in the special issue on "The Political Economy of Debt," *International Organization* 39(3) (Summer 1985): 357–534. An optimistic analysis by Irwin Kellner, "Developing Country Debt Bomb Defused?" appears in *Bankers Monthly Magazine*, 15 April 1984: 12–18.

17. For useful illustrative material see James Botkin, Dan Dimanescu, and Ray Stata, *Global Stakes: The Future of High Technology in America* (New York: Penguin Books, 1984); and Walter Goldstein, *The Changing Flow of World Trade, Jobs, and Investment* (London and Washington: British-North American Research Committee, 1985).

18. Contemporary analyses of the economic summit meeting and of the G-5 sessions in 1985 are to be found in *The Economist, Business Week*, the *Wall Street Journal*, and the *IMF Survey*.

19. The arguments between Japan and its commercial rivals are skillfully investigated by Kent E. Calder, "The Making of a Trans-Pacific Economy," *World Policy Journal* 2(4) (Fall 1985): 593–623.

20. A range of political explanations of labor and industrial problems in the United States is offered by the essays collected in George Cabot Lodge, ed., *U.S. Competitiveness and the World Economy* (Cambridge, MA: Harvard University Press, 1984).

21. A reasoned analysis of "Money and World Politics" is offered by Susan Strange in *Paths to International Political Economy* (London: Allen and Unwin, 1985). Also see Susan Hickok, "The Consumer Cost of U.S. Trade Restraints," *Quarterly Review* of the Federal Reserve Bank of New York, *10*(2) (Summer 1985): 1–12.

22. The imperative need of each national economy, and especially of the United States, to excel in the race for international industrial technology is argued in Robert B. Reich, *The Next American Frontier* (New York: Times Books, 1983).

23. The historical record of false models and untenable assumptions is imaginatively reviewed in Charles P. Kindleberger, *International Economics* (Homewood, IL: Richard D. Irwin, 1973).

24. On the "Triple Debt Crisis" facing the United States at home, overseas, and in the Third World, see Gerald Epstein, "Unshackling the World Economy," *World Policy Journal* 2(4) (Fall 1985): 625–58.

25. A partisan but considered analysis is given in Michael Moffitt, "Hard Landing Ahead? Economic Decline, Reagan-style," *World Policy Journal* 2(3) (Summer 1985): 387–414.

26. A troubled projection of the cost of carrying the U.S. debt is advanced by E. Gerald Corrigan, the president of the Federal Reserve Bank of New York in its *Quarterly Review* *10*(3) (Autumn 1985): 1–5, "Public and Private Debt Accumulation."

27. The cause for anxiety over the LDCs' debt is well argued in Donald R. Lessard and John Williamson, *Financial Intermediation: Beyond the Debt Crisis* (Washington, DC: Institute for International Economics, 1985).

28. Reagan's first-term achievements are appraised by Arthur F. Burns, "The American Trade Deficit in Perspective," *Foreign Affairs* 62(5) (Summer 1984): 1058–69.

29. A unique survey of U.S. economic failures and successes has been compiled by the former chairman of Reagan's Council of Economic Advisers, Martin Feldstein, in "American Economic Policy and the World Economy," *Foreign Affairs* 63(5) (Summer 1985): 995–1008.

30. See the classic essay by Fred Hirsch, "The Ideological Underlay of Inflation," in Fred Hirsch and John H. Goldthrope, eds., *The Political Economy of Inflation* (London: Martin Robertson, 1978).

13

The Strategic Defense Initiative: Candidate Technologies and Implications for the Atlantic Alliance

Gil Klinger*

> . . . What if free people could live secure in the knowledge that we could intercept and destroy strategic ballistic missiles before they reached our own soil or that of our allies?[1]

With these words, President Reagan announced on 23 March 1983 the start of the U.S. Strategic Defense Initiative. The SDI is a broad program of research and development that aims to eventually deploy a system of ballistic missile defenses. Supporters of SDI view it as the first step toward the creation of an extensive defense system. They have left without answer several longer-term policy questions, such as what effect SDI programs will exercise on the Western alliance or on the arms race between the superpowers. It is widely agreed that SDI will be one of the most momentous policy initiatives that President Reagan will take in his years in the White House. Whether this particular use of his leadership is wise or not is a hotly debated issue.

The present aims of the SDI program range no further than the technological goal:

> . . . to secure a thoroughly reliable defense against all incoming Soviet missiles, either intermediate or long-range, and to destroy, by non-nuclear means, those missiles before they get near any target.[2]

*The opinions expressed in this chapter are those of the author and do not necessarily represent the view of the Rand Corporation or any of its sponsoring agencies. The author wishes to acknowledge the assistance of Walter Goldstein and Chris Armstrong.

Various groups of scientists, military specialists, and policy lobbyists in Washington insist that the goal can eventually be reached and that the SDI research programs should be amply funded. New technologies such as laser and particle beams should be used along with existing technologies to intercept incoming enemy missiles, allowing the United States and its allies to shift away from the current strategy, based upon mutual assured destruction (MAD), to one based upon "assured survival" against the risks of a nuclear attack.

Critics of the SDI refer to the program as "Star Wars," asserting that the claim to protect large populations is not realistic and that a full-scale BMD project could led to a devastating escalation of the nuclear arms race. The critics argue that it will take decades to develop the necessary technologies to build the SDI and that the eventual cost could exceed hundreds of billions of dollars. They maintain that the initial research and the subsequent test programs will breach the constraints of the 1972 ABM treaty, leading to a breakdown in arms control negotiations between the superpowers. The debate over the SDI has divided Reagan's administration, the Congress, and the NATO allies, and the divisions might appreciably widen during his second term.

The SDI program has already forced changes in relations between the United States and its NATO allies. The cohesion of the NATO Alliance has been strained several times before by the deployment of new weapons systems. Most recently, the Alliance encountered popular protests against the deployment of INF systems in Europe. The SDI may generate an even more serious threat to the cohesion of the Alliance, since many European governments might come to suspect that an American BMD system will afford protection to the United States while leaving Europe unsheltered. Advocates of arms control in the United States and Europe also fear that SDI will breach the ABM treaty and eventually lead to a renewed offensive weapons buildup, thus demolishing the limits established by the SALT agreements of the 1970s. Leaders of Reagan's administration have not been persuaded by these criticisms, and the SDI program is moving forward, fueled by annual appropriations of $4 billion by the Congress.

This chapter will provide a brief description of the technical difficulties that must be mastered in intercepting ballistic missiles. A close examination will be given to the candidate or possible technologies for intercepting ballistic missiles and to the range of countermeasures an enemy could use to frustrate the SDI design. Finally, the possible effects of the SDI upon the NATO alliance will be assessed.

INTERCEPTING BALLISTIC MISSILES IN FLIGHT

Attempting to intercept a ballistic missile has been likened to hitting a bullet with a bullet. Until recently, technologies were too limited to build a large-scale BMD system. In the 1950s and 1960s new and more advanced radar and tracking systems were developed, along with higher acceleration and nuclear-armed interception weapons. By the late 1960s, defensive technologies had advanced sufficiently to permit interception of incoming warheads, using ground-based interceptors armed with nuclear warheads. Any large attack could still saturate a defense, particularly when multiple and independently targeted missiles were developed (in a MIRV format), rendering defense of large areas or cities technically unfeasible. The United States began to deploy an early form of ABM weaponry, most notably the Sentinel and the Safeguard programs; a lone ABM site was constructed at Grand Forks in North Dakota, but it was deactivated soon after its completion in 1975. The ABM treaty of 1972 restricted both superpowers to two ABM sites each, with a limit of 100 launchers and 100 interceptors emplaced at each site, though the limit was later reduced to one site in each country. The Soviets currently maintain one operational site, located near Moscow.

Since the early 1970s, advances in rapid data processing, sensor and tracking technology, rocket propulsion, and new interception technologies have revived interest in the creation of BMD systems. It is assumed today that high-technology industries will eventually be able to locate and track an intercontinental ballistic missile (ICBM) seconds after it has been launched, at a distance of 10,000 miles, and that it will be successfully intercepted as it moves at supersonic speeds through the four phases of a missile's flight:

- Boost
- Postboost
- Midcourse
- Terminal

Boost

Figure 13.1 depicts the flight of a ballistic missile. The boost phase begins with the ignition of the missile's first-stage booster engines, and it continues until all of the booster engines (usually in two or three stages) have completed firing. The boost phase typically lasts five to six minutes, at the end of which time the missile reaches an altitude of approximately 200 km. During the boost phase the missile has an intense infrared signature, generated by the extreme heat of engine exhaust gases. This heat signature makes a missile easy to detect and track, and the large size of missile boosters makes them vulnerable targets to intercepting weapons of the defense. The boost phase offers the defense a minimum number of targets, since no warheads or other penetration aids have yet been released, and a missile is a conspicuous target to intercept.

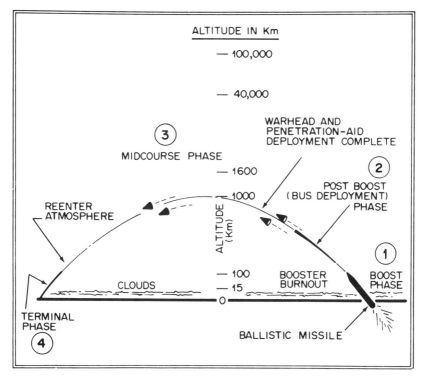

Source: James C. Fletcher, *The Strategic Defense Initiative Defensive Technologies Study* (Washington, DC: U.S. Department of Defense, 1984), p. 8.

Figure 13.1. Phases of a Typical Ballistic Missile Trajectory.

To take full advantage of the enemy's weakness, boost phase defense must be successfully carried out within a short time (in roughly five to six minutes) and against a relatively large number of targets. Table 13.1 depicts the vast number of U.S. and Soviet boosters and warheads that have already been deployed and that the defensive system will have to spot, track, and intercept. The tables in the chapter Appendix provide extensive details of the current strategic forces of the United States, its British and French allies, and the Soviet Union, along with the force levels that they are likely to acquire in the 1990s.

Postboost and Midcourse

Following the boost phase, a ballistic missile enters the postboost and midcourse phases of flights. During the five to seven minutes in the post-

Table 13.1. Missile Strengths of Each Superpower: Targets to be Intercepted
by Adversary BMD Systems

Type of Target	United States	Soviet Union
ICBM Boosters (land-based)	1,026	1,398
SLBM Boosters (submarine launched)	616	924
TOTAL Boosters	1,642	2,322
ICBM Warheads	2,126	6,420
SLBM Warheads	5,536	2,628
TOTAL Warheads	7,662	9,048

SOURCE. See footnotes to Tables A.1–A.6 in the appendix to this chapter.

NOTE. Deployment of single-warhead ICBMs such as the U.S. SICBM (Midgetman) or Soviet SS-25, or the deployment of dummy missiles would increase the number of objects confronting a boost phase defense system. Deployment of decoys and penetration aids (penaids) could increase the number of objects confronting midcourse and terminal defense layers by considerable orders of magnitude.

Force strength figures do not include strategic range manned bombers, cruise missiles, or other air-breathing weapons, since they would not be intercepted by the SDI program for BMD.

boost phase, the missile's postboost vehicle (PBV), or "bus," releases the missile's independently maneuverable warheads and a veritable "cloud" of penetration aids, including radar-reflecting chaff, decoys, aerosol clouds, and a number of dummy missiles, to confuse the defense. The warheads and penaids continue to fly on toward their targets during the five- to fifteen-minute midcourse phase, and they reach an altitude of approximately 1000 km prior to beginning their descent into the terminal phase of flight.

The postboost and midcourse phases afford the defense a longer time to attack incoming warheads. However, a number of factors complicate the interception problem during the two phases. The bright heat signature that simplified detection and tracking of the missile during the boost phase no longer exists. The PBV bus is equipped with only small maneuvering rockets or gas jets, and its independent warheads fly on ballistic (unpowered) trajectories after they are released. The smaller size of the postboost vehicles and warheads makes detection and tracking more difficult during the postboost and midcourse phases.

The most significant obstacle for the defense occurs with the release of multiple warheads and penaids during these five to seven minutes. Warhead and penaid release vastly increases the numbers of targets that must be detected, tracked, and intercepted. Identification and discrimination of real warheads from electronic decoys must be accomplished in the vacuum of space, where warheads and penaids travel at almost identical velocities. Postboost and midcourse discrimination pose great difficulties when a considerable number of objects must be continuously tracked and discriminated by the defense. These difficulties increase by several orders of magnitude the complex task of intercepting and destroying an incoming cloud of false and real weapons.

Terminal

In the terminal phase of flight, warheads reenter the earth's atmosphere above target areas and then detonate at predetermined altitudes, or they can explode at ground level for a surface burst. The terminal phase begins when warheads and penaids descend to altitudes of approximately 100 km.[3] During reentry, atmospheric drag begins to filter out decoys and penetration aids, thus reducing the discrimination difficulties encountered in the midcourse phase. In addition, defensive sensors and interceptors need to operate only at short ranges, rather than over the long distances encountered during boost phase interception. Nonetheless, effective terminal defense remains a difficult task. The terminal phase of flight lasts for only one to three minutes, during which time the reentering warheads achieve substantial velocities. Terminal defenses must intercept, in only a few seconds, the warheads that "leak" through the other layers of the defense, and they must eliminate the incoming missiles (probably with nuclear weapons) before the enemy warheads are detonated.

MULTIPLE LAYER DEFENSES

The SDI program assumes that a BMD system will be configured with single or multiple layers. A single-layer system would probably be a terminal defense comprising ground-based sensors, radars, and interceptors. It would engage incoming warheads prior to their reentry into the atmosphere (exoatmospheric interception), or within the atmosphere (endoatmospheric interception). The Sentinel and Safeguard ABM systems proposed during the 1960s provided early examples of single-layer terminal BMD systems.

The addition of midcourse and boostphase interception systems to a terminal BMD system would produce a multitiered system, and it should enhance the defense capabilities of a BMD. For a start, if some of the attacking missiles and warheads penetrated or leaked through any one layer of the defense, they would still have to pass through the remaining defensive layers prior to reaching their targets. A multitiered BMD system would raise the costs of evasion to the Soviet Union, because their offensive ICBMs could not be sure of evading all layers of the defense.

The primary aim of the SDI research program is to develop and test a multitiered BMD system that could provide area defense for the United States and its allies. Such a system might include an upgraded terminal defense layer, augmented by midcourse and boostphase defense layers. It is assumed that extensive and presently unknown technologies will be developed to transmit discrimination and tracking information to the terminal defense on the ground. All other functions would have to be fulfilled by radar tracking and battle stations that remained in permanent orbit in outer space.

The viability of the defense system envisioned by SDI depends upon the successful implementation of a boostphase interception system. In the last resort, SDI assumes that an enemy missile can be detected and aborted at an early stage of its flight path and clearly before it splits into a vast number of decoys and separate warheads.

> Because each booster is capable of deploying tens of reentry vehicles and hundreds of decoys, the defense, by destroying the boosters, has to destroy 1% or less of the objects it would have to cope with in subsequent phases of the missile trajectory.[4]

TASKS FOR ALL BMD SYSTEMS

Regardless of its form, a BMD system must perform three basic functions:

- Surveillance, acquisition, and tracking
- Interception and target destruction
- Battle management[5]

BMD systems must provide complete and continuous monitoring of all missile launch areas. The surveillance and tracking system must be able to reliably determine the size of an attack, and it must provide continuous tracking of all threatening objects in a manner that permits timely transfers from tracking to intercept systems. The tracking system must be able to discriminate between real targets and decoys or other debris; incoming warheads must be reliably intercepted, the destruction of targets must be confirmed, and surviving or missed targets must be attacked again. The layers and components of a BMD system must cooperate effectively and instantaneously during an attack, and complex information must be reliably and rapidly passed from one interception layer to another.

The organization of tasks to be handled by SDI, and their initial funding levels, can be listed under each functional activity. The budget and work load of the SDI organization in the defense department has been divided along these lines (see Table 13.2 for breakdown in dollars):

- Surveillance, acquisition, tracking, and kill assessment
- Directed-energy weapons
- Kinetic energy weapons

Table 13.2. SDI Organization Budget (in Millions of Dollars)

	Fiscal 1984	Fiscal 1985	Fiscal 1986	Fiscal 1987
Surveillance, acquisition, track, and kill assessment	10.0	545.9	1,386.3	1,874.9
Directed-energy weapons	9.5	376.4	965.4	1,195.6
Kinetic energy weapons	10.0	256.0	859.7	1,238.6
Systems concepts and battle management	10.0	99.0	243.3	272.5
Survivability, lethality, and key support technology	10.0	112.0	258.2	316.7
SDI management headquarters	.5	8.0	9.2	10.0
Total	50.0	1,397.3	3,722.2	4,908.3

Adapted from Eugene Kozicharow, "Strategic Defense Initiative Tries to Maintain Structured Funding Pace," *Aviation Week and Space Technology* 122(11), (March 18 1985), p. 35.

- Systems concepts and battle management
- Survivability, lethality, and key support technology*

INTERCEPTION TECHNOLOGIES: DIRECTED-ENERGY WEAPONS

Directed-energy, or *beam*, weapons, including both laser and particle beams, are critical to fulfillment of the BMD mission because they can, in theory, destroy many targets at great distances and with great rapidity. They would be especially useful for boost phase interception. *Laser* stands for "light amplification by stimulated emission of radiation." It denotes a device that generates a collimated beam of light in which all the electromagnetic waves oscillate synchronously as coherent light.[6] Laser beams cause damage by focusing this light on a target to cause overheating, melting, or vaporization of the surface material. Lasers could melt a hole in a missile booster's skin or use short impulses of energy to mechanically puncture the booster. Lasers vary according to power output, wavelength, lasing medium, and the mechanism for generating laser light. Variations in these

Source: U.S. Senate Committee on Foreign Relations, *Strategic Defense and Anti-Satellite Weapons*. (Washington, DC: Government Printing Office, 1984), pp. 17–18.

parameters determine which particular lasers will be used in a BMD system.*

A number of lasers are being investigated for possible use in a BMD system, and the hydrogen-fluoride (HF) laser seems to offer the greatest potential for near-term development. The HF infrared laser derives its energy from the chemical reaction of hydrogen and fluorine gases. Since its power is obtained from a chemical reaction, the HF laser does not require any external power supplies to operate.[8] As a result, HF lasers might be more easily deployed in a space-based system than other types of directed energy weapons.

Both excimer and free-electron lasers are high-power lasers operating in the visible wavelengths. An excimer laser receives its output when the excited states of a noble gas (such as xenon or krypton) react to form a lasing medium, whereas a free-electron laser utilizes an electron beam passed through a magnetic field.[9] Although operating at shorter wavelengths would permit the use of smaller optics to focus these lasers, both would also require the use of external power supplies with enormous power levels. Such power outputs have not yet been achieved, and the large size of the power supplies for such weapons could make space basing of excimer or free-electron lasers unfeasible. An X-ray laser would expose thin rods of material to the enormous X-ray burst emitted by a nuclear explosion. An X-ray laser would be more lethal than other types of lasers, and countermeasures to it would be difficult to devise.[10] However, an X-ray laser would be a single-shot system, because the nuclear explosion used to power it would be self-destructive.

Particle Beam Weapons

A particle beam weapon is essentially a large particle accelerator that charges particles to great energies. Stripping the charge from the particle as it leaves the accelerator results in the formation of a neutral particle beam.[11] Particle beams would strike a target with an intense stream of atomic or subatomic particles, penetrating the surface of a missile or warhead, igniting its missile propellant or causing thermal and radiation damage to its electronic guidance and other control systems. Their ability to penetrate the surface of a target would make countermeasures to particle

---

*The operating wavelength directly affects the laser installation's size, since the diameter of the optics required to focus the laser beam is inversely related to its wavelength.[7] Demands for high electrical power levels may require external power sources such as nuclear reactors, which also increase a laser battle station's size. Larger sized laser installations will be more difficult to utilize in a space-based BMD system.

beam weapons difficult to implement. Nonetheless, the current technical feasibility of these systems is unclear. Like high-power lasers, particle beams would require multi-megawatt power sources designed in size and weight especially for space basing.[12]

Deployment Schemes for Directed-Energy Weapons

A variety of directed-energy weapons could be deployed on the ground or in space as part of a BMD system. A constellation of orbiting infrared lasers could be linked with a system of pointing and tracking telescopes and an infrared sensor system to detect Soviet missile launches. Space-based particle beam weapons could also be deployed with a surveillance and sensor system. The systems could be configured to provide continuous surveillance and coverage of Soviet ICBM launch sites and the probable sanctuary areas for ballistic missile submarines (SSBN). An alternative technology could utilize ground-based free-electron or excimer lasers, together with a series of space-based mirrors, to direct the laser beams to their targets. These boost phase systems could be linked with midcourse or terminal interception layers to form a multitiered BMD system.

Kinetic Energy Weapons

Kinetic energy weapons are also known as *projectile weapons*. They include systems such as rocket-propelled interceptors (RPIs), electromagnetic launchers, and ground-based interceptors. In contrast with beam-directed energy weapons, kinetic energy weapons exert all of their destructive energy upon impact, using direct collisions or chemical explosions to destroy their targets. The simplicity of this kill mechanism and the relative maturity of many kinetic energy technologies are among the advantages that projectile weapons enjoy over beam weapons.[13]

RPIs are small missiles that utilize either kinetic energy or explosive kill mechanisms. The "hit-to-kill" RPI boosts a 5–10 kg mass onto a collision course with its target; the resulting collision destroys both the interceptor and the enemy target.[14] The present U.S. antisatellite weapon, a miniature homing vehicle, relies upon a hit-to-kill interceptor. An RPI armed with an explosive warhead could maneuver within a lethal range of its target and then detonate. Both of these systems could be equipped with advanced infrared sensor systems and sufficient maneuvering capability to home in on their fast-moving targets.

Electromagnetic Launchers

An electromagnetic launcher, or *railgun*, utilizes electromagnetic forces to accelerate a small projectile. This achieves much higher muzzle velocities than those of gas-driven projectiles, potentially reaching 5–25 km/s for

railguns, as against the 1.5 km/s velocity of a gas-driven projectile.[15] Like
the hit-to-kill interceptor, the railgun would destroy its target by collision.

Ground-Based Interceptors

Perhaps the most familiar weapon systems used for BMD are ground-
based interceptors. Like other kinetic energy weapons, ground-based interceptors utilize both hit-to-kill and explosive warheads. The homing
overlay experiment in 1984 demonstrated some of the advances in sensor
and homing technologies that have been achieved in ground-based interceptors. Future interceptors would require as yet undeveloped high acceleration vehicles to engage incoming warheads both outside and within the
atmosphere. Unlike previous systems such as Spartan and Sprint, these new
interceptors would rely on nonnuclear methods of interception.

Deployment of Kinetic Energy Weapons

Kinetic energy weapons and directed-energy systems could be deployed
in ground- or spaced-based systems. Large numbers of RPIs could be
deployed on board a constellation of satellites and linked to a surveillance
and tracking system.[16] A space-based RPI system might be of limited utility for boost phase interception systems, but it could be used for postboost
and midcourse interception. The relative maturity of RPI technology might
permit initial operational deployment for such a system in the late 1990s.
The development problems confronting electromagnetic launchers would
make any near-term deployment extremely unlikely.

A three-stage system has been suggested for future terminal defense systems. The exoatmospheric reentry vehicle interceptor system (ERIS) would
attack incoming warheads prior to their reentry into the earth's atmosphere.
Exoatmospheric interception at longer ranges would permit the ERIS system to be centrally located or to use a minimal number of interceptor sites.
The ERIS system would utilize advanced long-wave infrared homing sensors and a hit to kill interceptor system.

The high endoatmospheric defense system would intercept warheads that
penetrated the ERIS layer. It would rely on the detection, tracking, and
discrimination information provided by an airborne optical adjunct.
Infrared sensors deployed on board long-endurance aircraft would detect
arriving warheads late in exoatmospheric flight and continue tracking them
as they began reentry.[17] The information would be used to intercept the
arriving warheads prior to detonation. The system would utilize a high-
acceleration interceptor together with a short-wave infrared sensor and an
explosive warhead kill mechanism. Any warheads that penetrated the system would be intercepted by active radar homing interceptors utilizing the

small radar homing interceptor technology that would provide a low altitude "safety net" for the BMD system.

OBSTACLES TO DEPLOYMENT OF BMD SYSTEM

President Reagan has offered the vision of a world in which nuclear weapons would be made obsolete by the deployment of an effective BMD system. It is obviously attractive. However, despite the concentrated efforts of the SDI program, a large number of research and engineering problems must be overcome before deployment of a BMD system can even be considered. The high-power lasers necessary for a boost phase directed-energy interception system are as yet undeveloped. The U.S. Department of Defense has estimated that it will be fifteen years before a 10-megawatt, 10-meter, space-based laser (SBL) will be ready for deployment; and twenty to twenty-five years before a constellation of 100 twenty-five megawatt, 15-meter SBLs could be deployed.[18] The large power sources necessary for excimer and free-electron lasers, neutral particle beams, and kinetic energy launchers still have to be developed; so too have the pointing and tracking systems needed for directed-energy defense systems. Deployment of any space-based BMD system will probably require the development of a heavy-lift launch vehicle to place BMD components into orbit and to service them aloft.

Deployment of an effective midcourse interception system will first require a solution to the problem of midcourse discrimination. The inability to discriminate between real warheads and thousands of decoys could force the defense to expend many valuable laser "shots," or projectiles, in the attempt to destroy one warhead. This could result in exhausting a midcourse defense, placing an enormous burden on a terminal defense system. Many observers judge that the midcourse discrimination problem will not be effectively solved in the near future. Any future BMD system may have to depend only on boost phase and terminal interception layers if midcourse phase problems remain intractable.

The effectiveness of terminal defenses depends in part upon how early an interceptor can be launched and how fast it can fly toward its target. The high-acceleration vehicles planned for use in future terminal BMD systems have yet to be developed. The need for early discrimination of incoming warheads remains an obstacle to effective terminal defense, and, despite limited testing, nonnuclear kill mechanisms still remain to be perfected. In particular, homing sensors must be developed to withstand the tremendous acceleration achieved during the interceptor's flight, and nonnuclear interception must be perfected if a terminal BMD system is to be used for the area defense of cities.

Even if all of these development and engineering problems were to be overcome, a deployed BMD system would have to cope with numerous operational uncertainties and the threats posed by the countermeasures that the Soviets could quickly and inexpensively achieve. Inclement atmospheric conditions could affect the lethality of laser weapons; and nuclear detonations in the atmosphere could degrade the operation of the sensors, radars, and communications systems used by all layers of the system. More important, no full operational tests of a BMD system could ever be staged, and, after deployment, a BMD system might remain dormant for years. However, if an attack suddenly occurred, the whole system would have to instantly "turn on" and operate effectively on very short notice. There would always be uncertainty about whether such a technologically complex system could operate successfully in a hostile-attack environment.

The difficulties faced by the SDI program are numerous and daunting. Space is transparent, and any orbiting BMD components could easily be detected and tracked. The space-based components of an American BMD system would have to be defended against Soviet antisatellite (ASAT) weapons, space mines, and the space-based components of a Soviet BMD system. Meanwhile, ground-based lasers or interceptors would offer lucrative targets to the Soviets for a preemptive or suppressive attack. The survivability of a space or ground-based BMD system is therefore far from assured.

A survey of boost phase countermeasures suggests that a wide range of adjustments could be made by the offense to limit the effectiveness of a deployed BMD system. Ablative coatings applied to the missile booster or spinning of the booster in flight could limit the destructive capacity of laser beam weapons. Deployment of dummy missiles would complicate discrimination by the boost phase interception system, while the proliferation of single-warhead missiles (such as the Soviet SS-25) would increase the number of targets to be engaged by a boost phase defense. The effectiveness and cheap cost of most of these countermeasures would be ruinous to the defense. An increase in the number of space-based lasers would be required, and at considerable expense, if the system were ever to provide adequate shelter against attack.

If the Soviets deployed fast-burn boosters with low burnout altitudes, they would appreciably reduce the time available for U.S. boost phase interception. Their development of countermeasures, such as fast-burn boosters, would increase the number of U.S. space-based lasers needed to intercept simultaneously launched boosters. This countermeasure would make interception with either RPIs or neutral particle beams unfeasible. A shortened burn time would make the radius of action of RPI carrier satellites too small, while a low burnout altitude would nullify neutral particle beams, since they cannot penetrate even the thinnest atmosphere.[19] Offensive countermeasures taken by the Soviet Union could vastly increase the cost of building a defensive system, and they could seriously degrade the system effectiveness of BMD. The capacity to respond to both current and future Soviet offensive developments poses one of the greatest challenges to any form of American BMD system.

Apart from provoking disagreements over its technical feasibility or operational effectiveness, the SDI program has sparked a vigorous debate regarding the effects of BMD research and defensive deployments on the superpowers' strategic relationship. Supporters of the SDI acknowledge that the "astrodome" defense envisioned in President Reagan's speech may not be possible for decades to come. Nonetheless, political support for SDI research, and even for limited BMD deployment, persists. Advocates contend that deployment of terminal ABM systems to protect land-based ICBMs could improve stability by enhancing the survivability of ICBM forces. A defense for the MX could reduce Soviet incentives to attempt a preemptive attack, because Soviet planners could not be confident of destroying a sufficiently high percentage of American missiles. In addition, it is claimed, the pressures on the United States to "launch on warning" or "launch under attack" would be diminished, because terminal defenses would assure the survival of a greater portion of U.S. land-based offensive forces.

Critics of the SDI point out that even a limited deployment will require modification of the ABM treaty to permit the much larger number of interceptors required to protect even a small portion of each side's land-based offensive forces. Currently the ABM treaty restricts each side to 100 launchers and 100 interceptors. The testing of mobile, or space-based, BMD components, or the deployment of systems designed for wide-area defense of cities, would violate the ABM treaty and would probably result in its cancellation, thus leading to a defensive arms race.

In a defensive arms race, each side would proceed with development, testing, and deployment of its own BMD systems, while remaining uncertain of the status of its opponent's program. Each side would be likely to overestimate the capabilities of its opponent's defenses and to downplay those of its own. Advocates of the SDI assert that this uncertainty will lead to more cautious and conservative behavior in a crisis. The SDI critics disagree. They argue that uncertainty may lead each side to believe that it must strike first in a crisis because absorbing an enemy first strike would leave it with a degraded retaliatory force that could not reliably penetrate the other side's defenses. Deployment of defense systems, which are themselves vulnerable to attack and suppression, would only exacerbate these first-strike pressures.

A full discussion of the effects of the SDI upon the strategic balance and the arms control process is beyond the scope of this essay. Clearly, these issues will merit closer scrutiny as the summit talks proceed. It is hoped that one outcome of discussion of the SDI will be a greater understanding of the effects of defensive deployments upon the strategic balance between the superpowers and, therefore, upon the critical issues of crisis stability.

SDI AND THE NATO ALLIANCE

In many ways the SDI program could pose a considerable threat to the cohesion of the NATO Alliance. Several of the European members of the Alliance have advocated support for SDI research so long as it is conducted within the bounds of the ABM treaty. It is their hope to maintain Alliance unity in the conduct of arms control talks that include the SDI. The United Kingdom has reached agreement with the United States to participate in SDI research, and West Germany and other allies have expressed an interest in contributing to SDI research projects.

Allied support represents both an attempt to preserve alliance unity during the Geneva arms control negotiations and a recognition of the need to maintain a research program as "insurance" against possible covert Soviet BMD activity. Nonetheless, if the SDI should involve component testing or other actions that encroach upon the ABM treaty, Alliance consensus could begin to erode and European support for the U.S. initiative could decline.

The point has been stressed by the Reagan administration that the SDI program aims to create a defensive system that will provide protection to the United States and its NATO allies. Advocates of the SDI have suggested that an antitactical missile (ATM) system could be deployed to protect Europe against attacks by Soviet intermediate and short-range ballistic missiles and cruise missiles. An ATM system might consist of an upgraded Patriot air defense missile system or some modification of the low-altitude defense system that had originally been designed for mobile deployment with the MX.[20] Either system might be used to defend NATO's theater nuclear forces (Pershing II and cruise), its command and control centers, its airfields, and its other key military assets.

The deployment of an ATM system would supposedly strengthen NATO's theater deterrent. Defense of critical military installations would complicate Soviet attack planning, and it could improve the timely and effective responses that NATO could mount against any attack. The Soviets could try to overwhelm an ATM system, but this would require a massive attack on Western Europe, increasing the risk of retaliation by American strategic nuclear weapons against the Soviet homeland.[21]

It is unlikely that the European members of the Alliance would support deployment of an ATM or any other defensive system associated with the SDI. Experts on both sides of the Atlantic believe that the ATM interception problem poses a greater challenge than that associated with the interception of ICBMs and SLBMs. The slower reentry velocities of some Soviet theater weapons, such as the SS-21 and SS-23, would simplify interception of these systems. However, all theater systems have fairly short flight times and lower trajectories than intercontinental systems; they necessarily provide a shorter warning and response time to carry out successful interception.[22] In addition, existing technologies would require the use of nuclear-armed interceptors, because nonnuclear kill systems have yet to be perfected.[23] Any proposed ATM deployment would also have to overcome European skepticism about its technical feasibility, and objections would surely be raised to the deployment of more nuclear weapons in Europe.

Deployment of an ATM system would stir debates within and between Alliance members over the division of costs for the new system and over the choice of areas to be defended. An ATM system would require a fundamental change in NATO nuclear employment policy. The short response time available for ATM interception would demand advance agreement among the allies to allow the instant release of nuclear weapons, almost automatically and without political control, and this would provoke widespread insecurity in Europe.[24] It would certainly offend the long-standing preference of many Europeans to keep a tight political control over the use of nuclear weapons. Nor is it likely that many European members of the Alliance would consent to providing the United States with blanket authority to use nuclear weapons of any type over European cities or to launch them on warning, certainly not without any prior consultation.

Even if an ATM system should prove to be technically feasible, and if Alliance management problems could be resolved, a serious opposition to deployment would remain. ATM systems would utilize components identical to, or indistinguishable from, those used in an ABM system. The transfer of such components by the United States to its NATO allies would violate the ABM treaty, and several NATO allies have already criticized unilateral actions of the United States that might violate provisions of the ABM treaty.[25]

The potential for Soviet responses to a U.S. design for ATM deployment will also strengthen European opposition to its deployment. The Soviets may counter an ATM system by deploying more numerous and effective INF systems, thus increasing the number of nuclear weapons directed at Western Europe. Alternatively, they may assign SLBMs or ICBMs to the theater mission, forcing any ATM system to cope with intercontinental as well as theater systems.

Deployment of an ATM system or cancellation of the ABM treaty would certainly prompt the Soviet Union to accelerate its own BMD program. This would be seriously regarded, because any new Soviet deployments could undermine the effectiveness of British and French nuclear forces. The actual effects of Soviet BMD upon the allied nuclear forces would depend upon the future modernization of those forces and the extent of the Soviet deployment. At the very least, Soviet BMD would lower the perceived credibility of independent British and French nuclear weapons. Britain and France would oppose the United States if they believed that an expanded Soviet BMD was the result of the U.S. SDI.

European opposition to an ATM system, and eventually to the SDI as a whole, is based upon the different view of deterrence held by most Europeans. The United States has linked the credibility of deterrence to its ability to prosecute a war at various levels of escalation. Unlike their American allies, Europeans are not sanguine about NATO's ability to control or limit conflicts once they involve nuclear weapons. Moreover, the enhanced lethality of modern conventional weapons and the large number of nuclear weapons now deployed in the European theater render the distinctions, for many Europeans, meaningless among conventional, theater-nuclear, and general nuclear war. In all three modes of warfare, Europe would be devastated, but the United States might conceivably be spared. Thus the European concept of deterrence focuses upon the uncertain outcome and the potential for escalation in any war in Europe. The concept was articulated by McGeorge Bundy:

> . . . no one knows if a major engagement in Europe would escalate to the strategic nuclear level. But the essential point is the opposite; no one can possibly know that it would not.[26]

For Europeans, it is the possibility of escalation that could lead to the use of American strategic nuclear weapons and a resulting threat to the Soviet homeland. The coupling of American strategic weapons to the conventional defense of Europe is therefore central to the Alliance and to its conception of deterrence. But the enhancement of theater war–fighting capabilities, or the deployment of systems that tend to prolong conventional engagements, will only weaken deterrence and make conflict in Europe more likely.

Continued American efforts to develop sophisticated innovations in defense will exacerbate European fears concerning the American commitment to the defense of Europe. An ATM system deployed by the United States to protect NATO military assets and to enhance theater deterrence, paradoxically, might be interpreted by Europeans as an effort to "decouple" American strategic forces from the defense of Europe. The deployment of the INF has been seen as an attempt to create a "Eurostrategic" level of conflict, which Europeans have interpreted as an effort to confine a war to Europe. The creation of a BMD system for the United States could only revive similar fears in Europe.[27]

Even a limited terminal defense of MX or Minuteman missile silos is likely to elicit a negative reaction from Europe. Despite American claims that increased ICBM survivability would strengthen central and extended deterrence, Europeans would probably view such actions as an attempt to decouple American vulnerability from that of its NATO allies. At the present many Europeans believe that the unity of the NATO alliance depends not only upon the coupling of American strategic weapons to the defense of Europe, but also upon the maintenance of vulnerabilities shared between the United States and its allies. They argue that the SDI will afford full or partial protection to the United States, leaving Europe unprotected. Limited terminal defense of American-based ICBMs would feed these suspicions. It might also be viewed as the forerunner for an area defense of the United States, and that might leave Europe even more vulnerable to Soviet attack, because American cities could then be sheltered in a nuclear crisis.

European reactions to an ongoing SDI are likely to reflect the views that were once expressed by two prominent American observers during the ABM debate in the late 1960s. Abram Chayes and Jerry Wiesner expressed their criticism after moving from senior positions in Washington to Harvard and MIT. Their objection to BMD is still relevant today.

> . . . it seems inevitable that no matter how strenuously the Pentagon argues that the new ABM [BMD], by safeguarding our retaliatory power, will increase our capacity to deter any attack against the West. . . . many if not most Europeans will believe instead that the U.S. is increasing its capability to ignore some future Soviet nuclear threat which European nations cannot escape.[28]

In short, European allies might come to suspect that SDI will allow a future U.S. administration to take greater risks in Europe, as the fear of nuclear blackmail in the continental United States could eventually be relaxed.

EUROPEAN NUCLEAR FORCES

It may be helpful, given the debate over East–West proposals for arms reductions and over the impact of SDI on the Alliance, to provide a list of current British and French strategic forces and of the modernization plans that have been announced by both countries.

British strategic forces today include 64 Polaris A-3 SLBMs, which are deployed on four Polaris SSBNs. With three multiple reentry vehicles on each A-3 SLBM, the total number of British missile warheads is 192. British strategic forces are augmented by Buccaneer and Tornado aircraft.

France currently maintains its own strategic triad made up of 18 S-3 IRBMs, 80 M-20 SLBMs, and 34 Mirage IVA bombers. The IRBM force is deployed on the Albion Plateau in southeastern France, while the SLBM force is carried on five Redoubtable class SSBNs. French strategic forces currently number 132 warheads.[29]

During the mid-1990s, British strategic forces will be substantially upgraded with the deployment of four Trident submarines, each armed with sixteen D-5 SLBMs.[30] The deployment of the sixty-four D-5 missiles will add over five hundred hard-target missile warheads to the British and NATO arsenals.

French modernization plans include deployment of new land- and sea-based forces. Deployment of the MIRVed M-4 SLBM on a new submarine began in 1985, and eighty M-4s are planned for deployment.[31] Their longer range will allow French SSBNs to operate over larger areas and permit strikes against Moscow from the Norwegian Sea.[32] In the 1990s, both the M-5 MIRVed SLBM and the SX mobile IRBM are scheduled to enter service.[33] French strategic missile forces will total close to 600 warheads by the mid-1990s. Coupled with full deployment of the D-5 by the British, Anglo–French strategic forces could add over 1,000 warheads to allied nuclear arsenals.

APPENDIX

Tables A.1 through A.6 provide an inventory of the strategic nuclear forces currently maintained by the United States, the Soviet Union, Britain, and France and of the force levels that will be deployed in the 1990s.

Table A.1. Currently Deployed U.S. Strategic Nuclear Weapons Systems

Type	Number Deployed	Initial Deployment Date	Throw Weight (lbs.)[a]	Range (km)	CEP* (m)	Warheads	Maximum Yield†	Fuel Type[a]
ICBM								
Titan II	26[b]	1962	8,275	15,000	1,300	1	9 MT	Liquid
Minuteman II	450	1966	1,625	11,300	370	1	1.2 MT[a]	Solid
Minuteman III								
MK. 12	250	1970	1,975	13,000	280	3 MIRV	170 KT	Solid
MK. 12A	300	n.a.	1,975	n.a.	220	3 MIRV	335 KT	Solid
SLBM								
Poseidon (C-3) 19 Lafayette Class SSBN	304	1971	3,300	4,600	450	10 MIRV	40 KT	Solid
Trident I (C-4) 12 Franklin Class SSBN	192	1980	2,900	7,400	450	8 MIRV	100 KT	Solid
Trident I (C-4) 5 Ohio Class SSBN	120	1980	2,900	7.400	450	8 MIRV	100 KT	Solid
			Weapon Load (lbs.)			Weapons§		
Bombers								
B-52G‡	151	1959	70,000	12,000		12–24		
B-52H	90	1962	70,000	16,000		12–24		

*CEP (circular error probable) = the radius of a circle around a target within which there is a 50 percent probability that a weapon aimed at that target will fall.
†KT = kiloton, MT = megaton.
‡90 B-52G are outfitted with ALCM[c].
§Weapons loading depends on type of mission.
SOURCES.
[a]Congressional Budget Office, *Modernizing U.S. Strategic Offensive Forces: The Administration's Program and Alternatives* (Washington, DC: Government Printing Office, 1983), pp. 4, 84, 86.
[b]U.S. Department of Defense, *Soviet Military Power 1985* (Washington, DC: Government Printing Office, 1985), p. 29.
[c]Caspar W. Weinberger, *Annual Report of the Secretary of Defense for Fiscal Year 1985* (Washington, DC: Government Printing Office, 1984), p. 190.

NOTE. All other information from: The International Institute for Strategic Studies, *The Military Balance 1983-1984* (London: International Institute for Strategic Studies, 1983), pp. 118, 120, 122-123.

Table A.2. Currently Deployed Soviet Strategic Nuclear Weapons Systems

Type	Number Deployed	Initial Deployment Date	Throw Weight (lbs.)[a]	Range (km)	CEP (m)	Warheads	Maximum Yield	Fuel Type[b]
ICBM								
SS-111								
MOD 1	100	1966	2,200	10,500	1,400	1	950 KT[a]	Liquid
MOD 2			2,200	8,800	1,100	1	950 KT[a]	
MOD 3	420	1973	2,200	8,800	1,100	3 MRV*	100–300 KT	
SS-13	60	1968	1,500	10,000	2,000	1	750 KT	Solid
SS-17 MOD 3	150[c]	1975	6,025	10,000	450	4 MIRV	750 KT	Liquid
SS-18 MOD 4	308[c]	1982	16,500	11,000	300	10 MIRV	500 KT	Liquid
SS-19 MOD 3	360[c]	1982	8,000	10,000	300	6 MIRV	550 KT	Liquid
SLBM								
SS-N-6								
MOD 1								
23 Yankee I SSBN[c] (16†)		1968	1,600	2,400	900	1	750 KT[a]	Liquid
MOD 2								
4 Delta II	336[c]	1973	1,600	3,000	900	1	750 KT	
MOD 3								
SSBN (16†)		1974	1,600	3,000	1,400	2 MRV	200 KT	
SS-N-8‡								
MOD 1								
18 Delta I SSBN (12†)	292	1972	1,800	7,800	900	1	1 MT	Liquid
MOD 2		n.a.	1,800	9,100	1,300	1	800 KT	
SS-N-17								
1 Yankee II SSBN (12†)	12	1977	2,500§	3,900	1,500	1	1 MT	Solid
SS-N-18								
MOD 1	224	n.a.	2,500	6,500	1,400	3 MIRV	500 KT[a]	Liquid
MOD 2								
14 Delta III SSBN (16†)		1978	2,500	8,000	600	1	450 KT	
MOD 3		n.a.	2,500	6,500	600	7 MIRV	200 KT	
SS-N-20								
2 Typhoon SSBN (20†)	60	1981	7,500	8,300	n.a.	6-9 MIRV	100 KT[b]	Solid§
			Weapon Load (lbs.)			Weapons[d]		
Bombers								
TU-95 B/C Bear	120	1956	40,000			4		
MYA-4 Bison	45	1956	20,000			4		

*MRV = Multiple Reentry Vehicles, more than one warhead but not independently targetable.
†This figure refers to the number of launch tubes per submarine of this type.
‡SS-N-8 total includes 12 SALT-accountable missiles deployed on non-SALT-accountable submarines.
§This figure from *The Military Balance 1983–1984*.

SOURCES
[a]Congressional Budget Office, *Modernizing U.S. Strategic Offensive Forces: The Administration's Program and Alternatives* (Washington, DC: Government Printing Office 1983), p. 90.
[b]Robert P. Berman and John L. Baker, *Soviet Strategic Forces* (Washington, DC: The Brookings Institution, 1982), pp. 104–109.
[c]Organization of the Joint Chiefs of Staff, *United States Military Posture for Fiscal Year 1986* (Washington, DC: Government Printing Office, 1985), p. 19.
[d]Congressional Budget Office, *An Analysis of Administration Strategic Arms Reduction and Modernization Proposals* (Washington, DC: Government Printing Office, 1984), p. 64.

NOTE. All other information from: The International Institute for Strategic Studies, *The Military Balance 1983–1984* (London: International Institute for Strategic Studies, 1983), 1983), pp. 119, 121.

Table A.3. Future U.S. Strategic Nuclear Weapons Systems

Type	Initial Operational Capability	Number to be Deployed	Throw Weight (lbs.)[a]	Range (km)	CEP (m)	Warheads	Maximum Yield	Fuel Type
ICBM								
MX	1986[a]	100[a]	7,900	9,208[b,*]	93[a,*]	10 MIRV[a]	335 KT[a]	Solid
SICBM	1992[a]	400–1000	1,000	11,112*	130[a,*]	1[a]	475 KT[a]	Solid
SLBM								
Trident II (D-5)	1989[a]	†	5,075	7,400[a,*]	130–204[a,*]	8 MIRV[a]	475 KT[a]	Solid
			Weapons Load (lbs.)					
Bombers								
B-18	1985[c]	100	n.a.	n.a.		Weapons 22–38‡		
Advanced Technology Bomber(ATB) "Stealth"	1992[a]	132[a]	n.a.	n.a.		12[d]		
Cruise Missiles§								
ALCM	1982	About 1000 already deployed, total up to 3000[e]	2,800**	2,400	100	1	200 KT	Liquid[f]
SLCM	1984	n.a.	n.a.	2,400	n.a.	1	200 KT	Liquid[f]

*These figures converted from nautical miles.

†Number deployed depends on number of Ohio-class SSBNs built.

‡Number of weapons depends upon type of mission.

§ALCM deployed on B-52 G and H series, to be deployed on B-1. SLCMs deployable on attack submarines (SSN) through torpedo tubes or vertical launch system (VLS). Four to six SLCMs if mounted in torpedo tubes, 12 if mounted with VLS on SSNs. SLCMs deployable on surface ships in armored box launchers (ABL, 4 SLCM per ABL) and in VLS (64 SLCM per VLS on surface ships).

**This figure from *The Military Balance 1983–1984.*

SOURCES.

ªCongressional Budget Office, *Modernizing U.S. Strategic Offensive Forces: The Administration's Program and Alternatives* (Washington, DC: Government Printing Office, 1983), pp. 3–4, 9, 11, 84–85.

ᵇRichard Halloran, "Air Force, MX in Doubt, Speeds a Smaller Missile," *New York Times*, September 30, 1984, p. 26.

ᶜCommittee on Armed Services of the U.S. Senate, *Department of Defense Authorization for Appropriations for Fiscal Year 1985, Part 7 Strategic and Theater Nuclear Forces* (Washington, DC: Government Printing Office, 1984), p. 33.

ᵈCongressional Budget Office, *An Analysis of Administration Strategic Arms Reduction and Modernization Proposals* (Washington, DC: Government Printing Office, 1984), p. 63.

ᵉOrganization of the Joint Chiefs of Staff, *United States Military Posture for Fiscal Year 1984* (Washington, DC: Government Printing Office, 1983), p. 39.

ᶠ*Jane's Weapon Systems 1984–1985* (New York: Jane's Publishing Inc., 1984), p. 176.

NOTE. All other information from: The International Institute for Strategic Studies, *The Military Balance 1983–1984* (London: International Institute for Strategic Studies, 1983), pp. 118, 120.

Table A.4. Future Soviet Strategic Nuclear Weapons Systems

Type	Initial Operational Capability	Number to be Deployed	Throw Weight (lbs.)[a]	CEP (m)	Range (km)	Warheads	Maximum Yield	Fuel Type
ICBM								
SS-18 MOD 5	1985(?)	probably all 308 converted*	16,700	250	9,000	10 MIRV	750 KT	Liquid
SS-19 MOD 4	?	probably all 360 converted*	7,525	278[a],†	10,000	6 MIRV[a]	550 KT[a]	Liquid
SS-X-24	1985(?)	?	8,000	185[a],†	?	10 MIRV[a]	500 KT[a]	Solid[a]
SS-X-25	1985(?)	?	3,000	185[a],†	>11,000[b]	1[c]	500 KT[a]	Solid[a]
SS-X-26	?	?	estimated 10,000–11,000[d]	?	?	?	?	Solid[a]
SLBM								
SS-NX-23	?	?	>SS-N-18[c]	?	?	?	?	Liquid[a]
			Weapons Load			Weapons		
Bombers								
Bear H	1984[c]	?	@40,000*	?	@12,800*	20[e]		
Blackjack	1987[c]	?	n.a.	?	n.a.	12–20[e]		
Cruise Missiles‡								
AS-X-15 ALCM	probably 1984[f]	?	n.a.	n.a.	3,000[c]	1[c]	n.a.	n.a.
SS-NX-21 SLCM	probably 1984[f]	?	n.a.	n.a.	3,000[c]	1[c]	n.a.	n.a.

*Author's estimate.

†Figures converted to meters from nautical miles.

‡ALCM probably deployed on Bear H, to be deployed on Blackjack. SLCM deployable on "Victor II," new "Yankee," "Mike," and "Sierra" class attack submarines (SSN)[c].

SOURCES.

[a]Congressional Budget Office, *Modernizing U.S. Strategic Offensive Forces: The Administration's Program and Alternatives* (Washington, DC: Government Printing Office, 1983), pp. 90–91.

[b]Drew Middleton, "Soviet Said to Deploy A New Missile," *New York Times*, October 22, 1984, p. 3.

[c]U.S. Department of Defense, *Soviet Military Power 1984* (Washington, DC: Government Printing Office, 1984), pp. 23, 25, 28, 30.

[d]"In Focus," *Air Force Magazine* 67(7), (July 1984), p. 21.

[e]Congressional Budget Office, *An Analysis of Administration Strategic Arms Reduction and Modernization Proposals* (Washington, DC: Government Printing Office, 1984), p. 64.

[f]Seth Mydans, "Soviet Announces Own Deployment of Cruise Missiles," *New York Times*, October 14, 1984, p. 1.

NOTE. All other information from: The International Institute for Strategic Studies, *The Military Balance 1983–1984* (London: International Institute for Strategic Studies, 1983), p. 12.

Table A.5. Current British and French Strategic Nuclear Forces
(Tactical/Short-range Systems Not Included.)

Type	Number Deployed	Initial Deployment Date	Range (km)	CEP (m)	Warheads/ Bomber Weapons	Maximum Yield
IRBM						
French SSBS-3	18	1980	3,500	n.a.	1	1 MT
SLBM*						
British Polaris A-3	64	1967	4,600	900	3 (MRV)	200 KT
French MSBS M-20	80	1977	3000	n.a.	1	1 MT
Bomber						
British Buccaneer	45	1962	3,700		n.a.	
British Tornado	80	1981	2,800		n.a.	
French Mirage IVA	34	1964	3,200		1	60 KT

*British SLBMs deployed on four Polaris SSBNs, French SLBMs deployed on five Redoubtable SSBNs.
Robbin F. Laird, "French Nuclear Forces in the 1980s and the 1990s," *Comparative Strategy*, 4(4) (April 1984), p. 392.

SOURCE. The International Institute for Strategic Studies, *The Military Balance 1983–1984* (London: The International Institute for Strategic Studies, 1983), p. 122.

Table A.6. Future British and French Strategic Nuclear Forces
(Tactical/Short-range Systems Not Included.)

Type	Initial Operational Capability	Number to be Deployed	Range (km)	CEP (m)	Warheads/ Bomber Weapons	Maximum Yield
IRBM						
French SX	1996(?)	?	3,000–4,000	n.a.	3 MIRV(?)	n.a.
SLBM						
French M-4	1985	80	4,000–6,000	n.a.	6 MIRV	150 KT
French M-5*	1994(?)	?	n.a.		At least 6 MIRV	n.a.
British D-5*,a	1994(?)	64	7,400†	130–204†	8†	475 KT†

*British D-5 to be deployed on four new scaled-down "Ohio" type SSBNs, each with 16 tubes. Two new French SSBNs to be built, the latter perhaps with more than 16 tubes.
†This data from earlier tables.

SOURCE.
[a]Secretary of State for Defense, *Statement on the Defense Estimates 1984 Part I* (London: Her Majesty's Stationery Office, 1984), p. 24.
All other information from Robbin F. Laird, "French Nuclear Forces in the 1980s and the 1990s," *Comparative Strategy*, 4(4) (April 1984), pp. 397–401, 405–497.

NOTES

1. Ronald W. Reagan, *Weekly Compilation of Presidential Documents 19* (12) (Washington, DC: Government Printing Office, 1983): 423–66.
2. Caspar W. Weinberger, *Annual Report of the Secretary of Defense for Fiscal Year 1986* (Washington, DC: Government Printing Office, 1985), p. 54.
3. Ashton B. Carter and David M. Schwartz, ed., *Ballistic Missile Defense* (Washington, DC: The Brookings Institution, 1984), p. 53.
4. James C. Fletcher, *Defense against Ballistic Missiles: An Assessment of Tech-*

4. James C. Fletcher, *Defense against Ballistic Missiles: An Assessment of Technologies and Policy Implications* (Washington, DC: Government Printing Office, 1984), p. 19.
5. *Ibid.*
6. Dean A. Wilkening, in William J. Durch, ed., *National Interests and the Military Use of Space* (Cambridge, MA: Ballinger Publishing Co., 1984), pp. 141-47.
7. *Ibid.*
8. *Ibid.*
9. *Ibid.*
10. *Ibid.*
11. A space-based particle beam must be neutral because charged particle beams cannot propagate effectively in the vacuum of space. In addition, charged particle beams would have difficulty reaching distant targets due to bending in the earth's magnetic field.
12. Ashton B. Carter, *Directed Energy Missile Defense in Space* (Washington, DC: Office of Technology Assessment, 1984), p. 23.
13. Wilkening, in Durch, pp. 141-47.
14. *Ibid.*
15. *Ibid.*
16. Carter, *Directed Energy Missile Defense*, p. 26.
17. Fletcher, *Defense Against Ballistic Missiles*, p. 13.
18. Clarence Robinson, "Laser Technology Demonstration Proposed," *Aviation Week and Space Technology 114*(7) (16 February 1981): 16.
19. Carter, *Directed Energy Missile Defense*, p. 38.
20. David S. Yost, "Ballistic Missile Defense and the Atlantic Alliance," *International Security 7*(2) (Fall 1982): 159-61.
21. *Ibid.*, pp. 166-67.
22. *Ibid.*, p. 159.
23. *Ibid.*, p. 160.
24. *Ibid.*, p. 169.
25. Any alliance transfers would violate Article IX of the treaty: ". . . each Party undertakes not to transfer to other states, and not to deploy outside its national territory, ABM systems or their components limited by this Treaty." United States Arms Control and Disarmament Agency, *Arms Control and Disarmament Agreements* (Washington, DC: U.S. Government Printing Office, 1982), p. 141. Commenting on the expectations of many Europeans, Raymond Garthoff has pointed out: "The central political fact, however, is that the ABM Treaty of 1972 is widely seen not only as the crowning and principal surviving achievement of U.S.-Soviet strategic arms limitation efforts, but also as a symbol that détente between the U.S. and USSR is not completely dead and may be revived." Carter and Schwartz, *Ballistic Missile Defense*, p. 276.
26. McGeorge Bundy, "The Future of Strategic Deterrence," *Survival 21*(6) (November–December 1979): 271.
27. Yost, "Ballistic Missile Defense," p. 168.
28. Abram Chayes and Jerome B. Wiesner, ed., *ABM: An Evaluation* (New York: Harper & Row Publishers, 1969), p. 179.
29. Robbin F. Laird, "French Nuclear Forces in the 1980s and the 1990s," *Comparative Strategy 4*(4) (April 1984): 391.
30. Secretary of State for Defense, *Statement on the Defense Estimates 1984 Part I* (London: Her Majesty's Stationery Office, 1984), p. 24.
31. Laird, "French Nuclear Forces," p. 398.
32. *Ibid.*, p. 399.
33. *Ibid.*, pp. 399-400.

14

The Strategic Defense Initiative: Is It Technically and Strategically Defensible?

Steve Smith

Initial reactions to President Reagan's announcement of the Strategic Defense Initiative tended to concentrate on its technical limitations. Critics coined the term "Star Wars" to depict it as a futuristic, fictional ideal that for many compelling reasons could never work. Advocates of SDI came to Reagan's defense, and the debate with the critics has produced some remarkably useful literature. This chapter will discuss the technical problems raised by various SDI proposals, and it will review statements made in the literature with regard to major political and strategic disagreements over the initiative.[1]

The underlying theme of this chapter is that the SDI attempts to provide a technical fix for what is essentially a political problem. Furthermore, instead of improving political and strategic relations between the superpowers, SDI could lead to their significant degradation. The implication of this argument is that, unless the SDI is limited by arms control talks at the summit, it could begin to acquire a momentum of its own. Quite clearly, SDI will be the crucial issue of defense and foreign policy to be resolved in the second term of the Reagan administration. Its future development will affect relations not only with the Soviet Union but also with the Atlantic Alliance.

SDI is very much President Reagan's own initiative. When he first announced it, on 23 March 1983, there was little scientific consensus regarding the technical feasibility of space-based defense. An important chronicle has been written by George Ball, a former under secretary of state, to illustrate the key role played by the president.[2] In it he shows that Reagan has always opposed arms control as a way of dealing with the Soviets and that he has criticized every U.S.–Soviet arms control agreement that has ever been negotiated. His administration has relied on military might to influence Soviet behavior, and, as a new technical fix, SDI is supposed to utilize defensive armaments to reshape U.S.-Soviet relations. President Reagan's enthusiasm for Star Wars came from his many contacts with conservative organizations and individuals such as Edward Teller and Lt. General Daniel Graham. It was their "High Frontier" concept of ballistic missile defense (BMD) that led to the condemnation of the strategy of Mutual Assured Destruction (MAD) as "a mutual suicide pact" that would not deter nuclear war. Instead, the High Frontier proposed to build a defensive system based on available nonnuclear technologies, though it was later rejected both by Edward Teller and by a Pentagon study group led by the under secretary of defense, Richard DeLauer. Teller commented that, even though the project could be built for $100 billion, "the Soviets can get rid of High Frontier for ten billion dollars."[3]

The view of the Department of Defense was that the appropriate technology was not available and that it was "unwilling to commit this nation to a course which calls for growing into a capability that does not currently exist."[4] Despite this note of caution, Reagan was impressed by Teller and Graham's belief that a defensive shield should be built, now or in the future. This opinion was strengthened when Robert McFarlane, then deputy national security adviser, gave his support to the idea. McFarlane's reasons were different from those of Teller or Graham. He saw the SDI as a counter to the freeze movement and to domestic constraints on U.S. weapons developments; he thought SDI could gain bipartisan support and also serve as a useful bargaining chip in arms control talks.[5]

Reagan's move differed from the normal course of presidential initiatives, since it came from the top down instead of working its way through departmental channels. Apparently few people knew of the president's forthcoming initiative, including the leading officials concerned with BMD in the Pentagon and the president's own science adviser. When consulted, the Joint Chiefs of Staff gave the proposal only lukewarm support, but they did not formally recommend that the president should go ahead.[6] As one critic noted, if SDI had been forced to go "through the orthodox interagency review process, immediate objections would have either slowed its progress or stopped the plan altogether."[7] Clearly, the president announced the proposal before, rather than after, he asked for studies to evaluate its feasibility. For this reason, George Ball called the 1983 speech "one of the most irresponsible acts by any head of state in modern times."[8]

Reagan quickly became committed to the proposal and requested funding of approximately $26 billion over a five-year period. A critic of U.S. defense procurement might conclude that the $26 billion fund is supposed to prove that the SDI is feasible, and that, even if the required technologies are not attainable at present, there is a need to increase expenditure to achieve them. In the last year or so the debate has shifted away from concern with technological issues. It seems that SDI will not be feasible within the strategic and political parameters that operate today, though Reagan defended it at the Geneva summit as a nuclear imperative. The momentum gathered by SDI is likely to be unstoppable, even if it proves to be technologically unfeasible. This does not seem to matter, since the grounds for making a technical assessment are defined by wider political and strategic considerations. The definition of a workable technology depends on the goals that are ascribed to the initiative rather than on the doubts cast by skeptical scientists.

THREE CATEGORIES OF TECHNICAL PROBLEMS

It is useful to outline the major technical difficulties facing the research project. To better do so, the problems can be categorized under the three successive "layers" of BMD that the program must master. The three layers match the three stages that the trajectory, or flight path, of every ballistic missile follows: boost, midcourse, and terminal phases.

The boost phase lasts for from three to five minutes, as the missile accelerates with a powerful burn and its engines finally fall away, by which time it is well outside the atmosphere. In the post-boost phase, lasting up to five minutes, the bus of the missile splits off its MIRVs, together with a large number of penetration aids and decoys.

The midcourse phase lasts about twenty minutes for an ICBM or an SLBM on a normal, as distinct from a depressed, trajectory. After splitting away, the warheads coast through space without any additional form of propulsion.

The terminal phase lasts only one or two minutes, as the separate warheads reenter the atmosphere and fall toward their targets. The technologies needed by SDI to intercept Soviet missiles at each of the three stages are described in Gil Klinger's essay. As he carefully notes, the defensive system has to be ingeniously layered, but each layer suffers from distinctive, if not insuperable, difficulties. The major technical problems to be faced in each layer of defense can be briefly summarized.[9]

Boost and Post-Boost Phases

Although these two phases pose slightly different problems for any given defensive system, they involve common difficulties. It should be noted that five main technologies are being investigated to achieve boost phase interception: (1) space-based chemical lasers, (2) ground-based excimer lasers with space-based mirrors, (3) pop-up X-ray lasers, (4) space-based particle beams, and (5) space-based kinetic energy weapons. The scientific difficulties encountered by these technologies can be listed under each of the five categories.

Ground-based or space-based lasers. No one is sure how large a force would be required to build an effective SDI. One estimate, by the Union of Concerned Scientists, suggests that 300 laser weapons would have to be deployed for a space-based system, or 60 battle mirrors circling in low orbit for a ground-based laser system.[10] Forces of such size would be enormously expensive to deploy, and they would rise dramatically in cost if the Soviet Union ever chose to take countermeasures.

Generating energy for laser weapons. The major problem with either space-based or ground-based lasers is that of generating a sufficient amount of energy. There are extensive difficulties in developing perfect optical mirrors for ground-based sources, and there are severe technical limitations in using laser power in the atmosphere. The problems must be resolved if battle management controls are to determine, in only a few seconds, which battle station is to kill which one of hundreds of incoming missiles. To give an example of just one of the problems: The energy requirements for a ground-based excimer laser system would require between 20 and 60% of the entire electrical power output produced in the United States.

X-ray lasers. The problem with this technology lies in its basing mode. It cannot be located in the United States due to the curvature of the earth. An interceptor would have to climb to an altitude of roughly 1,000 km to hit a Soviet ICBM before it ended its boost and post-boost phases. Deployment of X-ray lasers would probably have to rely on pop-up weapons on U.S. submarines cruising near the Soviet coast, even though there are critical restrictions in communicating with submarines to give them precise targeting information. Moreover, submarines only launch one of their missiles at any one time. An orbiting system, circling either in low orbit or in geosynchronous orbit, would require one laser per booster.[11]

Space-based particle beams. This technology requires the use of charged-particle beams, even though they cannot work in outer space, as the beams are deflected by the earth's electromagnetic field. Research on neutral particle beams has barely started, and scientists refer to it as a very immature technology.[12] The energy requirements for particle beams are much greater than those for chemical or excimer lasers, and the deployment of any such system is likely to be retarded.

Kinetic energy weapons. This technology involves the firing of highly accelerated "smart rocks" from a railgun to destroy Soviet boosters. The system would have to be very large to cover low orbit targets, and it would be highly vulnerable. A scientific study found that it had an "extremely limited capability for boost phase intercept of present Soviet ICBMs, and no capability against future MX-like Soviet boosters, even if there is no Soviet effort to overcome the defense."[13] Because of the time required for the projectile to travel great distances to intercept the Soviet booster, some calculations indicate that it would have to be launched 53 seconds *before* the Soviets actually launched.[14] Moreover, the system could not be used for interception at the post-boost phase, because enemy missiles do not emit the large infrared plume on which smart interceptors home in during the boost phase.

In summary, the fundamental problems of boost and post-boost intercept lie in the size of the system required to intercept a large number of targets simultaneously and the number of battle stations that must be kept in place at any one time. In addition, there is cause to worry about the cost of such a system, about the split-second timing needed to carry out the interception, and about the vulnerability of the system to enemy attack.

Midcourse Intercept

The advantages of intercepting in the boost and post-boost phases are considerable. First, there is an infrared plume from the rockets to attract the homing sensors of the interceptors. Second, and more important, the target can be hit before it disperses its warheads, penetration aids, decoys, and debris, so that one kill can eliminate a large number of targets before they begin to disperse. In the midcourse phase the overwhelming problem is that of detecting the real targets, because they give off no heat plume and it is impossible to distinguish between reentry vehicles and decoys or chaff. Objects in space travel at the same speed, on the same trajectory, and they defy any foreseeable form of detection. The defense would have to hit each object in the "threat cloud" in case it was a warhead.

Candidates for defense weapons to be used in the midcourse phase have already been listed: X-ray lasers, particle beams, kinetic energy weapons, and lasers. But, in addition, there is the homing overlay experiment, which was successfully tested in June 1984, when a maneuverable steel "umbrella" destroyed a dummy Minuteman warhead in its midcourse flight across the Pacific. It was claimed that the experiment was misleading, as only one target was intercepted, while an attack in midcourse phase would need a large force of interceptors.

The use of nuclear-pumped X-ray lasers would interfere with other forms of defense management and sensing devices; and there are doubts that railguns could effectively propel interceptors at a sufficient velocity to kill their targets. Finally, an overwhelming of the detection systems would occur if the enemy launched a "threat cloud" numbering hundreds of thousands of objects, including reentry vehicles, decoys, chaff, and even balloons. The requirements for passive tracking of these objects would call for enormous computing facilities; the computers would have to handle 10 million lines of real-time programming.[15]

The budget for SDI for FY 1985 through FY 1987 reflects the priority of component requirements: $3.8 billion out of the first $8.8 billion would be allocated to sensor and battle-management development. It is assumed that the battle-management systems will work perfectly, on the first signal emitted in a hostile environment, and that no communications links will fail. One of the first studies made of the technological feasibility of SDI noted that the battle-management procedures would be so complex that any computer program to run it would require 50 million debugging runs before it would be battle-ready.[16] The purpose of a battle-management system is to instantly analyze billions of pieces of information, to determine which weapon should fire at which target, to communicate with all weapons at all times, and to verify kills for each use of each weapon on each target. These requirements seem to place midcourse interception in the realm of science fiction. Of all the three layers of interception, this one offers the greatest opportunity for the Soviets to deploy countermeasures to confuse and outflank the defense.

Terminal Interception

As a threat cloud begins to reenter the earth's atmosphere, it is easier for the defense to detect and discriminate among incoming targets. The chaff and light decoys burn up during reentry; and the friction of reentry causes objects to emit a glow that can be quickly tracked. The terminal phase had been the focus of earlier attempts at BMD, including the U.S. Safeguard and Sentinel systems and the Soviets' Galosh. The required nuclear technologies of interception are available, though they are publicly unpopular. New technologies are beginning to look promising, such as nonnuclear interceptors, improved sensor devices, and airborne optical systems. Despite these promising indications, two critical difficulties remain at the terminal interception stage. First, terminal effectiveness will depend on the completion of developments in the other layers. The second and most serious issue concerns the goals of SDI; is its aim to protect citywide areas or only hardened military targets such as silos? This choice has yet to be firmly determined.

If the SDI attempts to defend silos, it need only destroy 85%, maybe even 50%, of the attacking missiles as they pass through the three layers of interception. But, if the goal is to defend cities, would a "leakage" rate of 15%, or even 5%, be acceptable? The question is crucial. Should a Soviet attack include most of its ICBM force (about 6,000 warheads), leaving in reserve some 2,500 warheads on SLBMs and bombers, even a 95% success rate would allow 300 warheads to get through. In theory, up to 300 cities would be hit, although in operational circumstances the number would be much lower. The issue here is that a terminal defense for cities poses two problems that do not apply to the defense against a counterforce attack. First, the defense has more time to intercept a countersilo attack, since the weapons detonate either on the ground to crater the silo or very near it, while, in a city attack, the airburst is at a much higher altitude. Indeed, one Soviet countermeasure would be to build even bigger warheads, since they already have the throw-weight capabilities on existing missiles to carry them, so that the detonation could be set for an altitude of 30 km to destroy city targets.[17]

The second problem is that the defense of cities requires a much wider area of defense than defending against silo attacks. All of the United States would have to be covered by such a terminal defense system, while silos are concentrated geographically. Furthermore, the trajectories for city attacks can vary far more widely than trajectories aiming at concerted silo attacks. City defense would increase difficulties, since the point of impact could not be accurately predicted until very late in the flight of the reentry vehicle. The maneuverability of the reentry vehicles would make this task even more complex, and so, too, would Soviet efforts to "salvage fuse" their reentry vehicles. Obviously, protecting against attacks on cities is far more problematic than providing a defense against silo attacks.

When he proposed the SDI, President Reagan compared it to the Manhattan Project and the development of nuclear weapons in the early 1940s. Scientific opinion suggests that this is a misleading comparison. The Manhattan Project faced what were essentially engineering problems in adapting scientific knowledge to operational requirements. According to the report of a recent under secretary of defense for research and engineering, the SDI will require a breakthrough in eight key technologies, "every single one of which is equivalent to or greater than the Manhattan Project."[18] More important, SDI must contend with an opponent who is actively attempting to develop countermeasures. The technical literature indicates that it is not feasible to build a leakproof "astrodome"; yet this is precisely what President Reagan had in mind when he urged that SDI would give "us the means of rendering these nuclear weapons impotent and obsolete."[19] Although some officials talk of a defensive system that could "reduce significantly the military utility of Soviet preemptive attacks,"[20] the official position expressed by Caspar Weinberger and the president is that SDI will provide a "thoroughly reliable and total" defense.[21] Given the technical difficulties that have been listed, SDI is aiming for unrealistic goals.

POTENTIAL SOVIET COUNTERMEASUERS

It appears that the SDI has been evaluated in terms of *future* U.S. technology and against *current* Soviet systems. But by the time that any components of SDI would be deployed, it is certain that the Soviets would introduce some of the many countermeasures within their grasp. There are seven modes of countermeasures they could productively and relatively easily develop, and they can be simply enumerated.

Reducing Boost Phase

Current boost phases for Soviet missiles take roughly 300 seconds,[22] but the Fletcher panel on defensive technologies received evidence that, at the cost of carrying 25% less in payload, a missile could finish its boost phase in 50 seconds. This means that a missile would still be in the atmosphere at the end of burnout; a similar effect could be gained by altering the trajectory of the missile. These measures would reduce the time available for interception, and more laser stations would be required to extend interception capabilities. If the Soviets took such countermeasures, the kinetic energy weapons would lose some of their radius of action, particle beams would be unable to pursue the boosters into the upper atmosphere, and pop-up X-ray lasers would be significantly degraded in capability. As one critic concluded, reducing the boost phase would "be a potent or even decisive countermeasure against almost all concepts for boost-phase intercept."[23]

Shielding the Missile

Different techniques can be used to shield missiles from attack, and each would greatly increase problems for the defense. They include the coating of an ablative layer around the skin of the missile, spinning it in flight, placing a movable "skirt" to disguise the location of the booster above the flame, and varying the size and direction of the flame. These countermeasures would reduce laser absorption and require a ninefold increase in the dwell time that each laser spends on each target, as well as a ninefold increase in the number of battle stations deployed.[24]

Salvo Firing

Pressures on the defense can be increased by varying the levels of attack. A defensive system can better cope with a series of small attacks than with an all-out attack. In a full-scale attack the United States would have few stations in position, and new stations could not quickly be brought into range, as they would be if the Soviets prolonged their salvos.

Chaff and Decoys

The Soviets could overwhelm midcourse interceptors by increasing the number of dummy warheads and the amount of chaff released by their missiles. More advanced versions could transmit false radar signals in order to confuse the already enormously complex task of tracking hundreds of thousands of items in the threat cloud. Warheads could also be salvage fused so that if they were attacked, they would explode before the interceptor reached them. Finally, decoy ICBMs could be built and housed next to actual ICBMs, forcing the United States to destroy twice as many missiles in the boost phase and requiring twice as many battle stations to be deployed.

System Vulnerability

One of the greatest problems for a space-based defense system is its vulnerability. To guarantee coverage of targets, the orbits of the systems must be readily predictable, to both the attacker and the defense. The size of a space-based laser or particle beam battle station is likely to be considerable; and ground-based laser systems must put their most fragile components, the battle mirrors, in space too. All of these system rely on complex sensor equipment and error-free communications facilities to link space-based components with each other and with ground controls. The systems are therefore vulnerable to Soviet countermeasures, such as space mines positioned near U.S. battle stations. In fact, the United States would have to claim a sanctuary of several thousand kilometers to keep any Soviet space-based defense system out of operational range from each U.S. battle station. Even if the Soviets agreed to recognize sanctuaries, they could deploy either a system of pop-up X-ray lasers or a ground-based system with reflecting battle mirrors to counter the American defense equipment.

Clearly, the Soviets could potentially destroy a large percentage of U.S. boost phase interceptors, thus punching a hole through the defense just a few seconds before launching their ICBM force. The vulnerability of certain parts of the planned space defense systems is considerable. For example, a Soviet laser could blind and easily destroy such "soft" elements as sensors and laser mirrors, and a tiny steel pellet projectile could demolish the aluminum shield covering a laser mirror.[25] Above all, the communication facilities required for battle management are vulnerable to interception or disruption, or to a direct attack on the hardware that controls them.

Offensive Force Buildup

The danger in assessing tomorrow's U.S. technology against today's Soviet capabilities is nowhere more obvious than in calculating potential Soviet force strengths. The Soviets could obviously increase the challenge to the defense by simply multiplying the size of their missile forces or by placing more warheads on them. For a start, the SS-18 could carry 30 warheads as opposed to the ten currently deployed. It is estimated that, for every four extra Soviet boosters built, the United States would need to deploy one extra laser battle station to guarantee coverage of their orbital patterns.[26] The attacker would gain considerable cost advantages in a short time because its offensive proliferation could quickly overwhelm defensive capabilities.[27]

Systems Not Covered by SDI

The great defect of SDI is that it could not counter nuclear weapons that never leave the earth's atmosphere. These include cruise missiles, bombers, and SLBMs launched on a depressed or flattened trajectory. The Soviets' cruise missiles pose an especially grave threat, because a few can be destroyed, but in a salvo attack many would get through. The use of a depressed trajectory for SLBMs would sacrifice some accuracy, but it would still be useful for attacking cities and nonhardened military installations. It is unlikely that the Soviets would ever rely solely on their SLBMs, but they could probably combine an SLBM attack with attempts to blind U.S. reconnaissance satellites and knock out communications links.

Ideally, the advantage of a full-scale defense is that it would discourage a Soviet first strike by denying them the confidence to attack and destroy the vast majority of American ICBMs. But the question must be asked, Would they ever conceivably make so desperate a choice? Recent estimates by the CIA have indicated that Soviet ICBMs may not be anywhere as accurate as it claimed in the 1970s.[28] Even if the CIA's original figures on Soviet missile accuracy were correct, the technical feasibility of a first strike was dubious;[29] and strong reasons are now emerging for revising the methodology of Pentagon estimates of Soviet hard-target kill capability.[30] A first strike attack would be a foolish gamble by any Soviet leadership.[31] They would have to assume that all their missiles would work perfectly over brand new trajectories and the first time round, and that the U.S. president would accept a counterforce attack on U.S. silos as "only" a counterforce attack and not an attack on the American population. An estimate published by the Office of Technology Assessment held that between 2 and 20 million U.S. citizens would die even in a counterforce attack.[32] Thus the attack scenario depicted in the "window of vulnerability" argument should never have been seriously accepted. The possibility of a Soviet first strike does not pose a realistic threat, either militarily or politically, to the United States; and the stark choice between suicide and surrender offered by such an argument is no more than fiction.

POLICY CONSEQUENCES OF THE SDI

It is difficult to determine at this stage whether the Congress will appropriate funds for the SDI and whether the Atlantic Alliance will participate in its research. It is apparent, however, that serious policy consequences will flow from the SDI decision. These can be segregated into eight categories of development, to project possible changes in the relations between the superpowers and the Atlantic Alliance.

Soviet Defense Responses

The Soviets can be expected to match the U.S. SDI effort by developing their own strategic defense system. Though President Reagan continues to talk about eventually sharing the technology with the Soviets, it does not seem likely that this will soon occur. The key issue for any Soviet strategic defense system is not how well it will work in comparison with the American SDI but what effects it will have on U.S. defense efforts. As Caspar Weinberger admitted: "I can't imagine a more destabilizing factor for the world than if the Soviets should acquire a thoroughly reliable defense against these missiles before we do."[33] The United States would probably react with a further development of anti-satellite weapons (ASAT), after which the Soviets would deploy their own ASAT against SDI. This would lead to an arms race in ASAT and SDI weapons. It is difficult to imagine that either superpower would feel more secure than it had before the arms race escalated.

Effects on U.S.–Soviet Relations

It is possible that a generation of Soviet–U.S. relations will remain frigid and distrustful. The Soviet reaction to SDI has been uncompromisingly hostile. The defensive purpose that President Reagan claimed to be his goal was dismissed as "camouflage for a more sinister offensive aim."[34] The Soviets argued that, even if both sides built an SDI system, neither could survive a concerted first strike. They wondered whether the real U.S. intention was to perfect SDI and to remove their retaliatory strike capability after a U.S. first strike had been launched. Though hopes of improving U.S.–Soviet relations rose when the Geneva summit meeting convened, the

Soviets are deeply worried by the strategic threat that they perceive in the SDI thrust.

The question has been raised recently: How long can the United States pursue SDI before it breaks the terms of the 1972 ABM treaty? According to an extensive study of this issue, the United States will have to either abrogate the ABM treaty or gain Soviet approval to amend it by 1988–89.[35] There are thirteen areas in which the SDI could possibly breach U.S. compliance with the ABM treaty by the mid-1990s, and in which Soviet compliance might also break down. The treaty forbids many forms of component development, testing, and transfer, and SDI will have to breach these limits if it proceeds. It has been claimed that violations of the treaty have already been committed by the Soviets, including the building of a large radar installation at Krasnoyarsk. These claims have led to bitter disputes, and the Soviets have warned that they will not agree to any alterations of the treaty. The demise of the ABM treaty would signal a serious loss of confidence in arms control negotiations, and both superpowers insisted after the Geneva summit that they hoped to preserve it.

Arms Control

Apart from the ABM treaty, SDI threatens to undermine future arms control bargaining procedures. It was the aim of the Soviets to halt SDI research and testing before proceeding with talks about INF forces and a 50% reduction of strategic offensive forces. Their position was rejected by Reagan at Geneva. He had previously argued that agreements could be reached, independently, and that SDI would be needed even if the Soviets dismantled all of their nuclear warheads.[36] The U.S. goal at Geneva had been to reduce Soviet ICBMs, but this was unrealistic if these weapons offer the Soviets the best countermeasure response to any U.S. space-based defense system.

The Soviets' position seems to have shifted slightly. They now appear to be willing to distinguish between scientific research and development testing, and to allow talks to proceed on INF and offensive force reductions until the summit convening in Washington in 1986. The best hope for compromise is that the United States will accept a ban on testing SDI systems for a number of years in exchange for a set of deep cuts in Soviet ICBM launchers and warheads. It is likely that the Alliance could face a potentially divisive outcome if the Soviets proposed serious cuts in its INF and strategic forces in return for a ban on testing SDI-related components. President Reagan might eventually have to choose between arms control or SDI, and, if SDI were chosen, he might severely divide the sympathies of the Alliance.

Opportunity Costs

Predicting the cost of SDI is an impossible task when many of the technologies are not even on the drawing board. Estimates vary from $500 billion to $3 trillion, but the difficult assessment is that of calculating the impact on U.S. defense priorities and the enlargement of the budget deficit. With a defense budget running at $300 billion a year, the cost alone would not be an insuperable problem for SDI, though it would lead to further questions about the cost-effectiveness of the system. But there is also the issue of how to measure the U.S. and Soviet incremental costs. Since there have been grave problems and errors in estimating the costs of Soviet defense efforts in the past, it would be difficult to estimate the opportunity costs that each side would pay to build an SDI.

Effect on Crisis Stability

One of the most worrying consequences of SDI will be found in its impact on crisis-management capabilities. It is not yet known whether SDI is seriously intended to provide a leakproof astrodome or a hard-point defense for missile silos. There is little prospect that an effective leakproof SDI can be built or that SDI can provide for a silo *and* an area defense. The Soviets willfully maintain that SDI would make sense only if the United States intended to strike first. Perverse as this sounds, it probably resembles U.S. complaints that would be heard if the Soviets ever developed their own BMD. If there were an arms race to develop a Soviet strategic defense system, and to extend ASAT capabilities on both sides, crisis management and nuclear stability could be direly imperiled. In a crisis, each side would be looking for evidence that the other was "going first," because the advantage in striking preemptively would be considerable.

Transitional Problems

Even if it were assumed that SDI could offer greater security, there is still the problem of how to get from here to there — from the start of testing to the final phase of deploying defensive systems in space. If the United States and the Soviets were unevenly matched in a technological race, there would be intense insecurity between the superpowers. It is suggested that the Soviets might launch a first strike while they still could, together with deploying ASAT, using space mines, or building a great number of ICBMs. How the United States would respond to Soviet counterdeployments is difficult to guess. Obviously, the transition period poses dangers for stability and trust, and the period of uncertainty could last for many years.

Effects on the NATO Alliance

SDI threatens serious consequences for the NATO alliance. Some of the allies have strenuously objected to SDI, since they see it as a dangerous acceleration of the superpowers' arms race. Others are less critical and are willing to participate in the lavishly supported research program funded for SDI. Again, for the sake of brevity, the difficulties posed to the Alliance can be listed under eight brief headings.

Effectiveness of SDI systems. Whatever the effectiveness of the defensive systems, SDI would offer less to the members of the Alliance than to its leader in the United States. President Reagan stated initially that the system would protect not just the United States but also its allies. But, for compelling technical reasons, it is not possible to defend the European members of the Alliance to the same extent as the United States. Soviet missiles that threaten Europe travel on a much shorter time path to target, and in any layered defense system, tracking and interception capabilities would be greatly reduced. NATO also faces a sizable threat from air-breathing bombers, cruise missiles, and short-range nuclear systems that barely leave the atmosphere. SDI cannot possibly offer the same degree of protection to the Europeans as it does to the United States. It is no wonder that some Europeans view it as yet another attempt to "decouple" the United States from the defense of Europe.

Different levels of vulnerability. Because the European and American members of the Alliance perceive different levels of vulnerability of their homelands, what will this do to consensus values within NATO? The cruise and Pershing deployment strained the electoral position of some of the European governments and their links with U.S. contingency planning for the defense of Europe. One of the main arguments in Europe for the deployment of INF weapons was that they would make the United States as vulnerable to attack as Europe, because the use of Euromissiles under U.S. control would invite a Soviet retaliation against the United States. Some critics in Europe believe that SDI would allow the United States to retreat behind a defensive shield and to move away from its pledge to defend Europe. From the European peace movements it causes an opposite calculation: that the United States would be more willing to use nuclear weapons in Europe. Neither of these are realistic statements. But the point is that equal levels of vulnerability have been important in the past to maintain equilibrium and consensus within the Alliance. The SDI threatens to undermine this sense of equality and unity. It may even be that SDI would provide the Soviets with better options to retaliate in any conflict within central Europe.

The ABM treaty constraints. The restrictions of the ABM treaty should limit the ability of the United States to extend the SDI or its components to Europe. The treaty prohibits the placement of ABM components outside the national territory of the signatories (Article IX); thus any deployment of terminal defense systems, or of ATBMs in Europe, would be a serious violation. The agreed Statement G prohibits the transfer of "technical descriptions or blueprints . . . of ABM systems and their components,"[37] and this could limit European involvement in SDI-related research if it were strictly applied.

Soviet countermeasures. Of all possible Soviet countermeasures to the SDI, the option of increasing their ICBMs and warheads appears the worst threat to the European members of the Alliance. Large numbers of Soviet ICBMs are aimed at European targets, and an increase in their strategic arsenal might upset European perceptions of security. Further, were the Soviets to link U.S. behavior to European security, their strategic arsenal might be used to threaten reprisals in Europe as a response to any U.S. attack elsewhere.

Superpower relations. A less tangible but nonetheless important consequence for the Alliance would follow from deterioration in U.S.–Soviet relations following the deployment of SDI. For complex reasons of European politics, especially in inter-German relations, any increase in superpower tensions would increase European perceptions of insecurity. Possibly, if Europeans were to feel greater anxiety and insecurity, sections of European public opinion might call for the dissolution of the NATO alliance. This might occur if the United States were to shelter behind its defensive umbrella and then launch into angry confrontations with the Soviet Union. A deterioration in U.S.–Soviet relations could exercise ripple effects on Soviet relations with Eastern Europe, and this would stir uneasy reactions in Western Europe.

Europe's independent deterrents. Any Soviet strategic defense system would have a severe effect on the British and French nuclear deterrents. Though both are to be expensively modernized, the French and British nuclear systems would be less likely to penetrate to their targets if the Soviets perfected a strategic defense system, and the British and French deterrents would lose much of their credibility. This would cause serious reappraisals in London and Paris, and it might lead to a forced restriction of defense postures in both countries.

Economic effects. The Europeans fear that SDI is partly intended to preserve U.S. hegemony in key areas of high technology and to transfer research funds to U.S. industry. Many critics insist that the hidden goal of

SDI is to correct the U.S. decline in high technology, to induce another brain drain from Europe, or to pump research and development funding into emergent technologies. The French government has proposed a rival European research consortium, EUREKA, to compete with U.S. efforts and to provide insurance in case the United States inhibits European participation in high-technology areas of SDI research. Some Europeans suspect that Congress will not want to finance a potential European competition to American research and development; others view participation in SDI research as an attempt to rent support for the program. It may well turn out to be one of the most divisive projects that ever faced the Alliance.

NATO strategy. NATO does not rely on the United States for immediate nuclear defense of Europe in a conventional war, but it does expect that the U.S. strategic deterrent will hold the ultimate balance of power. Were the Soviets to develop their own version of SDI, they would call into question the credibility of the U.S. nuclear guarantee to Europe. This is critical. The Alliance was built on the belief that the United States would at all times use its nuclear forces to limit a Soviet conventional attack. A Soviet strategic defense system would threaten the credibility of the U.S. pledge because, in the last resort, U.S. nuclear weapons are stationed in Europe not to counter Soviet nuclear weapons, or to be used in war fighting, but to deter a Soviet conventional attack. The American SDI would open up to examination the doctrine of flexible response and all the necessary ambiguities and doubts that surround it. There has always been doubt as to whether the U.S. guarantee is truly credible, but a Soviet strategic defense system would intensify the questioning and stimulate a possibly divisive debate within NATO.

CONCLUSIONS

This chapter suggests three conclusions about SDI. First, it is above all a search for a technical fix to what is essentially a political problem. Soviet–U.S. relations are the problem and will doubtless continue to be so, but they cannot be solved by technological rather than political means. The SDI attempts to negate the Soviet threat in a manner that misses its essential character. It is not the technical threat of Soviet ICBMs that matters but the state of political relations between the United States and the Soviet Union, and these are more likely to be impaired than improved by SDI.

Second, much of the thinking on SDI reflects the "fallacy of the last move." It is tempting to see future U.S. capabilities as nullifying present Soviet capabilities; but by the time the SDI is deployed, the Soviets will have improved their capabilities and resorted to a wide array of countermeasures.

SDI will probably lead to a further round of the offense-defense contest, which the offense usually wins, leaving both sides infuriated and fearful.

Third, SDI will not enable the United States to achieve the goal stated by President Reagan, to make nuclear weapons obsolete and to replace nuclear deterrence with a sheltered peace. If the United States cannot render nuclear weapons obsolete, and if it cannot successfully replace deterrence with a BMD safeguard, the only alternative is to enhance nuclear deterrence. But there are better ways of achieving this, without starting an arms race in BMD deployments.

Deterrence is basically a psychological phenomenon, and it depends on the security perceptions of adversaries, and of allies. Given the likely impact of SDI on Soviet perceptions with regard to crisis management, political stability, arms control, the arms race in space, and the character of U.S.–Soviet relations, SDI is likely not to enhance, but to undermine deterrence. In aiming to improve U.S. defense, SDI may undermine U.S. security; and, after spending countless billions of dollars, the United States may end up being better defended but less secure.

The task that President Reagan faces in his remaining term in office is that of conjuring with four variables simultaneously: (1) his pledge to build a BMD shield, (2) Soviet perceptions of greater insecurity in a defensive arms race, (3) the anxieties of the Atlantic Alliance regarding the U.S. nuclear pledge to deter an attack on Europe, and (4) the "technological momentum" of the SDI that has been created by powerful forces of industrial and political pressure in the United States. If Reagan is to fulfill his aim to become the president who brought peace to the nuclear age, he will have to juggle these four factors against the stern political realities of negotiating arms reduction and control procedures with the Soviet Union in a series of summit and technical discussions. His plans for the SDI require many decades for development, while the four variables listed above must be handled in the short term. It still remains to be seen whether Reagan can move his own administration, as well as Gorbachev, to accept a set of transitional concessions and working compromise positions or whether he will persist with SDI regardless of all opposition and protest.

NOTES

1. There is a well-documented technical literature on SDI. On the critical side the best works include: for the Union of Concerned Scientists, John Tirman, ed., *The Fallacy of Star Wars* (New York: Vintage Books, 1984); Ashton Carter, *Directed Energy Missile Defense in Space* (Washington, DC: U.S. Office of Technology Assessment, 1984); Sidney Drell, Phillip Farley, and David Holloway, *The Reagan Strategic Defense Initiatives: A Technical, Political, and Arms Control Assessment* (Stanford, CA: Center for International Security and

Arms Control, Stanford University, 1984). Among the advocates of SDI see: Robert Jastrow, *How to Make Nuclear Weapons Obsolete* (Boston: Little, Brown & Co., 1985); Department of Defense, *The Strategic Defense Initiative: Defensive Technologies Study* (Washington, DC: 1984); Department of Defense, *Defense Against Ballistic Missiles: An Assessment of Technologies and Policy Implications* (Washington, DC: 1984). See also *The President's Strategic Defense Initiative* (Washington, DC: Government Printing Office, 1985). This chapter relies on much of the technical information cited in these sources.

2. George Ball, "The War for Star Wars," *New York Review of Books*, 11 April 1985, pp. 38–44. See also Laurence Barrett, "How Reagan Became a Believer," *Time*, 11 March 1985, p. 16.

3. Ball, "War for Star Wars," p. 38.

4. *Ibid.*, p. 39.

5. Barrett, "How Reagan Became a Believer," p. 16.

6. Ball, "War for Star Wars", p. 39.

7. Barrett, "How Reagan Became a Believer," p. 16.

8. Ball, "War for Star Wars," p. 38.

9. For detailed evaluations of the problems see Tirman, *Fallacy of Star Wars*; Carter, *Directed Energy Missile Defense*; and Drell et al., *Reagan Strategic Defense Initiatives*.

10. See Tirman, *Fallacy of Star Wars*, pp. 100–101.

11. Carter, *Directed Energy Missile Defense*, p. 57.

12. Drell et al., *Reagan Strategic Defense Initiatives*, p. 57.

13. Carter, *Directed Energy Missile Defense*, p. 35.

14. Daniel Graham, *High Frontier* (New York: Tom Doherty Associates, 1983), p. 153.

15. Department of Defense, *Strategic Defense Initiative*, p. 10.

16. Cited in George Church, "Explaining the High-Tech Frontier," *Time*, 11 March 1985, p. 23.

17. Tirman, *Fallacy of Star Wars*, p. 142.

18. Tirman, *Fallacy of Star Wars*, p. 42.

19. The sections of President Reagan's speech of 23 March 1983 dealing with SDI are reprinted in Drell et al., *Reagan Strategic Defense Initiatives*, pp. 101–102 (Appendix A); quote from p. 103.

20. Statement by Richard DeLauer before the U.S. Congress, House, Subcommittee on Research and Development of the Committee on Armed Services, 98th Cong., March 1, 1984. Reprinted as Appendix C in Drell et al., pp. 107–115; quote from p. 107.

21. Cited in Tirman, *Fallacy of Star Wars*, p. 39.

22. Carter, *Directed Energy Missile Defense*, p. 10.

23. *Ibid.*, p. 48.

24. *Ibid.*, p. 49.

25. Tirman, *Fallacy of Star Wars*, p. 123.

26. Carter, *Directed Energy Missile Defense*, p. 51.

27. *New York Times*, 18 May 1983, p. 11.

28. *International Herald Tribune* 20/21 July 1985, p. 1.

29. See Steve Smith, "The Mathematics of Counterforce," *Coexistence* 19(2) (1984): 126–141.

30. Steve Smith, "Problems of Assessing Missile Accuracy," *Royal United Services Institute Journal*, forthcoming.

31. See Steve Smith, "MX and the Vulnerability of American Missiles," *ADIU Report* 4(3) (1982): 1–5.

32. Office of Technology Assessment, *The Effects of Nuclear War* (Washington, DC: Government Printing Office, 1979), p. 84.
33. *Wall Street Journal*, 7 December 1983, p. 60.
34. See the excellent discussion in Drell et al., *Reagan Strategic Defense Initiative*, pp. 13–38; quote from p. 22.
35. Thomas Longstreth, John Pike, and John Rhinelander, *The Impact of U.S. and Soviet Ballistic Missile Defense Programs on the ABM Treaty*, 3rd ed. (Washington, DC: National Campaign to Save the ABM Treaty, March 1985), p. vii. See also the table on p. 51.
36. *International Herald Tribune*, 13 February 1985, p. 1.
37. Agreed Statement G to the ABM Treaty; the Treaty and the agreed statements are reprinted in *Longstreth* et al., *Impact of U.S. and Soviet Ballistic Missile Defense Programs*, pp. 80–88; quote from p. 55.

15
Congress and Foreign Policy: Noise and Politics in the Reagan Second Term

David Robertson

A distinguished British observer of the American political system in the last century, Lord Bryce, commented that the Congress was the most difficult institution for a foreigner to understand. The point still holds true, as I discovered while completing this study on Capitol Hill. It gradually became clear that this essay had to deal with two subjects. The first reviews the record of the Congress in making foreign policy in the post-Vietnam era. It provides a general survey of congressional maneuvers and foreign policy criticism, and it suggests a framework to appraise the difficulties that recent presidents have encountered in building majority coalitions on Capitol Hill. The second examines the sources of friction that are most likely to appear between Congress and the administration in President Reagan's second term. While the first part is unavoidably theoretical and historical, the second will attempt to interpret the internal political confrontations that influence America's statecraft today.

THE TRACK RECORD

Congress does not make foreign policy. A considerable level of noise and of political skirmishing has characterized the activity of formulating policy relations between the United States and the rest of the world. The critical forays and diversions emanating from Capitol Hill have confused many European critics and journalists. In previous decades the defense of isolationism allowed some room for Congress to determine policy, but its role was largely reactive. This is not to say that Congress left foreign policy initiatives entirely to the executive branch. On the contrary, in the period from Yalta to Vietnam it struggled to find a bipartisan support for a cold-war posture of containment, a policy almost as simple in conception as that of the isolationism that flourished in the 1930s. Congress tried to exercise its constitutional authority over treaties and executive agreements, but it failed to grapple with contemporary complexities such as arms transfers, foreign aid, or Third World insurgencies. In thirty years of containment, legislators learned to leave intervention decisions largely to the executive branch. Secrecy and subtlety were required, and the Congress deferred to the powerful energies of the executive branch. It basically deferred to the chief executive and his powerful agency chiefs, and it became relatively passive in allowing them free use of the war powers accorded to the executive by the Constitution.

The political balance changed once Congress began to doubt the wisdom of policy and process in the Vietnam war. Members of Congress no longer allowed the president unfettered discretion. Though it lacked the skill, the party discipline, or the power to control the executive agencies, Congress tried to reassert its authority.[1] It found difficulty in doing so, however, because its foreign policy decisions have to be filtered through deliberative procedures that are remarkably slow and factionalized in the House of Representatives and subject to filibuster delays in the Senate. Diplomats throughout the world confess that it is difficult to know whom they should consult or lobby in a system of multiple checks and balances. Some choose to lobby the leading committees of Congress, whereas others talk only to the White House or the State Department. Many of America's allies sympathized with a Soviet diplomat's reaction to the Senate debate on the SALT II ratification.

> With whom in America can we have dealings? If the President needs to coordinate his actions and stand with Congress, why isn't this done before any international agreement is concluded? . . . It appears that agreement with the Administration, even if it has a majority in the Congress, often counts for little. It comes out that having reached agreement with the Administration, one ought then to enter into separate external relations with the American Congress, and renegotiate decisions.[2]

Congress does not formulate foreign policy, but it also does not simply acquiesce in presidential policy-making procedures. What then does it do? As in domestic politics, members of Congress do many things simultaneously. They look after the interests of their districts, they respond to the more powerful lobbies, they pursue private goals that might lead to re-election and career enhancement, and they learn to use congressional power over foreign policy issues to win media coverage, personal recognition, and leadership roles in articulating public opinion currents.[3] They cooperate with other members of their party to promote "salient issues," particularly when the next presidential election looms near. They occasionally cross regional or party lines to pursue ideological causes and foreign policy issues that are highly symbolic, such as voting on aid to Israel or Central America, unless local constituency politics tend to modify their enthusiasms. Their basic responsibility is to help mobilize public opinion to support the national interest. It was Walter Lippmann who noted that congressmen are less interested in national than in local affairs, and that securing reelection is more pressing than national security. Though the U.S. Congress has long been noted for it parochial tendencies, it has not ceded its reserve of authority in foreign policy to the executive branch. It does not know how to use its authority effectively, but it is not lax in trying to do so during each of its brief two-year-term sessions.

Districts and Lobbies

Foreign policy does not provide many issues on which members of Congress can do much practical good for their constituencies. As the saying goes, "Afghanistan's not in my district . . . and voters don't know where Angola is." The House Committee on Foreign Affairs has never been important, and members with high seniority status choose to avoid it. It usually concerns itself with only one important piece of legislation a year, the annual foreign aid bill. If members of Congress are interested in external affairs, they opt for the Armed Services Committee; it combines a major role in determining defense posture with enviable opportunities to bring procurement contracts and services to the local constituency.[4] Members of subcommittees of the two appropriations committees can also help considerably in promoting local economic interest, thus strengthening their electoral base and their own political power in Congress.

Southern members of the Senate particularly have been distinguished by their ability to secure defense expenditures or military bases for their states. Stennis of Mississippi, Russell of Georgia, and Johnson of Texas were men who gathered political power and hardware contracts throughout their careers. So too did Henry Jackson, "the Senator from Boeing," who fought off Lockheed, McDonnell-Douglas, and the Salt II treaty. Senator Cranston of California is one of the few "single-issue" politicians on Foreign Relations, but, as a champion of arms control, he failed to oppose the B-1 bomber because it is built in his state. Senator Levin of Michigan, on Armed Services, has attacked many military procurement projects, but the army was forced to buy more tanks than it had planned because they were made in Detroit.

Military posture decisions affect foreign policy by sending signals to other countries that were not always intended by the State Department. The famed Nunn–Roth amendment on burden sharing in NATO was deemed unwise by the president and the National Security Council. So, too, was the decision to cut off financial aid to the Contras fighting to overthrow the government of Nicaragua. Interest politics are crucial on not only military but also trade policy. Congress has expressed a strong protectionist streak in defending the industrial base of America, even though its actions have endangered Alliance relations that the executive branch sought to nurture. Trade retaliation against the EEC and Japan became dangerously abrasive, while pressures were exerted to resume grain sales to the Soviet Union despite the antagonistic thrust of policy following the invasion of Afghanistan. Members of Congress from the Midwest had to pay attention to the farm vote, while limitations on Japanese car or Korean steel imports appealed to members of Congress facing reelection in a large number of industrial constituencies.[5]

Perhaps in no other Western democracy are such powerful lobbies formed by electors sharing ethnic ties with citizens of another country, and trying to change policy accordingly. The most dramatic instance occurred in 1917, when Irish and German immigrants criticized Woodrow Wilson's support for the British government and urged the United States to stay out of World War I. An upsurge of isolationist pressure occurred again in the 1930s, and the Congress wrote the Neutrality Acts specifically to stop President Roosevelt from pushing the United States back into war. Since then the strongest ethnic lobbying has come from Jewish voters over Middle East politics, Irish and Greek pressure groups, and, to a lesser extent, black and Hispanic groups.[6] In most cases these lobbies have pursued specific interruptions in foreign policy by influencing votes in one or the other house. Almost any military adviser in Washington, or any other major NATO capital, would admit that NATO's southern flank would be in better condition if the United States gave more military aid to Turkey, at the expense of aid to Greece, but the protests of the Greek lobby regarding Cyprus forbid it.

Another way for members of Congress to interfere with foreign policy has been developed by the Senate. Unlike the House, where few members are ever effective, the Senate allows members to wield great influence, particularly if they chair a committee or if they rank highly in the majority or minority leadership. At any one time several Senators will be toying with the idea of running for the White House, and most are eager to build up their public reputations and media coverage. Although voters usually tend to rank foreign affairs relatively low on the list of their concerns, foreign affairs provide glamorous limelight during the prolonged course of presidential primary elections. Senators sometimes win widespread attention for irresponsible views on foreign policy issues. As a result, policy remains at the mercy of members from either party who need to condemn the president on major issues in order to run against him. The renowned China lobby chastised the Democrats for "losing China" and prevented President Eisenhower from establishing normal relations with Peking. The Israel lobby has been conspicuously effective in shaping policy constraints in the Middle East and in identifying the leanings of all presidential candidates.

The U.S. Constitution gives enormous potential for harassment to the Senate, because the ratification of treaties requires the assent of two-thirds of the membership. A small number of swing votes has often been decisive. But there is a price to pay for the Senate's support, and, if the administration cannot or will not pay it, policies backed by a strong majority of the Senate can suffer. A recent example was given by Senator Baker, the former Republican minority leader, who almost single-handedly cost President Carter the ratification of the SALT II treaty. In 1978 Baker led Republican support for Carter on the two Panama Canal treaties, which passed the Senate by only one vote each. He had previously mobilized bipartisan support for presidential initiatives on foreign policy, but in 1979 he chose to change his position. When SALT II came to the Senate floor, it ran into serious trouble from the hawkish Democrats and Republicans on the Armed Services Committee, though it was backed by nearly the whole of the Foreign Relations Committee. Baker was planning to run for the Republican presidential nomination, and he suddenly came out against the Salt treaty. He had been severely criticized by conservatives for his Panama Canal role, and he needed a tougher image in order to combat Reagan in the primaries.

Many comparable incidents can be cited, including the dramatic shift made by Senators Fulbright, Javits, and Aiken during the Vietnam War. It took them many years, though, to shift their allegiances from a bipartisan support of foreign policy and to become outstanding critics. Senators are attentive to changing electoral moods, and they become gun-shy on quick or difficult issues such as combating the civil war in Angola or changing the status of the GDR or Taiwan. Of course, a seat on the Foreign Relations Committee wins prestige, but it is also electorally risky. Four of the five senators on the committee running for reelection in 1984 lost their seats, including the chairman, Charles Percy; his predecessor, Frank Church, was ousted in 1980.

Partisanship and Presidential Elections

So much is written about regional conflicts in U.S. politics and the lack of party discipline that the persistence of party competition in Congress is often overlooked. It is on foreign policy issues that partisanship and ideology occasionally matter, if only because vested or local interests do not have to be sacrificed by powerfully entrenched members. With the exception of Johnson and Ford, every postwar president has tried to make foreign policy a priority for political maneuver and electoral success. So, too, has the party that failed to win the White House. It will often take up and drop foreign policy positions with no great regard for consistency, simply to expose the vulnerable commitments of the administration. This was seen in the complex history of the MX missile. Opposition to arms reductions prompted leading Democrats in the Senate to desert the Democratic majority in both houses on the MX. They wanted Carter to tear off the "weakness" label that had been pinned to a president who had initialed the SALT II agreement and then cancelled the B-1 bomber. President Reagan recognized, on taking office, that the position had changed and that he could build less than half the 200 missiles planned. He therefore had to cancel the enormous funding for Carter's "mobile basing scheme" for the MX. The Democratic majority in Congress asserted itself, and it chose to vote for only 50 MX, regardless of the administration's advice. In the end Reagan appointed a blue-ribbon commission under General Scowcroft to devise a compromise on MX and arms control that the Democrats could not oppose. It is worth noting, paradoxically, that the authorizing vote for MX came shortly after the House had voted overwhelmingly in favor of a mutual freeze on nuclear weapons deployments.

Public opinion switched rapidly after Reagan revived the public from its sense of frustration after the hostage crisis in Iran. Yet, by the time of the 1984 election, it was Reagan who had to soften the hard-line reputation he had gained by accelerating the military buildup and talking tough to the Soviet Union. At the same time, Democrats in the House worried about looking too soft on a number of issues, varying from the nuclear weapons freeze to restricting aid to El Salvador and the Contra groups in Nicaragua. Neither party was sure whether the electorate wanted to preserve an intransigent foreign policy or if it had begun to look for a change.

Though partisan competition over foreign policy tends to be ideology free, foreign affairs have become a prime battleground for the conservative New Right. It finds containment too soft, and it usually equates arms control with defeatism. Just as the Moral Majority lobby targets liberal members of Congress on abortion and school prayer, the Far Right has become aggressive on issues of foreign policy. Jesse Helms chose not to take the chair of Foreign Relations because of prior commitments to his agricultural voters, but he held up numerous appointments to the State Department and ambassadorial posts until the administration abandoned its position on funding birth control and other disputed programs overseas. Senator Church attributed his 1980 election defeat to conservative anger at his support for the Panama Canal treaties. In 1984 his Republican successor as chairman of Foreign Relations, Charles Percy, found conservatives voting for his liberal Democratic opponent, in order to put Senator Helms into the chair. In 1978 Senator Helms persuaded the Senate to stop the United States from joining the United Nations vote favoring a trade embargo against Rhodesia, and he lobbied in 1985 to oppose an embargo against South Africa. In 1985 another prominent conservative, the Reverend Falwell, threw the support of the Moral Majority to the Marcos autocracy in the

Philippines, and he labeled Bishop Tutu in South Africa a fraud. He argued that the Nicaraguan government should be overthrown by a guerilla army of "freedom fighters," and he was instrumental in firing senior State Department officers who criticized his anti-Communist crusade in Latin America.

The possibilities for ideological intervention in foreign policy are limitless. They can sometimes be skillfully exploited by members of Congress, such as the late Joe McCarthy, who carry sufficient seniority in the system to win prestige committee assignments and extensive coverage in the mass media for themselves. There is another reason today to explain why congressional obstructionism will surely intensify during the rest of Reagan's second tenure in office. He cannot run for reelection in 1988; thus he can offer few inducements or threats of punishment to members who face a grueling race in 1988. Members of Congress do not need to hitch a ride on his coattails, nor do they particularly fear the withdrawal of his support in their next campaign, and hence they feel free to oppose his summit initiatives or his enthusiasm for SDI.

CONGRESS AND A LAME DUCK PRESIDENT

One statistic needs to be kept in mind. Though the Democrats have been the majority party in the House for most of the postwar period and have led in voter registration since the 1930s, they won the White House only once (1976) in the last twenty years. Party loyalty may not be the dominant factor in U.S. politics, as it is in Europe and Japan, but there are hard and practical reasons why Democrats want to capture the presidency. The literature today in political science theorizes about the realignment or dissolution of party allegiances. It frightens Democrats that they might lose their congressional majority and surrender all hope of winning the White House for years to come. Though Reagan was virtually unassailable on foreign and defense policy in his first term, following the sad disappointments of the Carter years, his second term will require bipartisan cooperation if his policy initiatives are to succeed. The choice for the Democrats is whether to rally their party together to win in 1988 by choosing to support or to oppose him.

The Republicans face a different problem. President Reagan has gained unprecedented personal popularity, but he has disappointed the influential sector of his own party that seeks to enlarge the conservative establishment and hard-line policy positions. The conservatives, like the Democrats, are tempted to attack administration policy on foreign affairs and not to be coopted. They resent the fact that Reagan has filled top positions with liberals rather than right-wing loyalists and that State is the department that conservatives have most failed to infiltrate. They tend to encourage the intransigent positions of Secretary Weinberger at the Pentagon, and they suspect that Reagan has been too swayed by his summit success in opening a dialogue with Gorbachev.

Anyone schooled in American theories of party competition can enjoy the minuetlike intricacies of electoral politics. Party platforms rarely ask what the public really wants. It appears that electors look for *both* a tough policy in East–West relations and a guarantee that arms control negotiations will lower the risks of war. In rather contradictory terms, electors favor a powerful military buildup and a determined reduction in nuclear forces through mutual and verified agreements. Many want protection for domestic industries that are being exploited by unfair European competition, and they also insist that the NATO allies have not paid their fair share of defense costs. There, balance of hard facts and particular demands will not sway the electorate. Support for Israel is almost limitless, but knowledge is hard to come by when electors are asked for an opinion about trade relations with the Pacific basin or to find a cure for the deficits that burden domestic and external accounts. In fact, what is basically required today is a balancing act by the administration so that it can adjust the military achievements of Reagan's first term against the changing political demands of the electorate in the second.

There is another factor that might provoke clashes between the administration and Congress. It stems from President Reagan's style in handling congressional relations. Most presidents fear an outright conflict with Congress, and they try to negotiate a set of overlapping compromises. If an absolute deadlock develops, policies are quietly dropped so that public friction can be minimized. Reagan's style tends to differ. He has sometimes denounced Congress, and he has often threatened to block appropriations or initiatives that he dislikes. But, when faced with a possible congressional defeat, he has quickly reversed his position. When Congress argued that the marine detachment in Lebanon should be pulled out in 1984, Reagan flatly refused. Only days before Congress threatened to invoke the War Powers Act, he gave in and withdrew the force, even though the evacuation created great problems for the British, French, and Italian governments that had loyally backed his policy of intervening. In the summer of 1985, as international demands mounted for trade boycotts against South Africa, the Senate prepared emergency legislation to impose a boycott. The White House denounced the legislation and insisted that the presidential policy of "constructive engagement" must stand. Once again, rather than negotiate a compromise, the administration firmly resisted. Then, overnight, it reversed itself. It announced its own boycott legislation to forestall the more stringent measures that Congress aimed to take against South Africa. There is no reason to expect a change in this style of confrontation and compromise in Reagan's second administration.

Where Will Conflict Emerge?

Given the shifting and opportunistic mode of congressional reaction to administration foreign policy, resistance will emerge when Congress senses that token or real victories can be won. It has fought the lame duck president to a standstill over tax reform, the budget deficit, arms transfers to the Middle East, Central America, and Southern Africa. It repudiated arms sales to Jordan, and it stalwartly refused to increase the budget for defense. It welcomed the summit meeting with Gorbachev in Geneva though members questioned if too much, or too little, would be conceded during the future rounds of summit discussions. Congress clearly perceived the dispute between State and Defense over the promotion of arms control negotiations, and members were eager to enter the fraternal conflict within the administration. Some members suggested that it might be advantageous to the Democrats if, in the next three years, Reagan failed to negotiate a formal arms control agreement; others were not so sure, as they saw a Congress that was reluctant to ratify another SALT treaty and that could finance an upturn in the arms race.

President Reagan recognized that the electorate was looking for an improvement in the superpowers' relations. He originally resented the diplomatic offensive launched by Moscow and its determination to concentrate the summit talks only on arms reduction and the SDI. He retaliated by condemning the Soviets' behavior in the Third World and in the area of human rights. He turned back Gorbachev's public relations campaign on SDI and, so, claimed a victory at the Geneva summit. Criticism in the Congress then focused on violations of the ABM treaty and the SALT II agreement that might be required by the Strategic Defense Initiative. SDI was never popular in Congress, even among the more hawkish members of the House Armed Services committee, and its funding has been bitterly disputed. Conceivably, it could be slowly and gently strangled by cutting off its funds.

Though there was skepticism about Gorbachev's proposal for a 50% cut in offensive strategic weapons, it was necessary for Reagan to face down the Democrats in Congress by proposing his own reductions. He could not afford to appear intransigent in the discussion of INF, strategic weapons, or the expensive and technologically dubious proposal for a Star Wars system of BMD. The administration has insisted that SDI is absolutely nonnegotiable, no matter how much it is criticized. It is likely that Congress will pare away some of the funding for SDI, however, or it might write limits into the authorization to restrict research and exclude testing. If the administration had chosen to regard SDI only as a valuable bargaining chip, Congress might have allowed the administration more leeway. Because the Democrats need good issues with which to fight in the elections of 1986 and

1988, they might still rally against SDI and force President Reagan to modify his idealist notion that the United States can protect itself against nuclear war.

Reagan senses a threat coming from the Congress and the electorate on various issues of defense policy, East–West understandings, and relations between Europe and the United States. Criticisms of European policy have come from scattered sources in the Congress, but the Republicans have, on the whole, been fairly conciliatory about European affairs. Secretary Weinberger has gone out of his way to ease criticism of European defense funding. The SDI office has invested considerable effort in selling Star Wars research projects to Europe, though with mixed results. Even the stalling by some European governments over the deployment of cruise and Pershing II missiles was treated with tact; the allies in Europe were neither hectored nor pushed around as tactical pawns in the INF and START discussions, and most of them came round to accepting U.S. policy positions.

Most of the Democrats and center Republicans see the European allies in NATO, for all their anxieties about maintaining the U.S. nuclear guarantee, as the vital element of a flexible response strategy. Since the Carter days, and even more strongly since Reagan's arms buildup, the Democrats have been searching for a viable defense policy. Their problem, and that of the more liberal Republicans, is to develop defense policies that are more acceptable than President Reagan's position in at least three respects. First, they must be cheaper and more cost-effective; second, they must be less liable to move the United States into dangerous confrontations with the Soviet Union and the Alliance; and third, though responding to popular demands for arms control, they must give no impression of weakness by modifying the U.S. military buildup or currying favor with the Soviet Union. They must also cope with the escalating threat of a war in Europe by raising the nuclear threshold, partly by confirming INF force assignments and partly by encouraging conventional rearmament on the part of European NATO governments.

It is remarkable that this has been a constant theme of Democratic defense policy toward Europe. Kennedy called in 1961 for a two-pillar structure in NATO, and Carter called in 1977 for an annual 3% increment in real defense expenditures. Most of the Europeans failed to meet these expectations, and influential Democrats have often expressed their impatience. The problem of burden sharing worries many of them too. They argue that the U.S. contribution to NATO is too expensive, that it is not justly shared, and that it distorts the global balance of U.S. military capabilities. The critics have ranged from Senator Nunn to liberal Democrats looking to trim the defense budget and to modify nuclear risks. The introduction of the Nunn amendment in 1984, which the Senate came close to passing, posed an explicit threat to withdraw U.S. troops from Europe if the administration did not force the European members of NATO to shoulder a larger part of Alliance defense expenditures. It is said that it was introduced because its defeat on the Senate floor was already assured, but nevertheless it fanned considerable anxieties in Europe.

Conflicts over Trade Policy

A second confrontation is likely to develop over trade policy. There is no doubt that the House, if not the Senate, will soon pass a series of tariff bills to retaliate against Japan and Europe for flouting fair trade procedures. Even the members of Congress who favor protectionism admit that the real problem lies with the federal budget deficit and the strong dollar, both factors that have seriously hampered U.S. exports and widened the trade gap and both able to be modified by American constraints. Members of Congress are not concerned, unfortunately, with macroeconomic analysis but with jobs and industrial development in their districts that have been lost to overseas trading competition. The shoe and textile industries insist that nearly a million people could lose their jobs, and many of them are concentrated in states that will turn out sizable voting majorities in 1986 and 1988. The issue is not that Reagan is a devout free trader and that leading Democrats are not, but that the industries needing protection are predominantly located in Democratic cities filled with blue-collar workers, while the high-technology and service sectors are often found in Republican towns and white suburbs. Trade control is a bread-and-butter, rather than a radical, issue. The internationalist beliefs in many states have been slowly displaced by a move toward trade protection and economic nationalism; the Congress has more often followed than led the change in preferences.

Obviously, if Congress began to pursue protectionist policies, it could hurt relations with Europe at a time when the president needs to gather support for SDI and his economic policy. The Europeans are worried about U.S. steel price controls, textile quotas, and agricultural export subsidies. Protectionism in the United States is especially worrying to them because the EEC countries rely on export trade to a greater extent than the United States and because they have to support a consistently higher level of unemployment. It is forgotten that European investment in the United States has now overtaken the sum of U.S. investments in Europe and that considerable sums of European money have been drawn into the United States. In fact, the capital inflow now pays for one-half of the federal deficit, and European business — though it profits from the transaction — does not look kindly on the Americans' spendthrift economy. The new mode of protectionism current among Democrats may be prompted by political concerns rather than sound international analysis. It is likely that the second Reagan administration will encounter stronger congressional opposition over foreign trade issues, whether it makes the European allies anxious or not about their trade and financial links across the Atlantic.

The greatest difficulty will stem from American disputes with the Pacific rim. Japan is regarded as the major sinner, in trade problems and in its failure to contribute to defense burden sharing, and its record is much worse than Europe's. There is clearly an increasing concern with the Pacific basin, rather than with Europe and NATO. The vital new economies of the Pacific are of greater interest to the Congress than the Old World, which hankers for welfare socialism, nuclear pacifism, and a relentless critique of American diplomacy. It is also apparent that U.S. friends in Asia are less aggressive in world affairs and more apprehensive about triggering U.S. economic trade sanctions. Though members of the Congress blame the Japanese, somewhat unjustly, for the poor performance of U.S. export trade, they are not caught up in stormy arguments over SDI, East–West relations, or redistributions of the U.S. defense program.

A minor issue of the past is fast growing in importance again, for both ideological and ethnic reasons. Domestic politics has raised pressures for the United States to intervene in the crisis created by South Africa. Liberal and black lobbies have lobbied for the imposition of economic sanctions and to change President Reagan's concept of "constructive engagement." The pressures are sharply different from those exercised in other regional or ethnic issues of foreign policy. On the Middle East it is difficult to stave off the influence of the pro-Israel lobby because it commands extensive sympathy in both parties. On Latin America the administration is hemmed in between Democrats looking to invoke a renewed mode of Vietnam protest, on one side, and right-wing groups who want to give military aid to anti-Communist groups in Nicaragua or El Salvador, on the other. The administration is also troubled by the currency insecurities and the fragile structure of Third World debt. Latin America is trying to stave off a potentially devastating banking crisis, but, since much of the debt is owed to commercial banks, the Congress is disposed to leave the rescue operation to the Wall Street money managers. This may not be wise, and Congress will have to take a greater interest in the near future in the affairs of the IMF, the Export–Import Bank, and the global alignment of exchange rates that can be negotiated by the leadership of the Western governments.

American intervention in many areas of the world, from Angola to Libya or Central America, looked extremely dangerous to the president at the midpoint of his second term. Yet failing to intervene could also be costly. The president realized his dilemma when indignation spread through American public opinion as the number of hijacking and terrorist incidents continued to multiply. It is in this context of activism and Third World order that movement is uncertain over U.S. action in South Africa, El Salvador, the Middle East, or Afghanistan. President Reagan was emphatic in his speech to the UN and at the Geneva summit in repeating that Communist activity in the Third World and terrorist attacks should be roundly denounced. But he is not sure what further measures should be taken to restore America's authority, and neither is the Congress.

Congress and President Reagan

It is sometimes thought that foreign policy does not need the active support of Congress. This is not correct. Technically, treaties and appropriations require congressional approval, and even executive agreements must be reported to Congress. In the Vietnam era, Johnson and Nixon managed to implement an aggressive foreign policy, ignoring as long as they could the rising and vocal opposition in both houses. Fortunately, the days of the "imperial presidency" are gone. Resolutions passed by the Congress finally cut off funds for the war in Cambodia, and funding authorization was withheld to arrest many of the other initiatives planned by Henry Kissinger. More important, the War Powers Act was passed by a restless Congress. It can be invoked after ninety days to call military action to a halt unless authorization is first given by the Congress. This restraint has inhibited policy in recent years in Southeast Asia, Lebanon, and Central America. It was also used to prevent major sales of aircraft to Saudi Arabia, to the delight of the British who picked up the contract, and to other Arab countries. Congress rarely defers to the executive branch today in criticizing or slashing expenditures or in trying to attach controversial riders to funding acts requested by the president. It is fair game to quash his funding commitments or to frustrate his procurement designs as part of the guerilla action to change his larger policy priorities.

Congress frequently uses its legislative and oversight roles to contest the president in a battle for public approval. Public opinion is carefully nurtured, both at home and in allied countries, and the support of key elites is constantly cultivated. For example, while preparing its stand on BMD at Geneva, the administration had to clarify its intentions in the NATO capitals and on Capitol Hill with regard to possible violations of the 1972 ABM treaty or the SALT II agreement. Angry questions were raised about the testing and development of ABM components, including lasers, directed-energy weapons, and multiphase radars. The administration's understanding of violations of the treaty was politically sensitive, because it had previously faulted the USSR for breaching various arms control agreements. The administration was determined to win approval for the $26 billion funding for SDI research and to line up assistance from leading members of Congress. Invitations were sent to leaders of the administration to testify before Congress, not so much to clarify details but so that Congress could try to exploit possible divisions over SDI between State, Defense, and the Joint Chiefs. Congress held numerous hearings to investigate the research and the political costs that might have to be paid in pursuing SDI programs, and its political exploration is obviously far from complete.

Instead of pursuing technical questions, it is customary for congressional hearings and resolutions to strike symbolic postures. Members supported Senator Nunn's amendment to withdraw U.S. troops from Europe because they assumed that it would never pass. Various trade bills and the nuclear freeze resolution were passed (only by one house) because they exercised no binding effect. Sending messages and scheduling hearings have long been established as essential rituals of congressional activity, even if, in the long run, they are basically ineffectual. Folklore assumes that "the purpose of the executive branch is to propose and of the legislative branch to dispose" of policy initiatives. There is no guarantee, however, that either branch will behave in a responsible manner. Both will probably play politics with foreign policy priorities and maneuver in mock debates, but that is characteristic of many democratic societies.

The Reagan administration needs to improve its popularity in the near term, as it might lose control of the Senate in 1986. Most of the Senate seats to be contested are now held by Republicans, and many of them are highly vulnerable. If President Reagan has to deal with a Democrat and not a Republican as the majority leader in the Senate, and with a Democrat as Speaker of the House, his lame duck position will be even further weakened. Moreover, if the chairmanship of important committees and subcommittees reverts to the Democrats, Reagan will find mounting conflict with Capitol Hill. Senator Nunn would become chairman of Armed Services, Senator Hart would chair the Strategic and Theatre Nuclear Forces subcommittees, the highly liberal Senator Pell would chair the Foreign Relations Committee, and critics of the Pentagon budget would extend their power in several subcommittees. Given the more liberal bias in the House, the last two years of the administration could see frequent clashes on arms control, delaying tactics over the defense budget, and disputes about NATO funding. A lame duck president could no longer intimidate congressional leaders over the slashing of expenditures or the curbing of budget deficits.

How much damage could a recalcitrant Congress do? Basically it depends on its success in rallying elite groups and public opinion. It also depends on the campaign strengths of rival candidates from Congress, or the governors of a few states, as they jockey for strong policy positions in the 1988 presidential primary elections. The election campaign runs for two years, and the president might sustain considerable damage during the protracted campaign.

Congressional opposition is usually moved by a mix of local interests, partisan maneuvering, ideological protests, and, occasionally, reasons of principle. The opposition could play havoc over the next three years if President Reagan lost some of his authority over foreign policy to the politics of congressional and partisan electoral maneuvers. One of the conflicts will surely involve the bargaining over SDI, the reduction of offensive and INF forces, and the promotion of arms reduction initiatives. The level of congressional influence over foreign policy bargaining was highly restrained in Reagan's first term. In his remaining years in office the president will have to pay greater heed to congressional questioning and obstruction, especially if it uses the Gramm–Rudman formula of budget cutting to overturn his policy priorities.

The U.S. Constitution provides for a system of checks and balances that allows Congress to exercise greater influence over foreign policy than any legislature enjoys in Europe. The doctrine of the separation of powers was designed to protect the investigative authority, the appropriation power, and the meddlesome ability of the legislature to limit the chief executive's domination of foreign and national security policy. In his second term Reagan will have to combat not only the growing assertiveness of Congress, but also the increasing fragmentation of the power structure of Congress itself. More and more members will defy party discipline as they try to promote their own policy positions in the years preceding a presidential election. Policy coherence might fall by the wayside as potential candidates or rival committee chairmen struggle to advertise their disagreements with the president's policy priorities. Governors and members of Congress running in the primary elections will be more concerned with the demands of their own campaigns than with long-term definitions of the national interest. That is their constitutional prerogative.

European critics tend to find fault with the fragmentation of political power that was enshrined in the U.S. Constitution. Americans have learned, over 200 years, how to cope with their constitutional difficulties and how to work out an effective *modus vivendi*. Though Reagan must leave the White House in 1989, there is no reason why he should forfeit his leadership power in the meantime. The prestige and authority of the president subsists until the day he leaves the Oval Office, and President Reagan is likely to exercise it in a vigorous manner. He enjoys the popularity to defy members of Congress or the host of presidential candidates who choose to contest the initiatives of his administration. Constitutionally, President Reagan will have to contend with an inevitable diminution of his power. But, as a popular and politically astute leader, he will probably complete his term of office as a highly enterprising and assertive chief executive.

NOTES

1. See the argument advanced by Coral Bell, "From Carter to Reagan," *Foreign Affairs* 63 (1984): 490–511.
2. Genrik Trofimenko, quoted in John Spanier and Eric M. Uslaner, *American Foreign Policy Making and the Democratic Dilemma* (New York: Holt, Rinehart and Winston, 1985), p. 208.

3. For a more extended analysis of congressional behavior, see Richard Fenno, *Congressmen in Committees* (Boston: Little, Brown, 1973).
4. Arthur Maas, *Congress and the Common Good* (New York: Basic Books, 1983), pp. 99–103.
5. The idea of the "reelection" constituency as the primary audience comes from Richard E. Fenno, *Home Style* (Boston: Little, Brown, 1978).
6. See the account given by a politician, Maryland's Senator Charles McC. Mathias, "Ethnic Groups and Foreign Policy," *Foreign Affairs* 60(3) (Summer 1981).

16
The Alliance and President Reagan: Future Prospects or Wasted Opportunities?

Walter Goldstein

The consensus emerging in this book is somewhat surprising. Many of the authors commented that they were at first alarmed by the militant rhetoric of the opening years of the Reagan administration. It took them some time to realize that the action was never going to match the words. They had not anticipated the popular appeal that Ronald Reagan would make to the American electorate with his chauvinist credo and his crusading determination to increase defense spending. Baffled by the mass media political techniques that Reagan had mastered, many Europeans suspected that his aggressive attitude toward the Communist world would lead him to abandon the twin doctrines of coexistence and containment that had moved U.S. foreign policy through the years of the Eisenhower, Kennedy, Johnson, Nixon, Ford, and Carter administrations. Fortunately, their fears were misplaced.

In the first years there were genuine causes for anxiety. President Reagan had denounced the détente delusions of Nixon and Kissinger's diplomacy and their program of arms control. He relentlessly castigated the Soviet "empire of evil" and attributed to its cunning strategies most of the crises that disturbed world affairs, from the nuclear arms race to Central America or the Middle East. It seemed that U.S. foreign policy was about to swing into an aggressive mode of cold war confrontation, discarding previous agreements for arms control and sharply accelerating the race to acquire nuclear weapons. The call by Reagan for Americans to "ride tall in the saddle" suggested that a new style of militancy and risk taking was about to be adopted. It would replace the moderation and continuity that had characterized U.S. foreign policy, or so it was said, since the 1950s. From the day that Secretary of State Haig left the administration, however,

197

it was evident that the hard line would largely be verbal and that the code of coexistence would remain basically intact.

The expression of surprise varies from one chapter to another in this book. The European authors were more often astonished than their American colleagues that the intransigent positions adopted by the first Reagan administration were only for a limited audience. Like the fabled "photo sessions" that replaced presidential press conferences, the Reagan team aimed to strike a vivid pose but not to take unnecessary action. Apart from the determined thrust to accelerate the buildup of U.S. military force strengths, no significant or vigorous initiatives were seized to dislodge Communist regimes and to reassert American power. In the exceptional cases of Lebanon and Grenada, U.S. troops were pulled out a few weeks after they had landed, while the covert wars in Central American never grew into the Vietnam-scale conflicts that had once been feared.

The point is made by most of the American contributors to this volume that the dual axioms of containment and collective security were never seriously challenged during Reagan's first term. Alexander Haig enjoyed a short spell of acting out the Hollywood vernacular of Reagan's expressions of activism in military and foreign policy, but he was replaced by people who could distinguish between hostile rhetoric and unthreatening behavior. Secretaries Weinberger and Shultz learned to pay more regard to the councils of the Atlantic Alliance, even when they disagreed with them. They also left no doubt that the policy of collective containment would remain unchanged as the keystone of American diplomacy.

Of course, there were critical disputes that came to divide the Washington administration as well as the members of the Alliance. Divisions over foreign and military policy materialized over four major issues, but no one ever suggested that President Reagan had tried to use them to *radically* change the U.S. commitment to alliance security and peaceful containment.

1. *The deployment of cruise and Pershing missiles*, paradoxically called Euromissiles, was approved after stormy debates in NATO countries. In the 1970s the Soviets had brought forward their SS-20 missiles to threaten Western Europe, and then they launched a propaganda campaign to inhibit NATO's response. Fortunately, the United States portrayed the initiative to deploy INF as a demand by NATO and not by Washington. As a result, the INF decision was resolved by the mainstream political parties in Europe, once the mass peace protests were exhausted, and a resurgence of anti-American sentiment in Europe was skillfully avoided.

2. *Alliance relations between Washington and NATO* were strained when the United States claimed that NATO should collectively increase its defense expenditures by 3 % ; and again when the United States urged its European allies to refuse to help build the Yamal pipeline bringing Siberian natural gas to Western Europe. In the event, the NATO allies resisted U.S. pres-

sure on both policy issues, and the Reagan team accepted a grudging defeat rather than provoke a serious split within the Alliance.

3. *The global police aims of the United States* provoked severe criticism from allies and adversaries, but there was no Vietnam-style intervention to mobilize mass protests or angry demonstrations against American power.* Intervention by the United States was kept at relatively low levels of visibility in Nicaragua, the Middle East, Southern Africa, and Afghanistan and in the selective bombing of targets in Libya. Indeed, conservative supporters of the president felt almost as cheated as his ideological critics on the left. His cautious actions invariably fell far short of his rhetorical threats, and both the hard-line enthusiasts and the peace marchers eventually lost much of their political following.

4. *The nuclear arms race* was the only significant issue on which the Reagan administration took forceful action. The military buildup planned during his first years in office escalated rapidly. The total cost exceeded $1.5 trillion, rising to nearly 7% of GNP, an increase in expenditure not matched since the Korean war. "To arm in order to parlay," Reagan insisted, required that the United States should rapidly extend its offensive and deterrent forces, no matter what the expense, and that it should add a BMD (the fabled SDI) to its vast arsenals. The future of his SDI proposals remains to be tested, however. Practically no one is enthusiastic about funding the SDI — in the U.S. Congress, in the public opinion polls, or in the NATO Alliance. Because Reagan is now committed to parlay with Gorbachev for the rest of his term in office, the SDI program may be whittled down, piece by piece, until it becomes simply another bargaining ploy in President Reagan's repertoire of hard-line maneuvering with Congress, with NATO allies, and with the USSR.

Leaving aside the SDI project for the moment, there is one other troublesome exception to the rule that Reagan talked aggressively but acted with caution. The exception is to be found in the conduct of foreign economic policy. In handling trade and financial matters, the administration chose an operational code of high-risk and unilateral pursuits. At no point was it conceded that political or economic injury might have been caused by its pursuit of economic nationalism.

A succession of annual summit conferences was held by the leaders of the largest Western democracies to try to harmonize economic policy. On each occasion appeals were made to Reagan to modify the priorities or to reverse

---

*Protests were later to intensify in 1986, when U.S. bombers attacked terrorist bases in two Libyan cities. Though opinion in Europe was strongly critical of the U.S. assault, and most Americans began to resent their allies' criticisms, it appears that arguments within the Alliance were politically contained.

the thrust of Reaganomics. The administration stalwartly refused to budge, claiming that the success of the U.S. economic recovery from the recession of 1981–1982 had been highly effective and should not be inhibited. It was angrily but uselessly pointed out that the success had largely been won by borrowing unprecedented sums of foreign capital, and that the expansion of U.S. job opportunities and consumption standards had basically been secured by running up giant deficits in foreign trade.

The startling deficits in the external account as well as in the government budget of the United States had been funded by investment credits drawn from industrial nations. These transfers had achieved a double effect; they had boosted the value of the dollar and they had stimulated the export earnings of a few nations, especially in Southeast Asia. But it was alleged that American policy had also retarded the course of GNP growth and capital formation in much of Europe and the Third World.

In its first term, Reagan's team was not moved by the stream of economic complaints and criticisms that came from foreign bankers, allied governments, or trading rivals. Nor was it influenced by the grievances vented by the more harassed groups of American electors, including millions of unemployed automobile, textile, and steel workers; family farmers who had been hammered into bankruptcy; and welfare recipients whose medical or benefit subsidies had been severely slashed. These were the critics, at home and overseas, who found in Reagan's policies cause for anger and vehement protest rather than welcome surprise, and he relentlessly ignored them. They were neither likely nor able to vote for him, and their opposition parties did not pose a serious political threat to his economic ideology, either in America or in Europe.

THE REAGAN SECOND TERM

The surprise of the first term can be simply stated. The most conservative president to enter the White House since 1932 was fundamentally, in his foreign and military policy, a chauvinist by confession and a hesitant pragmatist in behavior. He still looked and talked like the sheriff hero of his Hollywood cowboy movies, but his actions were basically devoid of passion, risk, and warring enthusiasm. The great exception, of course, appeared in the defense budget. Despite the growing burden of the federal deficit, President Reagan continuously urged the procurement of new weapons systems: the B-1 bomber, the MX, the Trident and Midgetman missiles and an armory of cruise weapons, tanks, and ships. The only omission, his critics noted, was in the pay and the operational costs for the 3 million men to use all this hardware.

More important, he urged the long-term cause of SDI. It was to be an ideal Utopian system, a leakproof astrodome, a perfect shelter that would one day render nuclear weapons worthless and thus liberate mankind from the terrible threat of war. Eventually, the Star Wars project might cost countless trillions of dollars, but it would not be operational in this century or even the next. Of course, it would antagonize the Soviets, foment severe anxieties among the NATO allies, and eventually exhaust the defense budgets of both of the superpowers. Nevertheless, it represented the one yearning exercise in idealism that Ronald Reagan hoped to bequeath to America in his legacy as a "peace president." His hero, Franklin Roosevelt, had planned to create a peaceful order at the opening of the nuclear era, and Reagan's ambition was to complete the task.

The considerable defects and dangers of the SDI program have been noted in many of the preceding chapters. Some of the analysis focuses upon the fictitious cost estimates, the science fiction technology, and the policy contradictions generated by the SDI project. Will it invalidate the use of nuclear weapons or provoke their early first use? Will the project eventually provide an area-wide or a hard-point defense to secure *either* the cities or the ICBM missile silos located in the United States? No matter which choice is made, it will leave Europe defenseless against an IRBM attack, and it will diminish the belief in stable deterrence held by U.S. allies in Europe. On all of these issues the authors raise questions of major significance. That no definitive answers are available at the present time is a matter for grave anxiety.

Whatever the ultimate aim of the BMD system for the next century, the fact remains that the basic technologies are still too primitive to contract out for research or to proceed with any major testing. So the key question remains: What opportunity costs will be paid, in terms of policy options that must be forfeited, if Reagan insists upon pursuing the SDI program and the U.S. military buildup in his remaining years in office? What mutual benefits might the superpowers conceivably negotiate if they chose to limit their arms race instead of multiplying their offensive and defensive capabilities?

These are difficult questions to pose to a president who seems to be on the point of reversing his beliefs about the benefits of détente, a concept he once despised. He argues publicly that understanding will spring afresh from his summit negotiations if he can only prove that SDI is a seriously funded project and not a token symbol to bargain away with Gorbachev. Reagan looks toward breakthrough agreements in 1987 or 1988 on matters of arms control. It appears certain, however, that he regards SDI as the great weapon that will force the Soviets to negotiate (and not repudiate) his proposals for arms control and disarmament. The success of his administration will eventually be judged by historians when they can determine, with the benefit of hindsight, whether his assessment of SDI was visionary in its daring or fatally flawed in its calculus of nuclear bargaining utility.

After years of icy distrust and propaganda warfare between the super-powers, there are a few optimistic prospects for disarmament and arms control negotiations that can be identified today. There is also reason for optimism in reviewing the course of strategic maneuvers both within the Atlantic Alliance and in the superpowers' deliberations at the summit. Serious offers have been advanced for a 50% reduction in offensive forces, for a phased withdrawal of INF weapons in central Europe, and for negotiated modes of on-site inspection or specified verification procedures. The prospects for discussion within NATO have improved, too. Bitter disputes over Air-Land Battle 2000, follow-on force-attack (a new ogre called FOFA), and flexible defense doctrines have been smoothed aside. NATO is still recovering from the intense political crises generated by the cruise and Pershing deployments that had lasted for over six years. It is content today to play a somewhat passive role over SDI and force reduction negotiations while the superpowers jockey over subcommittee agendas in Geneva. NATO's strategic position will be greatly influenced by SDI and the Geneva decisions, and NATO leaders are uneasy about the future of the Alliance. As general elections will come due in many allied countries in the next year or two, however, there is little drive to criticize or deflect the bilateral dealings of the two superpowers.

It now appears that there were two conflicting expectations that prompted the opening of negotiations with the Soviets during Reagan's second term. The first view, which has largely been adopted by the "hawks" in the administration, insists that both the Soviets and the NATO allies are amenable to negotiation today because Reagan was staunchly resolved in his first years to improve the force strength of the United States and the NATO alliance. "To avoid war," as Churchill is often quoted, usually out of context, "a nation must prepare for war." The slogan is cited by partisans of SDI; by Donald Regan, the powerful chief of staff in the White House; and by Secretaries Shultz and Weinberger. They hold that the $300 billion defense budget should be immune from the budget-slashing exercises devised by Congress; and that SDI development and offensive force buildup programs should move forward, even if they marginally violate restrictions of the SALT treaties negotiated in the 1970s by the détente gang of conspirators inspired by Kissinger.

The second view builds upon contradictory premises. The cost of weapons programs, it is argued, is likely to soar beyond all hope of constraint. Middle powers, like Britain and France, cannot afford to modernize their triad of nuclear forces for the 1990s if they are also to invest in high-technology industries and their depleted infrastructures. Strikingly, the superpowers face severe limitations in their allocation of resources too. President Reagan has been responsible for the doubling of the national debt from $1 trillion to $2 trillion in just five years, thus turning the United States from the world's largest creditor economy in 1982 to its largest debtor by 1985. He cannot allow the deficit financing of the U.S. economy to mount indefinitely, nor can defense spending be continually raised while all other budget items are cut. Gorbachev faces a far worse problem. The proportionate burden of military expenditures on GNP in the Soviet Union has reached enormous dimensions. The economic failures of the USSR have become more evident each year, and its GNP growth rate has flattened. Its need to divert resources from military to industrial purposes can no longer be brushed aside as the wistful hope of Western liberals and peace marchers.

A complex mix of motives has driven the two superpowers and their alliances to adopt more accommodating attitudes toward arms control and the revival of détente in the last few years. Both sides spend heavily to arm against each other's military buildup; both are aware of the crippling economic costs of escalating the arms race; and both have had to reach for agile political compromises because of the domestic stress with which they must contend. The stress that they face is intensely worrying. Any sign of premature concession is feared, lest it convey a signal that resolve is weakening at home or that alliance linkages are beginning to fray overseas. But the time to dare to make changes has come, and the leadership abilities of Mikhail Gorbachev and Ronald Reagan are likely to be pushed or pulled by rival groups. Each of their moves is analyzed with suspicion at home and partisan criticism abroad. If a new mode of entente is to emerge in the late 1980s, both will have to learn how to improve security for their own populations and also for the world power blocs they lead.

It is in this perspective that the title was chosen for this book. Though it was not clear when the authors wrote the first drafts of their papers in the summer of 1985, it now seems that Reagan stands virtually unchallenged as the leader of the Western Alliance. That he has used his powers firmly in the past is affirmed, though in a highly critical manner, by many of the American and European contributors to the book. It is open to question whether he will continue to do so in the future, or whether he will achieve the distinction of leadership to which he candidly aspires. The United States has regained its ascendancy in the Alliance on his watch, and he has successfully changed the agenda of negotiations with the Soviets and with the NATO allies. Many troubling matters still remain to be resolved, especially in the promotion of economic growth and the handling of enormous national debts. Though the political position of the United States has improved during the Reagan years, credit for the improvement should not be given too heavily to his personal powers of leadership. As the chief executive, he must rely on leaders in his own administration, in the Congress, and in various allied or adversary powers. It remains to be seen whether his capacity to provide constructive guidance to Western policy will survive until the day he leaves the White House in 1989.

THE MYSTIQUE OF LEADERSHIP

The surprise in this book is to be found in the unexpected consensus that has been expressed by a range of critical but fairly conservative analysts drawn from Europe and the United States. Some regretted the hard line President Reagan adopted in his first years, when he harshly criticized America's adversaries and paid little heed to its closest allies. Others pointed to the misleading thrust of his ideological pronouncements, to the erroneous objectives pursued by U.S. foreign policy in the Third World, and to the seeming disregard for arms control progress. His unremitting commitment to SDI and the U.S. military buildup was censured by several authors and so, too, was the self-serving conduct of U.S. foreign economic policy.

These criticisms are severe and cannot be lightly regarded. But neither, for that matter, can the accomplishments of Reagan's administration. He has established a *modus vivendi* in dealing with the Soviet Union and the Warsaw pact countries, and with the Chinese People's Republic, and he has helped restore the cohesion of the Atlantic Alliance. To a great extent, of course, his efforts were aided by the constant changes of leadership in the Kremlin and by the weakened position of Prime Minister Thatcher, Chancellor Kohl, and President Mitterrand. Had any of these leaders been more aggressive, or had the Congress been more determined to challenge his executive power, President Reagan's accomplishments might have been greatly diminished.

What will happen in the remaining years of the Reagan presidency? To try to draw straight-line projections is obviously absurd when it comes to plotting the future course of political action or foreign policy. Reagan's success in providing leadership to the Alliance, or in opening summit talks with Gorbachev, could rapidly crumble if a momentous crisis were suddenly to disrupt the global political order or its economic power base. A century ago it was anticipated that the maritime hegemony of Britain or the diplomatic mastery of Bismarck would preserve the stability of the European state system. Both expectations proved to be untenable. A similar shattering of expectations could occur in the 1980s or the 1990s. There are fewer than 700 weeks remaining in this century. Realistically, there could be a series of upheavals, starting with waves of economic unrest, followed by widespread social strife, irridentist wars, the proliferation of nuclear weapons, and the eventual clash of superpower interests. Systems changes occurred with astonishing rapidity in the tumults of 1914, 1939, and 1945 and in the financial crises of the 1930s and the oil "shocks" of the 1970s. A similar tumult could sweep aside the foundations on which we have built the assumptions that govern these last decades of the twentieth century.

The leadership role of President Reagan, the least thoughtful and yet one of the most innovative of the forty presidents of the United States, will not be objectively gauged until many years after he has left office. It will then be asked whether he sensitively anticipated the threats to global peace or prosperity that loom on the horizon today. Should he have paid more attention to the storm signals that are now flying, warning us that the structures of world order might not survive a storm? Or was he well advised in utilizing his own, personal popularity for short-run advantages and the boosting of defense preparations?

The balance of nuclear terror is terribly unstable, and severe distress warnings can be heard in the world's financial and trade markets. In the Third World there are regions of intense turbulence, economic despair, and murderous antagonisms. To name only a few problems of vital concern to U.S. foreign policy: Will Central America and the Middle East be embroiled in Vietnam-style wars; will there be bloodshed or an orderly transfer of power in the Philippines or South Africa; will a moratorium on the servicing of LDC debts force the Western banks to restrict further credit and world trade, bringing to a halt many hopes for GNP growth and stable expansion?

Reagan is hailed at the present time as the Great Communicator who personifies the national pride of the American people and the symbolic spirit of Atlantic unity. But it might be that future historians will see in him the articulate temporizer who courted acclaim, glamor, and cosmetic appearances while shrugging aside the troubling visions that displeased him. Will he be accused of scoring points in the public opinion polls by ignoring indicators of future turmoil? No objective judgment can be advanced while he is still in office. So far, the leadership of President Reagan has been appraised from the left and the right, by hawks and doves, by allies and adversaries. His economic and social policies have been praised by some and criticized by others; so too have his military enthusiasms. For the time being, he has been more highly praised by his contemporaries than any president in this century; and he has won the effective leadership of the security alliance that he palpably helped to preserve.

The success of the Reagan administration in holding together the Alliance can be attributed in some degree to the threatening measures taken by the Soviet Union, whether in Afghanistan or in deploying new weapons systems, and to the disorganized leadership in the rest of the NATO alliance. That the adversary was challenging and the allies divided, as indeed they were, will not detract from the conclusion reported by authors of the preceding fifteen chapters. During his years in office, President Reagan's leadership has secured a greater cohesion in the Atlantic Alliance than many critics had previously envisaged. He has exercised a more powerful charisma, or mystique of power, than any of his contemporary rivals; and his ascendancy in the public opinion polls has gone beyond challenge at home or abroad. This has allowed him to rally popular sentiment rather than to resolve complex policy dilemmas or to prepare for the crises that threaten to climax in the years ahead.

The mystic appeal to a mass electorate, or to an alliance of varied electorates, is an essential attribute of political leadership. It is in this regard that Ronald Reagan's contribution to the politics of the Western alliance can be positively judged. A less popular leader would never have matched Reagan's accomplishments in rallying the will of an Alliance that had lived through three decades of discord before he even entered the White House.

In his introductory chapter, Sir Frank Roberts wrote that the cohesion of the Alliance has been built upon the trust in American leadership and the capacity to discuss policy disagreements among member nations. His judgment has been confirmed by the wide-ranging discussion and the eventual consensus that forms the core of this book. The consensus was not easily reached, given the range of criticism that was expressed, and hence it stands as a remarkable conclusion.

About the Editor and Contributors

THE EDITOR

Walter Goldstein is Professor of Public Policy at the Rockefeller College of the State University of New York at Albany. He was a visiting professor at the London School of Economics, Columbia University, INSEAD, and on the management faculty of IBM and Royal Dutch Shell. His publications on energy policy, arms control, international trade, and NATO defense, include *Fighting Allies: Tensions within the Atlantic Alliance* (Brassey's, 1986).

THE CONTRIBUTORS

Guy De Carmoy is Professor Emeritus at the European Institute of Business Administration (INSEAD) in Fontainebleau, and formerly an officer of OEEC and a professor at the Foundation des Sciences Politiques. His numerous publications on European economic and energy policy, and on current political conflicts, include *French Foreign Policy, 1944–1968.*

Peter Corterier is a member of the Bundestag of the Federal Republic of Germany and of the Foreign Affairs committee of the Social Democratic Party. He is Vice President of the Atlantic Treaty Association.

Ellmann Ellingsen is Secretary-General of the Norwegian Atlantic Council and the author of several works on NATO defense policy.

Martin J. Hillenbrand is Dean Rusk Professor and Director of the Center for Global Policy Studies at the University of Georgia. He was formerly U.S. Ambassador to Hungary and the Federal Republic of Germany, and Assistant Secretary of State for European Affairs. His books include *Power and Morals*, *The Future of Berlin*, and *Germany in an Era of Transition.*

Gil Klinger is a graduate of the Kennedy School of Government at Harvard and of the Rockefeller College of the State University of New York. He worked at the Rand Corporation and for the Trident missile program, and as a research assistant in the U.S. Senate.

Zygmunt Nagorski is President of the International Leadership Center in New York, and a former professor at Columbia University. He served as a U.S. Foreign Service officer in Egypt, South Korea, and France; as program director of the Council on Foreign Relations; and Vice President of the Aspen Institute for Humanistic Studies. Among his many publications is his book, *The Psychology of East–West Trade*.

Robert E. Osgood is Christian A. Herter Professor of American Foreign Policy at the School of Advanced International Studies, Johns Hopkins University, and a former staff member of the National Security Council and the Policy Planning office in the State Department. He is the author of nearly a dozen books, including *Ideals and Self-Interest in America's Foreign Relations, Limited War, NATO: The Entangling Alliance*, and *Alliances and Foreign Policy*.

Otto Pick is Emeritus Professor of international relations at the University of Surrey and adjunct professor in the German graduate program of the University of Southern California. He has published widely on Soviet affairs; his most recent book (with Julian Critchley, MP) was *Collective Security*.

John E. Rielly is President of the Chicago Council on Foreign Relations, and formerly a consultant to the Ford Foundation, the Overseas Development Council, and the State Department. He is a member of the Trilateral Commission, the Council of the Harvard Graduate School, the American Council on Germany, and the editorial board of *Foreign Policy*. He has edited successive volumes of *American Public Opinion and U.S. Foreign Policy* in the last ten years.

Sir Frank Roberts is Chairman of the Standing Conference on Atlantic Organizations (SCAO), and was formerly the British Ambassador to Yugoslavia, the Soviet Union, the Federal Republic of Germany, and NATO. He has written about his experiences at Yalta in 1944 and in postwar diplomacy. He is a governor of the Atlantic Institute, Vice President of the Atlantic Treaty Association, and a member of the Trilateral Commission.

David Robertson is a Fellow and Tutor at St. Hugh's College in Oxford, and visiting professor in Canada, the United States, and Italy. His books include *Theories of International Competition, Superpower: A Dictionary of Modern Strategy and Defence*, and *A Theory of Party Competition: Class and the British Electorate*.

Robert Rothschild is former Ambassador of Belgium to Yugoslavia, the Congo, Switzerland, France, and the United Kingdom. His books reflect on his wartime experience in China and the pre-war politics of appeasement in the 1930s, including *Une Nuit de Sept Ans*.

Steve Smith is a lecturer in international relations at the University of East Anglia and at the State University of New York at Albany. His long list of articles and books includes *Foreign Policy Adaptation, Politics and Human Nature, Foreign Policy Implementation,* and *International Relations: British and American Perspectives.*

Stephan G. Thomas is Head of the Ostbüro of the Social Democratic Party in Bonn, and formerly of the Deutschlandfunk and of the international department of the Friedrich Ebert Foundation. He is Chairman of the Deutsch-Englische Gesellschaft.